PRAISE FOR *THE X-MANUAL*

"Peter Bellini combines biblical scholarship with psychological insight and practical experience in the ministry of deliverance. This is a rare combination that few can offer. *The X-Manual* is a most-needed practical help for Christians who are encountering a growing number of people who need deliverance.... I recommend *The X-Manual* as one of the best resources for Christians to utilize in the ministry of deliverance."

—RANDY CLARK, Global Awakening Theological Seminary

"Popular interest in demons and exorcism is on the rise, yet few US Christians are well-versed on a subject that has played a major role in church growth historically and globally today. *The X-Manual* offers a nuanced perspective, drawing on forty years of theological study and practical experiences. The book will be of interest to those who wonder whether demons exist or what to do if they seem to have encountered one."

—CANDY GUNTHER BROWN, Indiana University

"How timely! In my own thirty-eight years in inner healing and deliverance, I have witnessed a trend. As sin and the occult have increased, so has demonization. There is a cure.... Deliverance is made sure through repentance. As Pete writes, Satan's only hope is the lack thereof. But on behalf of those who bow to the deliverer of us all, Christ has given us authority to bring his works to an end."

—MARK SANDFORD, director, Elijah Rain Ministries

"This is a complete handbook of ministry for those who are ready to do more than offer perfunctory prayers over tough situations. It is full of meat and extremely practical, theologically sound, and accessible. If you're ready to get serious about spiritual warfare, this book is the place to begin. You will be encouraged by the stories and empowered by the principles. Thank you, Pete Bellini, for teaching us how to take authority."

—CAROLYN MOORE, vice-chairwoman, Wesleyan Covenant Association Council

"Peter Bellini . . . will equip you with biblical understanding, practical wisdom, and powerful tools to apprehend your authority, recognize bondage in others, and cast out demons. This is kingdom. There is no time to waste. Get the book. Read it. Do it. People are waiting for freedom. . . . I will be making this required reading for anyone doing ministry with me."

—KIM MAAS, president/CEO, Kim Maas Ministries

"*The X-Manual* powerfully brings the area of deliverance from demonic oppression back into the equipping and mission of the church in a biblically balanced and comprehensive manner. Bellini's life experiences sprinkled throughout this book reveal that he has been at this a long time and is now releasing practical tools to set captives free and keep them free. . . . This should be a part of every church's leadership curriculum."

—RODNEY HOGUE, author of *Liberated, Set Free and Staying Free from Demonic Strongholds*

"No other book is as *comprehensive* in bringing together so many important elements and dimensions related to the subject. . . . Most books on this subject are written by experienced practitioners directly involved in deliverance ministry. Very few have been written by seminary professors. Pete Bellini is a rare combination of both. He has written an extremely practical, user-friendly book that is easily accessible to any Christian who seeks to engage in deliverance ministry with someone."

—STEPHEN A. SEAMANDS, Asbury Theological Seminary, emeritus

THE X-MANUAL

THE X-MANUAL

Exousia–A Comprehensive Handbook on
Deliverance and Exorcism

PETER J. BELLINI

Foreword by Stephen A. Seamands

WIPF & STOCK · Eugene, Oregon

THE X-MANUAL
Exousia–A Comprehensive Handbook on Deliverance and Exorcism

Wipf & Stock
An Imprint of Wipf and Stock Publishers
199 W. 8th Ave., Suite 3
Eugene, OR 97401

www.wipfandstock.com

PAPERBACK ISBN:978-1-6667-3737-0
HARDCOVER ISBN: 978-1-6667-9672-8
EBOOK ISBN: 978-1-6667-9673-5

03/30/22

Contents

Foreword

In 1965, Harvard theologian Harvey Cox published *The Secular City,* a provocative, widely read book extolling the positive virtues of secular urban life in North America. Contrasting our secular, modern age with the former pre-modern age, as reflected in the supernatural world of the Bible, Cox had this to say about Jesus' ministry of casting out demons:

> Though it frequently embarrasses us today, Jesus was viewed by his own age as a great exorcist. His power to cast out demons was central to his ministry . . . as the personification of the kingdom he was recognized and feared by the demons he cast out . . . All this sounds extremely peculiar to modern ears. Most of us would prefer to forget that for many of his contemporaries, Jesus' exorcism was in no way peripheral, but stood at the heart of his work.[1]

Certainly, much has changed since Cox wrote that. Now, almost sixty years later, even in secular Europe and North America, Christians are slowly getting over their embarrassment and acknowledging what they wished to forget. Talk of demons and exorcism doesn't seem quite as "extremely peculiar" today as it did back then.

Several factors have combined to create a growing recognition among Christians of the reality of the demonic. In the last half century, we have witnessed a significant cultural shift in the West from a "modern" scientific, secular worldview to a "postmodern" worldview, which is more open to the spiritual and the mystical. As I was checking out of a grocery store a few weeks ago, I noticed that, along with the usual magazines for sale, like *Time*

---

1. Cox, *Secular City,* 149.

ix

and *People*, a special edition magazine, *Ghosthunters*, was also on display. Common now, that would have been unheard of when I was growing up in the 1960s.

We have also witnessed the phenomenal rise and growth of global Christianity. Today most Christians no longer live in the Northern Hemisphere (Europe and North America) but in the Southern Hemisphere (Asia, Africa, and Latin America). These "majority world" Christians have no problem at all believing in demons. As a Korean pastor and Ph.D. student explained to a friend of mine, "The only people who don't believe in demons are Western scholars." In their churches, deliverance ministry is commonplace, and no one questions its validity.

Finally, stemming from the sexual revolution, there has been a significant breakdown in the West of foundational family and community structures, which has led to an alarming rise in addictions and mental health problems and a growing involvement in various occult activities. As a result, pastors and Christian leaders are finding themselves directly encountering the demonic and demonic manifestations in the lives of their parishioners in ways that they simply cannot ignore.

That's how I got involved in deliverance ministry myself. I was a theology professor at Asbury Theological Seminary in the 1980s, trying to mind my own business. To tell my Wesleyan, orthodox faculty colleagues that I was involved in ministry with students that involved casting out demons was not the way to gain academic credibility or respect. No one denied the existence of demons, but no one talked or taught much about them either. So, I certainly didn't go looking for the demonic!

But in the early 1990s, because of some deep healing of childhood hurts in my own life, coupled with several profound encounters with the Holy Spirit, I found myself engaging regularly in a ministry of healing prayer to seminary students revolving around significant emotional and spiritual issues in their lives. Every now and then, as we were dealing with a person's emotional wounds, I found myself directly confronted by a demon or demonic activity in ways that I simply could not ignore.

Later I would learn a lot about deliverance ministry from Dr. Charles Kraft, and he would often say that "demons are like rats which are attracted to garbage." Generally, they like to hide and lay low. But sometimes, when you are joining with Jesus in seeking to heal and rid someone of their emotional garbage, the demons feel so exposed and threatened that they will directly manifest in ways you can't ignore. After all, by removing the emotional garbage, you are taking away their access to the person and what they thrive on. They don't like it and will do anything they can to hinder and shut down the garbage removal process.

That's how I initially got involved in deliverance ministry. In certain cases, deliverance became a necessity to affect emotional healing in a person's life. In order to deal with the garbage, I had to deal with the rats. So, I began to learn all I could from other practitioners and to read the few helpful books on deliverance that were available at the time.

Eventually, I became comfortable doing deliverance ministry, and when I wrote a book about the cross and emotional healing, I included a chapter on it. As a result of this, I ended up teaching a course on spiritual warfare, and continued teaching it for twenty-five years at the seminary. And since I always included a module on deliverance ministry in the class, I have probably read twenty to twenty-five books and manuals on deliverance ministry.

That's why I'm glad to have been asked to write the foreword for this book. The author, Dr. Pete Bellini, whom I'm pleased to say is a former student of mine, has written a book on deliverance ministry that is truly remarkable and unique. Relative to the many books on this subject that I have studied and read, no other is as comprehensive in bringing together so many important elements and dimensions of the subject.

The X-Manual is also unique because it is written by someone who is both a top-notch academic scholar and a seasoned practitioner of deliverance ministry. Most books on this subject are written by experienced practitioners directly involved in deliverance ministry. Very few have been written by seminary professors. Pete Bellini is a rare combination of both. He has written an extremely practical, user-friendly book that is easily accessible to any Christian who seeks to engage in deliverance ministry. Such persons are his target audience. All this, however, is rooted in his solid biblical, theological, and historical understanding. This comes through explicitly, as he weaves in biblical, theological, and historical material related to deliverance throughout the book. It also implicitly undergirds his approach to deliverance throughout.

Pete is truly a seasoned practitioner, someone who is called and anointed to Christ's ministry of deliverance. If you haven't been involved much in this ministry, you may read things in this book that seem sensational, weird, and beyond your pay grade. Rest assured, nothing that he describes seemed strange and foreign to me. I have encountered these things, too, and so have most of the practitioners I know who have engaged in such ministry.

The deep wisdom in Pete's approach shines through in so many ways. Some who are involved in deliverance ministry possess great zeal but lack knowledge and operate with an overly simplistic approach to deliverance. They tend to see a demon behind every problem. The truth is, however, that determining whether someone actually needs deliverance is often a profoundly complex process where much discernment is needed. The C-13 diagnostic tool Pete has developed takes this complexity into account and is an invaluable resource for anyone engaging in this work. So is his in-depth guide on preparing for a deliverance session.

Pete recognizes the great need for proper knowledge and training in deliverance ministry. Those who engage in it need a sound scriptural and theological framework coupled with practical strategies and methods. They also must be careful to attend to their own spiritual formation in seeking to grow in holiness and walk in the power of the Spirit.

I especially appreciated the profound emphasis on the Cross of Christ woven throughout the book. "When Satan attacks you," E. Stanley Jones often said, "command him in the name of Jesus to bend his neck. On the back of it you will find a nail-scarred footprint." By his death on the cross, Jesus soundly defeated and triumphed over all the demonic powers. There, too, as we learn from the rich discussion of Romans 6, we also died with Christ so that we can be set free, not only from the penalty but also from the power of sin. Our authority in deliverance ministry is rooted in the cross.

Often as I was reading the manuscript, I found myself thinking, "This is actually a book about sanctification. It's about practical sanctification, setting people free from demonic bondage so they can grow in holiness and run the race of discipleship to which they have been called." This book, reflecting the author's deep roots in the Wesleyan theological tradition, is written from the conviction that holiness of heart and life is the supreme end of the Christian life. Ultimately, that's what shapes his understanding and approach to deliverance. And that's what makes *The X-Manual* such a rich, needed resource which will produce much good fruit—fruit that will remain.

STEPHEN A. SEAMANDS
Emeritus Professor of Christian Doctrine, Asbury Theological Seminary

Preface

Why would anyone want to be a deliverance minister? It is a dirty job, but someone has to do it. Your ministry consists of cleaning out spiritual sewage infested by invisible rats and roaches. Better to be an exterminator or work for Roto-Rooter. I never went looking to be a ghostbuster. It found me (see chapter 1). But I do not regret the call because it brings glory to God to set a soul free, and nothing gives me greater joy!

No, I did not seek to be a ghostbuster or an exterminator. I am a United Methodist ordained minister, a seminary professor, and a recreational power-lifter and heavyweight boxer on the side. I also teach a boxing class, which is a ministry. I received my first pair of boxing gloves when I was six. I was born into a rough neighborhood and was taught never to start a fight; however, if someone started one with me, I learned never to back down. I think this is also how I got started in deliverance ministry. Satan threw the first punch.

One of those punches looked like this. Back in the 1980s, I was the leader of a campus evangelism team at The Ohio State University. We would go out every Friday and Saturday night from nine p.m. to three a.m., or later. Students would make a pilgrimage to the campus clubs and bars religiously every weekend. At that time, the campus had around five blocks of clubs on High St. Hundreds of students would flock to the clubs to do the things that college students do on the weekend, and preachers preach against on Sunday. Our evangelism team would station ourselves right before the first block of clubs, so students had to pass by us.

We would set up a booming public address system. One of us, usually me, would preach in the open air, while the others would have conversations with intrigued passersby, usually hecklers. At the end of one of our typical nights of evangelism, after the bars let out at around 2:15 a.m., something peculiar happened. Two rough-around-the-edges teenagers, a young man and woman, broke away from the pack that they were hanging out with and approached us. They were dressed like punkers or today's goths. They were curious about what we were doing. We told them that we were sharing the good news of Jesus Christ.

The young man challenged our Christianity, specifically mine as the leader. He prodded me with a host of, "If you are a real Christian, you would. . .." type of demands. He asked for my coat. He claimed he was homeless. I gave him my leather coat. He asked for my Bible. I gave him my Bible. He said he and his girlfriend were hungry and asked me for food. I said, "Let's go to McDonalds for breakfast." And we went. After we finished eating, the two ragged fifteen-year-olds said they had nowhere to stay that night. They wanted to stay with us. Our ministry had several fellowship houses, at least one for single men and one for single women. I lived in the single men's house at the time.

We brought the teens back to our ministry houses. The young man, named John[1], and I stayed up through the early morning past sunrise talking. I did most of the listening. I wanted to hear his story. I learned that the tattered bunch he was hanging out with were Satanists. And he was one of them. I asked to hear the rest of his "testimony." He informed me that he knew all about the Christianity that I was preaching on the corner. He said he had "been there and done that." I was intrigued and asked to hear more. John said he was raised in a Pentecostal church. He went every Sunday morning and night, as well as every Wednesday for years. I asked whether his family brought him to church. John's voice grew louder. He cried out, "My dad was the preacher, and he molested me for years—all that time!" My jaw dropped. He began to weep profusely. I was crushed. He had been crushed. I could not speak or move.

He continued: "One day I met a girl. She was a Satanist. She introduced me to other Satanists. They reached out to me with unconditional acceptance and love. They didn't judge me. I had no one, but now I have someone. So, I ran away from home and joined them. They are my family. They are my church." Whoa! I learned that many of his friends shared a similar story of family abuse. My heart was broken. Needless to say, I could not sleep that morning.

The next day we talked again, through the night until dawn. This time I talked, and he listened. I shared about the real Christ, not the hypocritical faith of his father. I told him that God had nothing to do with what had

---

1. Throughout this book, I will share true stories of deliverance from my ministry. Identities and related information at times are changed or not mentioned to protect the privacy and dignity of those involved.

happened to him, and that Jesus had wept over him during those horrid times. I shared the good news of God's love, and then I shared my own radical testimony. I had not been abused, but my story had its own drama and gripping content; I had been converted as a former atheist and a wannabe gangster to an on-fire revivalist.

By the end of the night, the Spirit had really moved on John. He was under heavy conviction and wanted to be delivered from Satanism. The Spirit was doing a work of inner healing, and his heart was softening. He was ready. I explained deliverance to him, and we had a session. We prayed late into the night, and by early morning he was set free and received Christ into his heart! Praise the Lord! That week I spent hours daily with him, reading scripture, discipling him, and praying with him. The weekend came. Our team prepared to go out and evangelize on campus, as we did every weekend. But this time, we attracted a new worker. John wanted to come out with us on the streets.

We had been out on the corner preaching for about two hours when a group of young teens approached us. They were John's Satanist friends. They started talking with John. They questioned why he was with us. John shared in so many words what had happened to him. Not surprisingly, they did not take it as good news. His friends became irate. The hostile pack began to mock John, me, and the rest of the group. They finally left, but not without threatening that we "would pay." The rest of the night was uneventful, but the following weekend was different.

Our ministry assembled at our regular location and began to preach and share the gospel. Soon the same group of Satanists that had threatened us the previous week came to stand directly in front of us, specifically in front of me. One young livid teen began to scream in my face that I was going to die. He informed me that his people were holding black masses for my death daily until I died (See chapter one for another such occasion). The Spirit of God immediately rose up inside me, and, not missing a beat, I said, "Fine, but Jesus has the keys of Hell and Death, not you. Try getting them from Him. If you can get them from Him, go for it, but good luck!" And then I chuckled. The Satanists were not expecting this response. They were hoping I would cower in fear. I was pumped. My adrenaline was flowing, but deep inside I was imagining what my next week would look like.

My ministry team and I would pray nightly throughout that week. We were engaged in intense spiritual warfare. But the Greater One lives inside me. Of course, I did not die. I am here writing this book. After a few weeks, I would see that band of broken teens no more. I share this story as a preface to the book because it is one of the many reasons why I am in deliverance ministry and why I wrote this book.

I am a United Methodist minister and professor and have been in ministry since the 1980s. I can honestly say that I do not know many of my denomination's insular and ill-equipped churches or many churches outside of my denomination that would have reached out to John on the streets, taken him in, and further, been equipped to cast out demons from him and to lead him to Christ. Many in our churches hide safely within the four walls: "a mighty fortress is our church." They are fearful or unprepared to encounter broken and battered people on the streets who need Christ.

The average churchgoer needs to get saved and be lit on fire until their flesh screams and their spirit shouts. We need flammable people who will demonstrate the gospel in a blaze of Holy Spirit fire. We need equipped believers who can reach the Johns out on the streets.

Nonetheless Pete Bellini didn't do anything. It was Christ in me that led me to work with this young man. Jesus gave John his coat, Bible, and home. I do not have that kind of love. The Holy Spirit wept when John shared his story. And the Holy Spirit hung in there with him, delivered him from bondage, and brought him to Christ. Pete was dumbfounded by what he heard and witnessed. Like anyone else, I did not know what to say to a young man who had been raped regularly by a preacher, who was his father. There was nothing I could say. I had to move out of the way and let Christ deliver, save, and heal him.

Let me digress for a moment and give God glory for our campus ministry as a whole. During my tenure as a campus minister at the Ohio State University, we prayed regularly that God would remove those five blocks of clubs where sin was so prevalent, including sexual assault, drug trafficking, vandalism, violence, and rioting. After about four years of concentrated prayer, *every* club on those five blocks was torn down and replaced with more community-friendly establishments (see footnote for news article)[2]. Praise God! Believe big! Believe in a big God, and big things will happen!

This book is about moving out of the way, letting Christ find the least, the last, and the lost, and allowing the Spirit of the living God to arise and set the captives free.

REV. PETER J. BELLINI, PH.D.
November 6, 2021
On our granddaughter Costanza's birthday.

---

2. Gill, "Missing: Campus Bars and Clubs"; Bench, "The High Street Evolution;" and "University Square."

Acknowledgments

I would like to the thank the many students and graduates from United Theological Seminary who I have trained in deliverance and healing ministry. Many of them are pastors on the frontlines of ministry. I have discipled them as spiritual daughters and sons in the faith. Their hunger to learn more and more about the person and work of the Holy Spirit has fueled my teaching ministry and inspired the idea to make my teaching on deliverance accessible in book form.

I would also like the thank my wife Mariuccia, my adult children Aaronne, Paola, and Zac, my granddaughter Costanza, and the rest of my family for their love and support. Throughout the COVID 19 pandemic, we have held house church regularly. They have been the ears that have heard and tested my preaching and teaching, including some of the ideas in this book. I also want to thank my editor Erin McKenzie for her skills and keen eye.

Above all, I thank Christ my Lord for his love for the world and even for me. It was the Father's holy love that sent Jesus to deliver me. Forgiveness of sins and salvation are unfathomable blessings that I will spend an eternity contemplating in praise and thanksgiving. The Lord has given me an unspeakable joy to participate in healing broken hearts, a labor of love of which I will never grow tired. I pray that my service and yours will always be acceptable to the Holy Spirit. Let us fight for the weak and broken, and may God deliver many from the kingdom of darkness. Blessed be God—Father, Son, and Holy Spirit!

Introduction

The title of the book, *The X-Manual,* is taken from the first syllable of the word *exousia,* which is part of the book's subtitle. *Exousia* is the Greek word for authority. *Exousia* is pronounced *ex-oo-see-a,* accent on the '*see.*' The word is used throughout the New Testament. For our purposes, it is used to express the divine authority or right to cast out demons (Luke 10:19—NIV)—"I have given you authority (*exousia*) to trample on snakes and scorpions and to overcome all the power of the enemy; nothing will harm you." Jesus gives us authority to cast out demons. This book is about spiritual authority over evil. *The X-Manual* is a practical handbook for clergy and laity on deliverance and exorcism. Most of the book comes from my nearly four decades of study and experience in deliverance ministry.

Currently, I serve as Professor of Church Renewal and Evangelization in the Heisel Chair at United Theological Seminary, a United Methodist affiliated institution in Dayton, Ohio.[1] I am an ordained United Methodist Elder. Before teaching in seminary, I served in many capacities, including inner city senior pastor, church planter, turnaround pastor, missionary, revivalist, prison minister, and campus evangelist, among other roles. In all these settings, I have ministered in deliverance and healing. As a professor, I hold a bachelor's, master's, and Ph.D., but no one I know has a Ph.D. in deliverance ministry from a legitimately accredited school. Such a degree, to my knowledge, does not exist. I learned from my own study and experience. Most deliverance ministers have likewise.

I read all the best material on the subject from the Bible and the church fathers to today. As a young believer, I went to conferences on healing and

---

1. The church must really be in need if the Methodists are teaching the body of Christ how to cast out demons.

deliverance. I had mentors who taught me as well. I even took the 51-session course on *Demons and Deliverance* from the late Lester Sumrall, the pioneer and apostle of deliverance ministry. No one exhibited the manifest authority to cast out demons like Dr. Sumrall did.

I learned from a variety of sources and instructors. One learns along the way, but most of all, I learned from the Holy Spirit, who has taught me from the beginning about the spirit world, authority, and deliverance. It has been quite the ride. You name it, I saw it and dealt with it. Nothing shocks me anymore. The devil knows his time is short, and so he is desperate. But in the end, Jesus is Lord and has crushed Satan under his feet!

In the first chapter of this book, I describe how I entered deliverance ministry. I was not looking for it. It found me. I never wanted to be a spiritual exterminator. Ever since, deliverance ministry has continued to find me either by chance or by appointment. My calendar of cases is never empty, which is one of the reasons I am writing this book.[2] The harvest is plenty, and the laborers are few (Luke 10:2).

The X-Manual is a follow-up to another book I wrote on deliverance, entitled *UNLEASHED!—The C1–13 Integrative Deliverance Needs Assessment: A Qualitative and Quantitative Probability Indicator.* It's a long title. *Unleashed* was an apologetic or defense of deliverance ministry. I wanted to establish the legitimacy of this type of ministry in the church and world, basing it on biblical and scholarly grounds. *The X-Manual* is not an introduction or defense of deliverance ministry nor an introduction to demonology (see *Unleashed* for an introduction to deliverance). This book assumes you know about demons and deliverance and want to learn to cast them out.

The X-Manual is more of a how-to guide or primer. One reason I wrote the book is that so few understand and/or operate in deliverance ministry. And some who do tend to be unbiblical, extreme, or imbalanced. The reasons are often ignorance, fear, malpractice, and lack of sound training, which I address in chapter two. Nowhere is the church more inadequate or excessive than in deliverance ministry.

My goal was to offer a simple (not simplistic), clear, balanced, biblical, and interdisciplinary training manual from a scholar practitioner. I am currently developing *The X- Seminar* which will be a one-day annual training

---

2. Throughout the year, I receive numerous requests for deliverance from clergy and laity who know someone in need. Sometimes people call me directly for help. However, my case load goes off the charts between September first and November first. This period marks the witching season when concentrated and intentional occult practice is rampant. Some of it is even directed at the church. Witches will go into churches on assignment and pray against the pastor and the people. We need to be aware of the devil's wiles and tactics.

course on deliverance and exorcism. I hope to launch it at the time of publication of this book. The book will be the course manual.

As wickedness has increased in its intensity and creativity, the need for deliverance has increased as well. There are numerous books on the subject. In my opinion, some of these are also insufficient. They are either incomplete, unbiblical, impractical, or imbalanced. However, some high-quality and resourceful material does exist.[3] Let the buyer beware!

It has been said, "Those who can, do. And those who can't, teach." The adage does not apply here. The uniqueness of *The X-Manual* is that it comes from both a scholarly and a practical viewpoint. And the theoretical framework of the book is interdisciplinary, which means, in this case, it works with theology and the hard and soft sciences. The hope is that what is offered is biblical, practical, sound, balanced, effective, and relevant. The reader will be the judge.

Much of my work is academic, meaning I write for the scholarly community. The subject matter is abstract, highly specialized, and abstruse to the average person. Other aspects of my work are written for pastors, leaders, and the graduate students I teach. Nevertheless, this book intentionally has less of an academic edge and is intended for a broader audience. Hopefully, it contains fewer abstract concepts and complex philosophical arguments than my other work and is more accessible. This is not to say that all the ideas will be immediately understood by all, but the overall message and content of the book are geared toward the everyday reader.

It is advantageous for the reader to know upfront the presuppositions and terms used by the author. Christ and his disciples ministered deliverance, and we are called to as well. Deliverance and exorcism ministries are based on the Lord's Prayer: "Lead us not into temptation but deliver us from evil." Satan is real, and so we pray for victory over temptation and deliverance from all forms of evil. The Father also gave us the answer to this prayer. He sent his Son to exercise his authority to deliver people from demonic influence and possession.

There is a difference between the terms "possession" and "degrees of demonic influence." In chapter four, I address the distinction between possession and degrees of demonization or oppression and the controversial question of whether Christians can have a demon. Possession is quite rare. Possession involves complete and total demonic control of human agency or will. A possessed person cannot act freely by their own will in any circumstance. Christians *cannot* be possessed by demon. They are born of and

3. See books on deliverance by Randy Clark, Francis MacNutt, Lester Sumrall, Pablo Bottari, Carlos Annacondia, Charles Kraft, John Eckhardt, and James Goll, among others.

indwelt by the Holy Spirit. Possession is uncommon in general. Most deliverance ministries will never deal with a case of possession.

On the other hand, there can be *degrees of demonization or degrees of influence* by a demon over a person. Demonization or levels of demonic influence are quite common in unbelievers and even in believers. Unbelievers can be oppressed or possessed. Believers cannot be possessed, only oppressed.[4] Deliverance is administered for degrees of demonic influence like oppression. Exorcism is administered for possession when the unbeliever no longer has agency to act freely. Many Spirit-filled deliverance ministries do not use the term "exorcism." They more commonly use the terms "deliverance," "oppression," and "obsession."

With either degrees of demonization or possession, the penultimate goal of demons is to inhabit and manifest their work through a habitation or vessel (human souls and bodies). There is debate about whether demons can inhabit non-agentive objects (that do not have a will): objects like a mask, a statue, or even a house. I speculate that they can. But they still need human agency to manifest from object to person. Their ultimate goal is then to operate through that vessel to steal, kill, and destroy.

The X-Manual recognizes that demons can have an influence on unbelievers and believers, beginning with temptation, leading to sin, and eventually habitual sin or a stronghold, if not resisted and broken. I call these *degrees of demonization*.[5] Though even with degrees of demonization, deliverance is often not necessary. In chapter two, we learn that the biblical and normative way to deal with sin and Satan is to resist the devil and temptation, and Satan will flee from you (James 4:7). Deliverance is *not* needed. Growth in grace and sanctification are worked out not through deliverance but through the cross. When Christ died, he took the sinner (Rom 6:6). Paul commands us to acknowledge that we already died to sin as believers (Rom 6:11). Break the sin, and you break the devil's hold. Keep the sin, and the devil keeps his hold.

So, when the devil, the voice of temptation comes, we submit to God and resist the devil, and he will flee from us (James 4:6–8). In resisting, we acknowledge that we died to sin, and by the Spirit we put to death that

4. The Roman Catholic Church also makes the distinction between possession and degrees of demonization (oppression). The RCC uses the terms "major exorcism" (possession) and "minor exorcism" (deliverance) or liberation prayer. Only a priest by permission from a bishop and using the Rite of Exorcism can administer major exorcism on behalf of the person under possession. However, trained priests and laity can administer deliverance prayer for minor exorcism. See the course "Exorcism and Prayer of Liberation" that is offered by the Sacerdos Institute at the Regina Apostolorum Pontifical Atheneum.

5. Some use similar categories, such as oppression and obsession.

temptation and its power and thus overcome sin and Satan (Rom. 8:13; Col 3:5). We crucify the flesh (Gal 5:24). By the spirit, we put to death the misdeeds of the body and do not yield our bodies to sin but to righteousness (Rom 6:12–19; 8:13). This is the way of the cross. It is the biblical and normative path to victory.

However, every believer does not always have victory over sin. Who is without sin? Some even fall into habitual sin by which Satan establishes a stronghold in their life. There is a degree of demonic influence in their lives that they cannot control or overcome. It often comes in the form of sinful habits or addictions. This believer is not possessed. But an area of their life is under the dominion of sin and the tempter. An attachment has formed. The attachment is to the sin and to the demonic influence that have tempted and seduced the person. The demon does not *possess* them, but through the attachment, the demon has *influence* over them. They become connected, person-sin-demon. They are experiencing a degree of demonic influence or demonization. The word *demonization*, or *daimonizomai* in the Greek, is the New Testament word that sometimes gets wrongly translated as *possession*. *Demonization*, I think, is a better translation, implying degrees or a process of demonic influence. It is not all or nothing.

In *Unleashed* and in this text, I employ four variables or factors to determine the degree of demonization—**generational, duration, frequency, and intensity**. These factors determine to what extent a person is bound (see chapters three and four). The four variables are used in the C_{1-13} instrument, which I developed, to try to determine if someone needs deliverance as a last resort. Sometimes the problem can be solved by a pastor, a small, group, a spiritual director, a recovery group, a healing ministry, an accountability group, a medical doctor, a therapist, or by another professional. But if nothing else seems to work, we invite people to take the C_{1-13} assessment to determine if deliverance is needed. Note that it is not always needed. If deliverance is needed *The X-Manual* will prepare both a deliverance team (X-Team) and a seeker of deliverance for a deliverance session(s).[6]

Here is an overview of the book. Chapter 1 tells the story of how I was first exposed to deliverance ministry. Chapter 2 lays a theological foundation and framework for deliverance. Chapter 3 unpacks the Four Laws of Deliverance that are essential for effective deliverance ministry. Chapter 4

---

6. I make a distinction between an emergency deliverance session and a formal deliverance session that includes preparation and a protocol (the C_{1-13}). Even though an emergency session may at times bypass the lengthy preparation and C_{1-13} protocol due to pressing circumstances, both the emergency session and the formal session will employ the Four Laws of Deliverance, the 5-Step Method, and follow-up involving a renewal of the mind.

prepares both X-Teams and seekers for deliverance, laying out biblical qual-ifications for selecting team members and strategies for an effective session, including: involving prayer, fasting, repentance and forgiveness. Chapter 5 teaches us the proper, caring way to do deliverance with a special sensitivity to pastoral issues that arise. Compassion and care are essential. Chapter 6 explains the deliverance session itself, utilizing the 5-Step Method of deliv-erance. Finally, chapter 7 provides a post-deliverance strategy that involves renewing the mind with the Word of God through *Truth Therapy*.

Let me plainly state that *every* pastor and minister should know how to cast out demons. And *every church* should have a deliverance ministry. Further, *every disciple* should know how to cast our demons (Matt 10:7–10; Mark 16:17; Luke 10:19–20) simply because they are a disciple of Christ. Everyone should be equipped, even if they do not have the gifts of healing. All they need is faith in God's Word. There are no excuses!

Key teachings, like the cross and repentance, are often repeated throughout the book. However, you may come to this text with prior expe-rience. Feel free to skip familiar sections and move ahead to what is needed for your learning and preparation.

Due to the heavy subject matter of the book, I sporadically try to lighten up the tone with some humor. Deliverance is serious business, but it can be overwhelming for some. If it is your type of humor, feel free to laugh. If it is not, then pray for me.

Lesson 1

They're Real!

THIS IS THE BRIEF story of my baptism into deliverance ministry almost four decades ago. My unforeseen initiation into spiritual warfare and deliverance began while I was an open-air campus evangelist. Outdoor preaching was a longstanding tradition at the Ohio State University. Students waited for the warm weather when the campus preachers would arrive. They would eagerly cut class and flock to the Oval (OSU's version of a quad) to hear and heckle the outdated, over-the-top, Bible-banging preachers. Witches, warlocks, and Satanists attended our preaching events and were ready to stir up a firestorm of opposition at the first syllable of the good news.

Back in the 1980s, following the first week of my conversion to Christ, I felt the call to share the gospel with my fellow Buckeyes. I would set out for the Oval daily to preach repentance and faith in Christ for the forgiveness of sins. Old time, revivalistic, fire-baptized, Holy Ghost convicted preaching seemed to stir up the sleeping sinister sprites in those days. Or perhaps the mere oddity of proclaiming the truth outdoors at a major secular university day in and day out in the twentieth century rubbed some the wrong way.

In any case, my colleague and I found ourselves regularly accosted by a group of self-proclaimed witches and Satanists. Two stood out: an older and a younger woman, both self-proclaimed witches. They informed us that they were cursing our ministry and holding black masses for our death (see preface for another such occurrence). What did I do as a young Christian to deserve this attention? I sure felt special. In that season, my friend and I prayed more intensely in our devotional time. We meticulously "put on the armor of God" and interceded with prayers of divine protection. Undisturbed, we continued our regular outdoor routine. John Wesley would have been proud. Nonetheless, the harassment and threats continued, until a startling incident happened to my friend one night. He called me in a panic and related what had occurred. It went something like this:

> I was in my bed trying to fall asleep, when I saw an apparition at the foot of my bed that scared the @#X* out of me. Those two crazy witches who have been praying curses against us appeared in my room. I am not kidding. I freaked out and began to pray. Then, they disappeared. Then shortly after the phone rang. I answered it. I heard a female voice say, "Did you see us?" and the voice began to laugh. It was a shrieking, menacing laugh, along with another cackling female voice in the background. I quickly hung up the phone.

Needless to say, as a young believer, I was a little shaken. For a moment, I questioned the veracity of my colleague's "ghost story." Maybe after hearing the frequent threats, he had become paranoid. Yet, in my spirit, I felt he was truly sharing what he had experienced. His alarmed and frightened tone had a ring of truth to it. I began to pray for discernment as to what our next move would be. They had already planned theirs.

One Sunday, we were aghast to find them at our church parking lot, sitting in their car. They began regularly attending services on Sundays and Wednesdays, especially evening services. We had heard stories of occult members sent on assignment to pray against churches and pastors, but we took those tales lightly. Besides, those sorts of things always happen to other people.

The women managed to fit perfectly into our small, non-denominational, charismatic congregation. It was as if they had rehearsed this methodically, almost like they had performed it before. They were clothed conservatively in dresses or long skirts. They clapped to the praise music and lifted their hands when the music shifted from high praise to deep worship. They warmly shook everyone's hands and hugged every neck when the preacher told the congregation to go and greet each other. During the sermon, the ominous pair would "amen" at the right moment and shout along with the best of them. During ministry time at the altar at the end of service, they would routinely come up front with hands lifted high, ready to receive prayer and even a word from God. The whole charade was eerie. It was something I had never witnessed before or since.

The good people of the church did not suspect anything. In fact, some of our friends in the church rebuked us when we refused to embrace the two "visitors" during greeting time. We were stand-offish with the ghoulish guests. We knew the truth, and they did, too. This went on for weeks. They arrived an hour prior to every service, camped out in their powder blue

Trans-Am. We assumed that they came early to pray against the service, the pastor, and the people of the church. Their part was well rehearsed and their performances stellar . . . until the revivalist came to town.

We were holding revival the next few weeks, as any Spirit-filled church would do in the summer. The evangelist was a powerful African American preacher who was also a seasoned prophetess, fluent in the gifts of the Spirit and dripping with spiritual authority. The sanctuary was packed one evening with many new faces, as is customary during revival season. Our stealth sorceresses blended in well, and the service proceeded as usual. At the conclusion of her preaching, the prophetess began to operate in the word of knowledge. She called out people who had various problems and health issues. Again, this is customary in a Spirit-filled service. However, this time was different for both the prophetess and our two friends.

Following the word of knowledge, both pernicious performers came forward with hands raised, the elder standing in front of her apprentice. Immediately, as the woman of God laid hands on the elder witch, the prophetess boldly exclaimed, "We have two witches in the house!" At that very second, the spellbound, startled woman hit the floor and began to scream with a deep howling shriek. She began to writhe on the ground like a snake. The prophetess followed her to the floor, rebuking the spirit of witchcraft as she commanded the slithering figure to repent and surrender to Christ. The angry woman screamed, "No, no, my power!" and would not yield. My friend and I, enthusiastic, young, and insensitive, were elated and energized, as we shot up out of our pews and ran to the altar behind the fallen witch, almost waiting for the prophetess to retrieve a bucket of water to pour on the two women to melt them, like in *The Wizard of Oz*. (Jesus would have clearly rebuked us. We would later repent for our misguided zeal). For us, the events leading up to this Elijah vs. The Prophets of Baal smack-down was both an adrenaline blitz as well as a comic conclusion.

After lying on the carpet for a few minutes, the elder witch, still screaming and squirming on the floor, managed to get to her wobbly feet. She snatched the wrist of her whimpering apprentice and made a mad dash for the door, never to be seen again. We hoped and prayed that one day those two souls would heed the call to repent of their dark arts and come to Christ. This was my glorious baptism into deliverance.

After nearly four decades of deliverance ministry, I have seen every type of demonic manifestation imaginable. I have heard growling, husky male voices speaking through petite women. I saw one man levitate. I have observed both eyes roll back until only the whites were showing, then smoke coming from the person's mouth. I watched an oppressed woman go into a violent rage and take on a whole team of ushers. I witnessed all the twitching, shaking, hissing, foaming, screaming, and flailing conceivable.

And some still ask, "Are these invisible beings that the Bible calls demons or evil spirits real?" I could tackle this question from a scientific perspective. We can examine complex concepts like causal closure and the hard problem of consciousness, emergence of intangible properties and downward causation, quantum indeterminacy and quantum non-interventionist divine action, and dark matter and dark energy, etc. And I have done so elsewhere. These discussions all challenge the notion of reductionistic physicalism (the idea that only matter exists) and posit the reality of immateriality. Of course, that would not "prove" in a hard, Cartesian sense that invisible beings like demons and angels exist. But if science can entertain the possibility of invisibility and immateriality, theology can possibly entertain angels unaware.

The scriptural notion of an invisible realm of spirit beings cannot be unequivocally ruled out. Science admits invisibility at the least. Where science wants proof, scripture assumes. The biblical worldview assumes a notion of divine and even spirit agency, which is held by most Christian denominations and other world religions—in other words, spirit beings with a will, such as angels and demons. Everything is not provable by hard reason, nor does it have to be. We are justified by faith, not reason. Reason is instrumental in the pursuit of truth, but it works in concert with faith, "faith seeking understanding."

As believers, we take scripture by reasonable faith and believe what it reveals about God, angels, demons, heaven, hell, miracles, the supernatural, and other invisible realities. The Bible calls us to believe in a God we have never seen who saves us from a hell we have never seen. Scripture offers us eternal life in a heaven where we have never been. Reality is not just material or matter. We walk by faith and not by sight, like Moses, "who saw Him who is invisible" (Heb 11:27). Our five senses apprehend the rational, empirical world (the world in front of us). But faith is the sixth sense that apprehends the invisible world. What we believe, though, is not irrational but revealed from the suprarational mind of God.

Colossians 1:16 states that the Son of God created all things "visible and invisible." When we acknowledge the doctrine of creation in holy writ, we are admitting a worldview that encompasses both material and spiritual realities. Scripture is filled with accounts of divine agency working in both the invisible and visible worlds. We also note invisible beings such as angels and demons working in the visible world. On the other hand, we see visible beings, such as women and men, interacting through prayer and worship in the invisible realm, as their prayers are lifted to heaven. The traffic of agency flows both ways.

There is divine-human interaction in the invisible and visible realms, which are interconnected. For example, in Genesis 28:12–13 and John 1:51, "Jacob's ladder" resembles a staircase between the invisible and visible worlds depicting angels descending and ascending from heaven to earth. Angels are ministering the will of God in the world, while demons are seeking to thwart it. In Revelation 12, Michael the archangel casts Satan and the other fallen angels out of an invisible heaven to visible earth. In Luke 10:18, Jesus said that he "saw Satan falling like lightning from heaven" to the earth. Conversely, a good portion of Christ's ministry was "to heal all of those oppressed of the devil."

Scripture is replete with exchanges between the invisible and visible worlds. We observe this in the life of Jesus who spoke to his heavenly Father, was filled with the Spirit beyond measure, was ministered to by angels, healed the sick, worked miracles, raised the dead, and cast out demons. Jesus interacted with spirit beings in the heavens and earthly beings in this world. In fact, Jesus was an exorcist, as New Testament scholar Graham Twelftree reminds us. Jesus cast out demons and commanded his disciples to do likewise.

Was Jesus operating merely out of a premodern worldview? Is the evil that he faced hermeneutical (only in his own interpretation) rather than ontological (real, existing beings)? Was Jesus wrong in his interpretation? Stated another way, was Jesus ministering to the afflicted with healing and exorcism, because the ailments and treatments were interpreted through a pre-modern worldview? And if Jesus were living with our post-enlightenment worldview, would he really cast out demons and lay hands on the sick? Would he instead refer such people to medical professionals, since we know that demons are not real and that no one can supernaturally heal the sick?

Modern interpretations of demonic encounters in the gospels are frequently demythologized or explained in scientific terms as mental disorders or physical illnesses. The assumption is that today we are more enlightened and aware of the exact physical nature of these first-century afflictions. We do not need to resort to demonology.

This line of thinking is problematic. Today, we are *not* aware of the exact neurobiological causes of mental disorders, nor do modern treatments offer "cures"; they merely provide symptomatic relief that attempts to ameliorate one's condition. Similarly, there are many physical diseases that have unknown origins and remain incurable. Of course, that is not to take away the advancements of medical science which has performed its own "miracles" that first-century Palestinians could not have imagined. Simply put, although our biomedical model is the best that science can put forth at this time, it is limited.

In our scientific worldview, if we cannot perceive something with our five senses, then we cannot understand it with reason, and thus we dismiss such things as not real. Simply, we cannot see demons; therefore, they do not exist. On the other hand, this is also not to say that every ailment is demon-caused, including mental disorders. (I parse this and other problems, like multiple levels of causality, in my book *Unleashed!*)

The question remains: does our modern, post-enlightenment worldview, with the advances of medical science, understand what Jesus and his disciples were facing any more than people in the first-century Greco-Roman world? Scientifically, yes, but not exhaustively. Explain a man levitating when going through deliverance. I have seen it. Explain how a person can be delivered instantly of sexual addiction. I prayed for such people. My contention is that perhaps scientism has exorcized demons from its worldview, but it has not exorcized them from the world. Only the Spirit can do that. Science cannot heal the soul of pride, adultery, murder, or any other deadly sin. These are matters of the spirit.

Thus, we still have the problem of spirit or immateriality. Does it exist? Many scientists would say no. Some philosophers, theologians, and scientists would say yes. The scriptures clearly say yes. Remaining modern intangibles and uncertainties related to etiology (the origin of a disease) and cure, sin, and the problem of evil are understood by scripture in terms of broader moral concerns related to spirit. God is Spirit. Angels and demons are spirits. Humans are spiritual beings capable of relating to God. We are made in the image of God. God the Holy Spirit indwells our hearts. The Bible understands the problem of evil and its collateral damage in the world in terms of demonic agency and temptation, human freedom and sin, the universal fall, and redemption in Christ.

Scripture does not have a problem with a spirit worldview, spirit beings, divine and angelic action, supernatural miracles, deliverance from demonic powers. It does not see the need to prove these realities. It assumes a worldview that includes supernatural occurrences, as does the majority worldview outside the West.

The great tradition of the church from the apostles to today also affirms the invisible and visible nature of creation.[1] Many traditions have practiced exorcism and deliverance through their rites; most have incorporated it into their baptismal liturgies. The early and medieval church as a rule ministered

---

1. Twelftree, *In the Name of Jesus*.

exorcism rites.[2] This is illustrated most notably by St. Francis of Assisi.[3] Spiritual warfare against evil spirits was also a standard feature of Puritan sanctification.[4] The scientific revolution and the deism of the enlightenment period challenged the notion of interaction between the supernatural and natural realms. However, revivalists during the age of reason, such as John Wesley, regularly encountered and battled the demonic.[5] Exorcism continues to be a *charism* in the modern church. Roman Catholicism and Eastern Orthodoxy have practiced exorcism rites since their inception.[6] Pentecostal-Charismatic and global Christianity of all stripes recognize deliverance ministry as normative. Along with the witness of the major Christian traditions, I call upon the numerous testimonies of my vast array of colleagues who have ministered in deliverance and add those to my own. Demons are real, alive, and well!

Yet that is not my ultimate point. Above all, Christ on the cross has defeated the power of the devil. We do not fear demons. He has given us his power (*dunamis*) and authority (*exousia*) to set captives free and put the enemy under our feet. The name of this book, *The X-Manual*, refers to the *exousia* we have in Christ to combat and attain victory over the devil. The *X factor*, or the key to victory, is authority, Christ's authority. He has given us his authority to bind and cast out demons. Many are bound and oppressed by deception, witchcraft, the occult, false systems of belief, addictions, trauma, fear, confusion, and other afflictions. They need to be set free. God calls us to do it. Will you?

During the dark times we live in, we need more than ever to revive the healing ministry of deliverance. We will learn four simple laws of deliverance in the next few chapters that will equip us with the weapons we need to set the captives free:

THE FOUR LAWS OF DELIVERANCE

1. The Law of the Cross: The power of sin, death, and the devil were broken and defeated at the cross; it is finished.

2. Daunton-Fear, *Healing in the Early Church.*

3. Forcen and Espi, "Demonic Possessions and Mental Illness," 258–279.

4. Gurnall, *Christian in Complete Armor.*

5. Jennings, *Supernatural Occurrences of John Wesley,* and Webster, *Methodism and the Miraculous.* Many fell "thunderstruck" by the convicting power of God's Word as demons would manifest through them. Through breakthrough prayer, they were delivered of demonic strongholds under Wesley's deliverance ministry.

6. See Appendix B.

2. The Law of the Will: To the degree a person submits to sin/the demonic or Christ, to that degree sin/the demonic or Christ has authority over the person.

3. The Law of True Repentance: True repentance breaks the legal authority that sin and Satan have over an individual.

4. The Law of Authority: Christ gives us power of attorney to use his authority and name to defeat and cast out devils.

Lesson 2

A Theological Foundation for Deliverance

WHY ANOTHER BOOK ON DELIVERANCE?

THERE HAVE BEEN NUMEROUS reasons why deliverance and exorcism have been avoided by the church. I think the top reasons are *ignorance, fear, malpractice,* and *lack of sound training.* By *ignorance,* I mean the lack of understanding concerning several facts. First, the devil is real. Jesus and his disciples dealt with demons. Demons didn't ride out on dinosaurs into extinction. Satan and his friends are still around. Second, he can influence unbelievers and believers to various degrees. Third, the devil is defeated. Fourth, Christ has given us his authority to combat the devil and deliver the captives. Many in the church do not realize that Satan holds unbelievers and many believers captive to sin. Similarly, many believers in the church are not aware that Satan is defeated, and that we have been given power and authority to put him under our feet. Many perish for a lack of knowledge (Hos 4:6).

Fear pertains to the church's attitude toward the demonic. Due to misunderstanding in the church and caricatures and distortions in culture (for example, in popular movies like *The Exorcist*) people believe that the devil is equal to or greater than God. In *The Exorcist,* although the priest called on the Lord to deliver the young girl, God could not deliver her. Satan was too strong. In the end, the priest had to beg the demon to come into him. Once the demon left the girl and entered the priest, the priest jumped out the window believing if he killed himself the girl would be delivered, and the devil defeated.

There are several false ideas portrayed in this movie. One is that the devil is greater than God. Another is that the church, in this case the priest,

9

is powerless against the devil. And finally, that demonized people are without hope. All three of these conclusions are false. However, such portrayals have instilled fear in people. Unbelievers and even believers are afraid of the devil. Some imagine that the devil has equal power to God's, and that they are locked in eternal combat—good versus evil—awaiting a final outcome. This is nonsense! God created and defeated Satan, end of story!

I remember hearing of an incident at a strict conservative Wesleyan Holiness church I used to attend. Like many Wesleyan Holiness churches, the people knew about the Holy Spirit's work in sanctification and healing, but they did not know much about charismatic gifts or deliverance. Most conservative Wesleyan Holiness churches separated themselves from the Pentecostal-Charismatic movement after the Azusa St. revival. Coming out of the Azusa St. revival, classical Pentecostal denominations identified speaking in tongues as the initial evidence of Baptism with the Holy Spirit.[1]

By contrast, the Wesleyan Holiness movement held that entire sanctification was the true evidence of Baptism with the Holy Spirit.[2] As a result, many separated themselves from Pentecostals and their practices, including speaking in tongues and casting out devils. Personally, I believe in both entire sanctification and the supernatural power of the Holy Spirit. Why pick and choose, when you can have it all!

1. Some classical Pentecostal denominations, include The Assemblies of God, Church of God Cleveland, Tennessee, Church of God in Christ, Open Bible Standard Churches, International Church of the Four Square Gospel, International Pentecostal Holiness Church, United Pentecostal Church International, and the Pentecostal Assemblies of the World, among others.

2. Entire sanctification is a doctrine of holiness that was a hallmark of John Wesley's teaching and preaching in early Methodism. It was later redeveloped and promulgated by the various writers, evangelists, and churches within the Wesleyan Holiness movement.

Following regeneration and initial sanctification, believers were convicted of inbred or birth sin that remained in their hearts. Inbred sin prevented Christians from fully walking in perfect love and growth in grace. Wesley believed as one is justified by faith, so also one is sanctified by faith. One can be fully sanctified through faith because it was God's will. God promises entire sanctification in scripture. He is also able to perform what he promises. Further, he can accomplish entire sanctification by faith in an instant. And in that moment the believer can know that the work has been done. See Wesley's sermon "The Scripture Way of Salvation."

Upon believing, the Christian experiences full cleansing of inbred sin by the blood of Jesus, is freed from the inward struggle with the principle of sin, and is filled with the Holy Spirit. The perfect and holy love of God and neighbor are the fruit of the sanctifying experience. Although Wesley did not equate the experience of entire sanctification with the Baptism of the Holy Spirit, his would be successor John Fletcher did make the connection. Likewise, the Wesleyan Holiness movement would follow Fletcher, equating entire sanctification with the Baptism of the Holy Spirit.

At one evening service, the Wesleyan Holiness church had an altar call. People came forward. Workers at the altar began to pray for them. One person began to manifest, roaring with an unnatural growling shriek for a long period of time. Most of the people in the church dashed in a furious frenzy out of the building. They were terrified of the devil. Sadly, that person did not receive deliverance due to fear among God's people. Since Satan is already defeated, and we have been given authority over him, we have no reason to fear. Jesus said in Luke 10:19, "I have given you authority to trample on snakes and scorpions and to overcome all the power of the enemy; nothing will harm you."

Malpractice relates to the unbiblical, unpastoral, abusive, traumatic, sensational, or ineffective ways in which so-called deliverance ministries or lone ranger, self-appointed exorcists have abused the practice. In itself, deliverance can be a frightening experience for the seeker. Imagine coming to terms with the reality that an evil spirit is working through you—a terrifying realization. Deliverance needs to be administered as carefully as surgery.

When I was a young Christian, I had heard about a church that was known for its deliverance ministry. I was a novice in my deliverance apprenticeship and was eager to learn from trusted authorities. In the pre-internet days, it wasn't like I could search for "deliverance and exorcism ministries" on Google or even in the Yellow Pages. You heard by word of mouth. So, I visited that church to observe their deliverance practices.

I was shocked at what I witnessed. They had garbage cans in every room. Nothing alarming there. But they were used for deliverance sessions. Sure, I have noticed that once in a while people get nauseous during sessions and at times want to or do vomit. However, this ministry made vomiting an imperative and a goal. For them, it served as evidence that someone was truly delivered. In other words, if you vomit during the session, then the devil(s) has been expelled. If you had a demon but had not vomited yet, then you were not delivered. So, this church had a vomiting ministry? I am being facetious. They did not call it that.

Yet, the truth is that many deliverance ministries have standardized such unbiblical practices. This is an example of malpractice. Other examples of malpractice that I have observed include, laying hands on private parts of the body, holding deliverance sessions in public during church service, sharing someone's identity or personal information about a deliverance session without consent, extended conversations with demons, forceful and physical aggression toward the seeker, allowing people to be in compromising positions during deliverance, etc. There is no shortage of Sons of Sceva deliverance ministries. We need proper teaching, balance, and deliverance etiquette.

Finally, there is a *lack of sound training*. This lack is ultimately the cause of the other three problems. Pastors and laity are ignorant, fearful, and ineffective because they have not been trained properly. I am not condemning the church. Some of the problem is rooted in the nature of deliverance and exorcism. The Bible does not clearly spell out the details entailed in this ministry. It does not provide a step by step set of instructions on how to cast out demons. We merely get some highlights of Jesus or the disciples in action. Deliverance is portrayed in a narrative, not enumerated in an instruction manual. We have to study the scriptures, glean, and analyze the data, and prayerfully construct a sound theology of deliverance. We are attempting that project here.

Another difficulty is that deliverance deals with evil spirits. Since normally we cannot empirically observe demons directly with our five senses, it becomes problematic when we try to analyze them and make rational conclusions about them. In other words, deliverance tends to be *more of an art than a science*. We cannot scientifically detect, identify, prove, or measure demonic activity or deliverance. This isn't to say that we cannot use the hard or soft sciences to detect or identify *indirectly* that people may be influenced by demonic behavior. Although locating such behavior ultimately in the demonic still begs the question of proof.

In my book *Unleashed*, I deal with the validity of deliverance ministry from a scientific and theological perspective. The best we can do is to operate by the Holy Spirit to detect, identify, and "measure" demonic activity and deliverance *directly*. Then we operate by scripture, discernment, sanctified reason, and the soft sciences like behavioral psychology to detect, identify, and "measure" demonic activity and deliverance *indirectly* through sinful human behavior.

The idea is that behind every sinful act is a demon , at some point, that has tempted and persuaded the person directly or indirectly. Deliverance requires people to be trained and seasoned in walking with the Holy Spirit, discerning the demonic, understanding the demonic through a sound scriptural and theological framework, and practicing good strategies and methods that flow from such a theological framework. The bottom line is that we need sound theology and training to equip the saints in the practice of deliverance. Sound theology begins with the Triune God.

THE TRIUNE LOVE OF GOD

God is Trinity, one divine being in three persons Father, Son, and Holy Spirit. In the beginning God created the heavens and the earth. Why? I believe it is because God is love, and love reaches out to express and share itself. Love is God's nature. So, God created. God freely creates out of love. He does all of his work out of love. In fact, the Trinity is a divine community of shared love. The Father eternally begets the Son out of love that is reciprocated back to the Father. The Father through the Son eternally breathes the Holy Spirit out of divine love, and this love is reciprocated to the Father through the Son. The heart of the Triune God is holy love that is shared, Father, Son and Holy Spirit. And God wants to share this love with us.

Holy and perfect love is at the core of everything God does, within the Trinity and outside the Trinity, in creation and new creation. God brought all things into being out of divine love. And God sent his only Son into the world to save it from itself, all because of perfect love. The Father's heart is to set the captives free and heal the brokenhearted (Ps 147:3). The mission and ministry of his Son Jesus Christ clearly embodies the Father's heart (Isa 61:1–3). Jesus is our Deliverer!

In Luke 4:18 (KJV), Scripture reveals to us that Christ was anointed with the Holy Spirit to "preach the gospel to the poor," "to heal the broken-hearted," "to preach deliverance to the captives," "recovering of sight to the blind," "to set at liberty them that are bruised." The supernatural love of the Father is motivating the work of Christ to deliver us from sin and bondage. His love delivers and heals; it never fails (1 Cor 13:8). Christ accomplished our deliverance on the cross.

Christ promised his disciples that after he finished the work of salvation, he would go to the Father and ask him to send the Holy Spirit in Jesus' name (John 14:26). The Comforter will bear witness to the person and work of Christ. The Spirit will be poured out upon us and fill us with supernatural love that we may share the *agape* that comes from the Father and the Son (John 17:21–23, Rom 5:5 Gal 5:22, 2 Pet 1:4). God's love delivers and heals the brokenhearted, and it welcomes the redeemed into the family of God.

The love of God bears and endures all things (1 Cor 13:7). God's love is not saccharine or our favorite sweetener we use to cover the taste of life's bit-ter seasons. God's love is real, and it is tough. He relentlessly pursues us. No enemy can stand in his way as he is tracking his beloved. His love is stronger than death (Song 8:6). The Son of God left heaven's eternal perfection to come into a broken world, tasting death and hell to find us.

True love fights! Around eight years ago, my brother-in-law Todd was in a horrible motorcycle accident. His right leg and three fingers were sheared off his body. The EMTs found him on the road dead, no response. One of the technicians had been an EMT in Afghanistan during the war. His split-second timing and skill resuscitated Todd's heart. They brought him to the ER. He was in a coma fighting for his life. The doctors did not give him much chance. One doctor said less than 25 percent. Several of his vital organs were shutting down, and he was clotting throughout his body.

We received a call from my sister Sheila. She was rightfully in despair. She informed us that Todd had only a slight chance of surviving. I told her we would make the three-hour drive to the hospital and pray for him. I got off the phone and began to pray. As soon as I began to pray, I felt the power of the Holy Spirit, and he spoke to me Psalm 118:17 that, "He will live and not die and declare what the Lord has done." I knew I had heard from God, and that the Lord would continue to lead me.

When we arrived at the hospital, family and friends were in the waiting room consoling each other. The atmosphere was somber. My sister led me into the ICU room, where Todd lay in a coma, unresponsive. She told us that we could pray, but we had to be quiet per the doctors' orders. Todd was in a precarious place and could not tolerate any loud noise or sudden movement. We agreed.

However, the Spirit of God rose up on the inside of me. God was taking me in a different direction. I did not want to go there, but I had to obey God. My prayer turned from a solemn hush to fiery, booming preaching. God was speaking through me. I was exhorting Todd, "Fight and don't quit. Fight, fight, fight! This is a matter of life and death. Resist the devil and fight, Todd!!!!!" I sounded like Mickey in Rocky V when Rocky was knocked to the ground in a street fight. Rocky has a vision of Micky, who had passed away, yelling at him to get up and fight. To the dismay and shock of everyone in the ICU, I was shouting and coaching Todd to fight. I was on one side of the bed, and Todd's son Nicky was on the other side of the bed.

The doctors, nurses, attendants, and Sheila threw me out of the ICU room. I was somewhat embarrassed, but I knew God was leading me to do what I had done. I shared the Word God gave me with Sheila that Todd would live and not die (Ps 118:17). She had received the same scripture but had her doubts. Todd was in a coma for nearly two months. I had mustered up an intercessory team of several thousand people to pray. To the glory of God, after several surgeries and procedures, Todd came out of the coma alive. He did not remember the accident or anything after that. He told my sister that there was only one thing he remembered, and it was urgent that he speak with me. He said, "Only your brother will understand. Only Pete can explain to me what I saw."

Sheila informed me of Todd's request. I drove to the rehab facility. I walked in and saw Todd in a wheelchair. I gave him a pair of boxing gloves as a gift. Todd recounted to me all that he remembered.

I was lying down. You were on one side of me, and Nicky was
on the other side. I knew I was going to die. I was fading away
toward a great light, but then suddenly, the light faded as well,
and the devil appeared. He was condemning me and telling
me that I would die. But he assured me that if I gave him my
son, he would let me live. I was terrified! Then all of a sudden
out of nowhere, I heard you shouting at me and coaching me
to fight, fight, fight! You instructed me to resist the devil and
were preaching the gospel at me. I began to fight the devil with
everything I had and called out to the Lord for help. The devil
and I wrestled back and forth for what seemed like an eternity.
I finally broke through, and the devil left. At that point I woke
up out of the coma and here I am! You coached me back to life.

Wow!!!!! While in a coma on the edge of life and death and eternity,
Todd saw and heard what was going on in the ICU room, which was really
going on in the Spirit. No further explanation needed. The Lord fought for
Todd. Todd fought for his life, and I was in his corner. Todd fought for his
son and still does today. Love fights. Love is stronger than death.

The healing love of God pursues and fights for us! The Father's love
poured out through the Spirit brings deliverance and victory, for where the
Spirit of the Lord is, there is freedom (2 Cor 3:17). Deliverance is a triune
operation. All three persons of the Trinity work together in deliverance. The
Father sends his liberating love through the Son and the Spirit. The mission
of Christ and the Spirit work in tandem. Christ defeated sin and Satan at the
cross *objectively* in history. It is finished.

And the Spirit bears witness to the *objective* work of Christ by applying
it to our lives *subjectively*, here and now. He downloads Christ's deliverance
to our lives personally, making it real for us. The anointing of the Spirit
breaks the yoke and chains of sin and death in our lives (Isa 10:27). Romans
8:2 declares that "the law of the Spirit of Life in Christ Jesus has set us free
from the law of sin and death." The lifegiving Holy Spirit delivers us from
condemnation and sets us free to experience abundant life.

THE TRIUNE GOD AND ABUNDANT LIFE

The Triune God is also a life-giving God. In Genesis 1:1, God created the
universe and brought all life into being. In 1 John 1:1, the second person of
the Trinity is called the "Word of Life," because he is life, and he gives us life.
In Romans 8:2, the Holy Spirit is called the "Spirit of Life." In the Nicene
Creed, the Spirit is described as "the Lord the Giver of Life." The Lord gives

life and restores life. After humanity succumbed to temptation, sin, and evil, the Lord had a plan of restoration. God sent his only Son to deliver us from the bondage of sin and death and give eternal life.

In John 10:10, Jesus said he came to bring "abundant life." In John 11:25, Christ declared that he is "the resurrection and the life," and reiterates the same claim in John 14:6 as "the way, the truth, and the life." The words he speaks are Spirit and life (John 6:63).

Similarly, the Holy Spirit, who is also called "the Lord," "the Spirit of Life," and "the Spirit of Truth" brings liberty and life to all who are oppressed (2 Cor 3:17). The Spirit regenerates and restores our soul with new life in Christ (John 3). Scripture witnesses throughout to the life of the Triune God, and to God's desire to impart life to all of creation. God's heart is to free us from darkness and death and to grant us divine life (*zoe*).

The Triune God is eternal life in three persons. The Father declares life through his Word and breathes life through the Spirit, as evidenced in creation (Ps 33:6) and the new birth (John 3:5). Through creation and the new creation, we are made partakers of the *same* divine life that is in God (2 Pet 1:4). Nothing less. In God there is fullness of life, life that quenches human thirst. It is living water that springs up to eternal life. Living water heals and makes us whole. The world is seeking such life, but they are blind to its source. The Kingdom of God is infused with abundant life, and Christ is its source (John 1:4; 1 John 5:11–12).

THE KINGDOM OF GOD: THE RULE OF RIGHTEOUSNESS, PEACE, AND JOY

God created all things to bring him glory. He also created all things to participate in his Kingdom and to enjoy fullness of life. His Kingdom is his rule of righteousness. It is where God's Word is the law of the land. In our world today, God's Word is not the law of the land. Often it is not even taken seriously as an option to follow. But God's Kingdom will increase, outlast, and overtake the kingdoms of this world (Rev 11:15). God created all things to participate in his glorious Kingdom.

A prelude to our theology can be summed up in Genesis 1: "In the beginning, God created the heavens and the earth . . . and it was good." Everything was created exactly according to God's will. It was good and fitting for his purposes. The universe was crafted to be the holy temple of God's presence, rule, and work. All things were fashioned in perfect *shalom*, or holy order, ready to fulfill God's kingdom purposes.

The final touches on his masterpiece were man and woman, the crowns of creation. Humanity was made in the image of God, capable of communing and fellowshipping with him. Humanity was given God-capacity. Adam and Eve were shaped in the rational, volitional, moral, and relational image of God. That simply means that God gave humanity a mind, will, emotions, and a spirit to relate to him.

Scripture also indicates in Genesis 1:28 that humanity was made in the *functional* image of God, specifically to be an agent of his righteousness, peace, and joy in the world. Humanity has a divine purpose. We were called to extend God's righteous rule, or dominion, to all creation. Of course, Adam fell. And Christ the King, who is the true image of God, would come and restore God's Kingdom in the world. But originally, God chose our primordial parents to be God's agents of dominion and blessing to all creation.

However, with the fall, Adam and Eve became subject to a foreign, despotic ruler under a tyrannical law. The evil one, Satan, became "the god of this world" (2 Cor 4:4). He rules by the law of sin and death (Rom 8:2). The whole creation has groaned in travail and suffering ever since (Rom 8:22). And the annals of human history record the evil and complicated wickedness that exude from every page under the reign of sin and death. As Paul cried out in Romans 7:24, "Who shall deliver me from this body of death?" Deliverance is the need of the ages. As the angel cried out in search of a deliverer, "Who is worthy?"

Is God's hand too short to save us from sin and death? Can he break the vice grip of pride, greed, envy, lust, gluttony, sloth, and death that choke the soul of the entire human race? One of the elders in heaven responded, "Do not weep! See, the Lion of the tribe of Judah, the Root of David, has triumphed . . . "

Where Adam failed, Christ succeeded. Jesus, the Lion of the Tribe of Judah, the Mighty Warrior, has soundly and forever defeated temptation, sin, guilt, shame, death, the world, and Satan. All of his enemies are his footstool. Christ the King rules and reigns over heaven and earth. Christ is our Overcomer (John 16:33). He is our victorious champion, *Christus Victor* (Christ the Victorious One). On the cross, the King of kings and the Lord of lords destroyed the power of the enemy and delivered his people from the kingdom of darkness and into the kingdom of light.

Christ has established his kingdom of righteousness, peace, and joy (Rom 14:17). Every knee will bow, and every tongue will confess that Jesus Christ is Lord (Phil 2:10–11). Kingdoms and nations will bow before him, and he shall reign forever and ever (Dan 7:13–14; Rev 11:15). He will minister peace and healing to the nations who have spent their years suffering and at war (Ezek 47:12; Rev 22:2). The coming of the Kingdom in its fullness is the culmination of God's work in history. The Lord invites us to participate in his mission of setting the captives free and establishing the Kingdom of God. Christ the King is the Alpha (the start) and Omega (completion) of our deliverance and our deliverance ministry.

THE FALL AND THE LAW OF SIN AND DEATH

God's mission is to establish his Kingdom on earth as it is in heaven (Matt 6:10). Satan's mission statement is to "kill, steal, and destroy." Who is this Satan, this adversary?[3] He was originally named Lucifer (the light bearer) and was debatably responsible for worship in heaven (Ezek 28:13). Satan, a fallen angel, fell when he was lifted up by his own pride (Isa 14, Ezek 28, and Rev 12).[4] He deceived himself that he could ascend to the throne of God.

---

3. He has various names. The most common names, Satan or the devil, mean the adversary (one who opposes) or the slanderer (liar).

4. Like any soldier (2 Tim 2:3) in battle or a fighter in the ring (1 Cor 9:26–27), saints need to know their opponent. Scripture says that the devil is extremely cunning (Gen 3:1; 2 Cor 11:3) and even uses the scriptures (Matt 4:6), false signs and wonders (Mark 13:22; 2 Thess 2:9), pleasure (Prov 5;6:20–35; Rom 1:25–27; 1 Cor 6:9–10; 1 Tim 1:10; 2 Tim 3:4; 2 Pet 2:14), and clever disguises (2 Cor 11:3) to blind people's minds. These tactics are combined with false religion and philosophy, the occult, addictions, and various ideologies in order to lure his prey. The devil traps, binds, and destroys his victims with sophisticated, well-crafted, tailormade lies specifically and personally designed to bait and hook you.

Demons, as former angels, have intelligence and power even in their fallen state. They thoroughly understand and control the intricacies and machinations of sin. They also have a detailed profile of their prey and a track record of which strategies of sin and temptation have worked on you. And thus, their bait is tailormade to entice and trap you (e.g., Proverbs 7). How do we know this? How Satan tempts and attacks the faithful in Scripture, history, and how we are attacked today give us clues about how customized, well-crafted, well-informed, and precise his strategies and tactics are.

Pardon the loose analogy here, though the story is a classic. When I was a teenager in the 1970s in my neighborhood of Little Italy, there was an ongoing war between the organized crime syndicate that ran our neighborhood and Irish gangster Danny Greene who wanted to move in on the family. Greene and his Italian mob partner John Nardi put a serious dent into the family business, territory, and personnel. Eventually, an all-out war erupted with thirty-six bombings occurring in Cleveland in 1976 alone, more than in Beirut that same year during their civil war.

The stalemate was broken when the Cleveland mafia tapped Greene's phone and obtained intelligence. They learned the time and place of Greene's next dentist appointment. They hired two hitmen from out of town to take Greene out with a car bomb, and they did, ending the war. However, the local mob would soon vanish due to sentencing.

The true story was captured in the film, *To Kill an Irishman* (2011). The insider intelligence gave the mafia an upper hand on their enemy. The devil seeks such an advantage on us, but the gifts of the Holy Spirit release discernment, knowledge, and wisdom to the church so that we can have the winning edge.

The attempted overthrow led to a war in Heaven, where Michael the Arch-angel and his armies defeated Satan and the rest of the fallen angels. The accuser and the one-third were then banished to the earth, where they seek to devour its inhabitants. The enemy began his earthly mission of temptation in the Garden of Eden.

Evil as an option for us has been around since the Garden. There, lodged in the possibility of human freewill was the choice to rebel against God's way. God told our first parents to eat freely from the tree of life and live forever under God's blessing. He also warned them of the alternative, the choice of disobedience. The forbidden fruit hanging on the Tree of the Knowledge of Good and Evil represented disobedience to God. In order to partake of the fruit, man and woman would have to turn their backs on God and his blessing and defy his commandment.

God loved Adam and Eve, so he forbade them not to rebel. He cautioned them that such a decision would result in death. As we know, the couple was seduced by the serpent. They were deceived. They believed that the forbidden fruit would be profitable for food and wisdom and would make them like gods. The serpent told them the same lie he had told himself before he fell. It is the same lie he has been telling ever since. The devil has gotten a lot of mileage out of the flim-flam sales pitch, "You will be gods." We were already like God, made in his image. After the fall, we became less like God. Adam and Eve's eyes were opened to sin and death. The law of sin and death has ruled humanity ever since.

Although God gives abundant life freely to all of creation, we resist God's grace and love and turn from his goodness. We refuse to partake of the tree of life but instead indulge from the tree of the knowledge of good and evil. We eagerly choose to be our own gods and obey our own wills. Satan has cunningly seduced humanity to do what is right in its own eyes (Judg 21:25). Proverbs 14:12 instructs us that "there is a way that appears right to human eyes, but in the end, it leads to death." Romans 6:23 declares, "that the wage of sin is death." Sin enslaves us and leads us to death. Death is the "reward" or cost of sin.

In Romans 7, Paul vividly describes in detail how the will is bound and enslaved to sin, no matter how much it desires to do good. When one attempts to do good, one discovers that evil is present. The evil that one does not want to do, one finds oneself doing. Paul recognized the dynamic of how sin enslaves the will; I do what I don't want to do, and I don't do what I want to do. In Romans 7:21 he identified it as a "law" at work within us that counteracts every good intention with an inward response of evil (Gal 5:17). I am sure you have felt this personal civil war inside you between flesh and spirit.

In Romans 8:2, we note that the cost of sin is death, the "law of sin and death." The law of sin and death rules over humanity with an iron fist. No one escapes its unbreakable clutch. Without grace and the power of the Spirit, we cannot overcome the dominion of sin (Rom 6:14).

THE CHOICE IS OURS

Although sin and death act on human behavior with the consistency and power of a law, they do not act alone or deterministically. We have a choice in the matter. We are free to choose. We cannot blame the devil or someone else. The devil didn't make us do it. In fact, we thought he had a wonderful idea and partnered with him. Our will freely cooperates with sin. Sin seduces our will, and we concede. James 1:14–15 clarifies that one is tempted because of his or her own lust, and when one gives into lust, it conceives, and it conceives sin. So, sin is birthed when the tempter is successful at tempting us.

The devil exists, and he tempts. He attempts to lure us away from God into rebellion. Satan tempts our will with the *deceitfulness* of sin (Heb 3:13). Sin blinds and deafens. Sin is seductive, and his witchcraft is captivating. But he does not show his hand. When he tempts you, he does not expose how hideous he is. He does not reveal how treacherous his plan is. He does not disclose the consequences for sin. No, he camouflages sin with a glossy, gold plating that appears real and attractive but is as fraudulent as he is. Originally, you only wanted just a taste, but sin and Satan will take you farther than you intended to go.

True, sin can be pleasurable for a season (Heb 11:25). Satan will let you have enough enjoyment and success to hook you. But sin will take you farther than you want to go. You will find yourself believing and doing things that you had never planned to when you first started doing business with the devil. Eventually, the devil will take away the pleasure and replace it with bondage, torment, emptiness, and heartache Once sin drains and sucks the life out of you, Satan comes back to collect. Now, it is time to pay the piper. And it will not be pretty. The enemy will imprison you in chains to pay off your debt for the rest of eternity. He will no longer work for you. Now, you work for him, and he is a cruel taskmaster.

So, intercept the devil's schemes at the temptation phase, which is spiritual warfare. Beware and be vigilant. His insidious voice subtly and frequently visits our ears to allure and antagonize us. The voice of temptation was present at creation and in the first choices made, as our original parents were seduced by the evil one to disobey God. Even our Lord, who was fully divine and also fully human, was tempted as he walked the earth, though he did not yield to temptation. Satan tried to lure Christ away from the will of the Father while he was in the desert, through the opposition of the religious leaders, through the unbelief of the people, and through suffering in the garden of Gethsemane and on the cross. If the devil tempted Christ, you can be sure that he will tempt you. Christ was tempted as any person, but he was without sin (Heb 4:15). And scripture indicates that it is not a sin to be tempted.

How does sin seem to have its way so easily with us? Why are we so readily given in to sin? Sin is able to allure us because of our temptable human nature. We are weak, limited, and susceptible. And we have been given the overwhelming and complicated freedom and responsibility to choose. God does not pre-program us to obey. Since we have freedom to choose, the enemy tries to seduce us to choose against God. He plays off our natural human needs that were meant to be fulfilled in God's order. The devil tempts us to fulfill them in a way that is out of God's plan, leading to disorder and chaos.

The devil overplays our needs. The psychologist Abraham Maslow identified our needs as psychological, safety, social (love and belonging), esteem, knowledge, aesthetic, and self-actualization. As humans we have needs that, when rightly ordered by God's will, enable us to live a fruitful life of purpose and meaning. Take our passions, for example. God created us to be capable of passion or desire. However, our passions can be attracted to all types of stimulation, even sinful stimulation. At times, such stimulation can be overwhelming and overpowering. That is why our passions were meant to be subject to Kingdom order.

But when passions are not subject to Kingdom order, they become sinful and can lead us to destruction. Another God-given need is for companionship. Scripture lays the guidelines for lifelong covenantal companionship within the context of marriage between a man and a woman. The needs and passion we have for companionship, attraction, reproduction, and intimacy are drives given to us by God, not the devil. In their proper order and place, they are good and holy. Keep the fire in the fireplace. It is productive. Out of the fireplace, fire will burn the house down.

Outside of God's order, these pursuits become self-serving, divisive, self-destructive, and sinful. Pleasure and people become objectified. The bond of love that holds each person faithful to the other may be easily broken when marriage is not held as a holy covenant from God. The birthing and raising of children without the resources of a stable family may also be detrimental to parenting. God has a distinct purpose for marriage and family. However, in a fallen world, marriage and family structures can experience the same destructive patterns as relationships outside of marriage. Divorce and dysfunction occur in Christian homes as well as non-Christian homes.

These concerns and others arise when companionship or any other God-given need or capacity is pursued outside of the purpose and order of God. God created us in his image with agency and the choice to follow his way or our own way. This choice is God's gift to us and must be strongly factored into any analysis of deliverance. We often make choices that misuse our freedom and fall outside of God's order.

We can make grave choices of obedience or disobedience, life or death (Deut 30:19–20). We can choose to open the door to God's reign or the reign of sin and Satan. When Christ comes to deliver us out of the kingdom of darkness and into the Kingdom of light, he liberates our will from the power of sin so that we can choose to obey God's will. He defeats both sin and Satan. With evil defeated and judged, the world is being restored to God's proper order.

Thus, both sin and Satan need to be judged and defeated. Where humanity failed, Christ succeeded. Jesus judged and defeated sin and Satan on the cross. Jesus chose to obey the Father and overcame temptation by the power of the Holy Spirit (John 12:31). On the cross, he defeated sin, death, and the devil on our behalf, so we may be delivered and walk in victory. On the cross (John 19:30) Jesus declared, "It is finished." He meant the power of sin, death, and the devil is finished. At the cross, the power of evil is destroyed. The finished work of the cross is truly our basis for deliverance and victory.

THE CROSS: THE WAY OF THE CROSS IS GOD'S WAY OF DELIVERANCE

God is a Deliverer. Historically, he has consistently set his people free from sin and oppression. After the fall, the Lord revealed his plan to deliver and save the human race through Eve's seed, the Messiah Jesus Christ (Gen 3:15). In Genesis 6:5, when humanity was steeped in wickedness, and the thoughts of their hearts were only fixed on evil, the Lord told Noah to build an ark. The Lord provided an opportunity for all to be delivered from sin and the impending judgment. Later, God raised up Moses to deliver his people from the tyrannical hand of pharaoh and the bondage of slavery in Egypt. Still later, God would deliver his people from exile in Babylon.

These are only a few scriptural examples of God's deliverance. And of course, the great and final deliverance was wrought at the cross by Jesus Christ, the Son of God. *Christus Victor*, Christ the Victor, delivered humanity from sin and death and defeated the power of the devil through the power of the cross. Our God is a deliverer, and he has commissioned us to participate in his ministry of deliverance (Matt 10:7–8).

Deliverance begins and ends at the cross. There, Christ defeated sin, death, and Satan. Law #1 of our four laws of deliverance is The Law of the Cross, that Satan was already defeated at the cross. "It is finished" (John 19:30). The use of the term, "the cross" or the "work of the cross" in this context is shorthand for the death, burial, resurrection, and ascension of Jesus Christ, and all that these events theologically entail. Christ's work on the cross is the means by which God has dealt with sin, death, Satan, and all evil. He took sin and death in his own body and destroyed its power, so that we may be free from its tyranny (Rom 8:3). Deliverance begins and ends at the cross. The basis, authority, and power for all exorcism and deliverance, either general or specialized, stems from the cross. If we are to be effective in spiritual warfare and deliverance ministry, we must forever settle this fact in our hearts and minds.

IT IS FINISHED

Victory in deliverance ministry over sin and the devil is grounded *solely* in the finished work of Calvary, not in our practices, strategies, ability, experience, thoughts, or feelings. In deliverance, our eyes need to be fixed on Christ the alpha and omega of our faith (Heb 12:2).

Satan has already been defeated at the cross. His power was destroyed when Christ died on the cross (Heb 2:14, 1 John 3:8). This fact is an objective, finished, absolute fact. In John 19:30, Jesus cried out, "It is finished!" What did he mean? Sin is finished. Death is finished. Satan is finished. The power of the world is finished. The work of salvation is finished. We must see that Satan has already been defeated. That is our starting point. All that we are called to do is enforce and implement what has been finished at the cross.

But, sin, death, the world, and Satan *seem* to be alive and well. "They do not *seem* finished," you may say. For those who have accepted and walk in Christ's finished work of the cross, the power of sin, death, the world, and Satan *are* finished. For unbelievers and believers who do not know their full authority in Christ, these powers are still alive, well, and active, using deception to keep people in bondage.

Like the Roman church in Romans 6:3, many do not know that they have died to sin. The word "died" in this verse is in the past tense. It had *already* happened. But the god of this world blinds our minds from seeing the full light of Romans 6. The work has been done. The gospel is centered on

Jesus Christ and his cross, not on my destiny and prosperity, as some would have it. The cross alone is our solid basis for deliverance and exorcism. It is imperative to be utterly convicted that when you begin a deliverance session that you are beginning from a place of victory. You are not struggling to attain victory. You start with victory. The battle has already been won!

ROMANS 6—THE KEY[5]

Why is it, though, that many do not receive victory? Why are so many defeated by sin? Because often, believers do not understand the cross. They wear it around their necks. They see it hanging in their sanctuaries. But still they do not know what really happened at the cross *objectively*. And often they have not received *subjectively* through the Holy Spirit what happened at the cross. I encourage you to read Romans 6 several times carefully.

It is noteworthy that the doctrines of the cross and deliverance from sin, found in Romans 6, were the leading teachings that fueled the great Welsh Revival, one of the greatest revivals in history. The Welsh Revival also ignited the powerful Azusa St. Revival. I hope that is motivation to get these teachings into your heart. I will frequently hammer these teachings home throughout this book. Let us examine these two essential teachings.

Remember, *dead people are delivered people*. We died with Christ, so that our bodies will no longer be controlled by sin (Rom 6:6). Whoever is dead is free from sin (Rom 6:7). This is a finished fact that we need to believe and receive. The cross is the *objective* ground for deliverance and victory, while the work of the Spirit based on the cross is the *subjective* implementation and manifestation of deliverance and victory. *Objective* here means outside and apart from us. It is a fact independent of us. It is not based on my experience or feelings.

Jesus died for our sins as a historical fact, regardless of our experience. It was accomplished in history. It is finished. When Jesus died for our sins, he also took the *sinner* with him to the cross. We experience this objective reality subjectively once we believe. *Subjective* here means a reality that we experience personally. When we believe the gospel, the Spirit applies what has occurred objectively in history to our hearts subjectively. We personally experience death to the old self.

Consider the founder of Methodism, John Wesley. He grew up in a devout Christian home. He understood Christianity biblically, doctrinally,

---

5. For a thorough and practical exposition of Romans chapter 6, two of my favorites are Lloyd-Jones, D. Martyn, *Romans: The New Man*, and Jessie Penn-Lewis, *The Centrality of the Cross*.

and historically. He knew the faith as an objective fact. Though when asked by a Moravian Christian if he knew Jesus Christ, Wesley replied, "I know he is the Saviour of the world." The Moravian quickly responded, "But do you know He has saved you?" "I hope He died to save me," Wesley said. "But do you know yourself?" the Moravian pressed. "I do," said Wesley. Wesley later confessed, "But, I fear those were vain words."[6]

Wesley understood Christianity as an objective fact on paper, but he had never experienced forgiveness and assurance subjectively in his heart. In other words, he knew the menu inside and out but never ordered the food and ate it. He never tasted personally that the Lord was good until his Aldersgate Experience on May 24, 1738. He then experienced forgiveness and assurance.[7] At that point, what he knew objectively, he also came to know subjectively as an experience that would strangely warm his heart. Wesley penned in his journal, "I felt my heart strangely warmed. I felt I did trust in Christ, Christ alone for salvation, and an assurance was given me that he had taken away my sins, even mine, and saved me from the law of sin and death."[8] Wesley's knowledge of forgiveness moved from objective to subjective.

The Spirit works from the objective ground of the cross and applies the experience of deliverance and victory to our lives. The Spirit works in unison with the cross. What Jesus did on the cross, the Spirit applies to our hearts. He bears witness and implements, or puts into effect, the work of the cross in our lives. The Spirit makes the cross real to us. He lifts it off the pages of history and scripture and applies it to our heart. The Spirit leads us to Christ; that is the Spirit's ministry. The Spirit leads us to the cross. He executes this ministry as the Spirit of Truth. He leads us and guides us into truth about our sin, truth about Christ, and truth about our need for a Savior.

The Holy Spirit convicts us of sin, righteousness, and judgment and leads us to Christ as our deliverer from sin (John 16:8). The Spirit gently but firmly points out our sin and points to Christ. It is often a still, small, but firm voice deep in our heart. In leading us to Christ, the Holy Spirit leads us to the cross of Christ, where God has destroyed the power of sin and death. Jesus not only took our sins, but he also took you to the cross. He took us. I died with Christ. You died with Christ. We died on that cross two thousand years ago. "Died" is *past* tense. It is already done.

6. Curnock, *Journal of John Wesley*, 151.

7. Wesley scholars tediously debate the interpretation of Wesley's Aldersgate experience. Was the experience for salvation, assurance of salvation, entire sanctification, or a moment of deeper growth in his salvation journey?

8. Curnock, *Journal of John Wesley*, 475–476.

Romans 6:6 declares that "the old self *was crucified* with Christ, so that sin's power would be destroyed." Stop struggling in your own strength with sin. We died to sin. The cross is the parking place for your flesh. Leave it there. The Spirit reveals the power of Romans 6 to our hearts: When Christ died, we died. When Christ was buried, we were buried. When Christ resurrected, we resurrected. When Christ ascended, we ascended and are seated with him in heavenly places (Eph 1:20). There, our enemies are his footstool (Heb 10:13).

HOW IS THIS POSSIBLE?

Now, you may ask, "What does the Bible mean that 'I already died with Christ'—in what way? I, me, my body, is still alive." Here is my best biblical explanation of what is called our union with Christ. When Christ died on the cross, he took our sins and the sinner (me and you). Our old sinful self (whom we used to be before Christ in Adam) died with Christ, so that we can resurrect with Christ as a new person. We are a new person but remain in an old body awaiting our death and resurrection. We are like a new butterfly that is still in the cocoon, waiting to burst free and spread our wings.

God takes away our sin and our old sinful self. Otherwise, what is the sense of just removing the sins, if we are the same old person? We will go back to sinning again. What is the sense of a criminal serving time in prison for his crimes, if he is not penitent, rehabilitated, and reformed as a citizen? Sure, he paid the price, and did the time for his crimes, but if he does not come out a new person, then he will leave prison only to commit the same and maybe worse crimes. If he wants to be a reformed law-abiding citizen, then crime *and* criminal must be dealt with entirely. Jesus paid the price for sin and served our sentence of death, but he wants to deal with the sinner too. On the cross the old sinner dies, and a new person is risen!

The cross of Christ deals with both sins and sinner. So, now we know *what* dies—our old sinful self. We know *where* the old self died—on the cross. We know *when* the old self died—over two thousand years ago. Scripture informs us of these facts, and we believe God at his Word. But Scripture does not tell us fully *how* we died. Yes, we died by co-crucifixion like Paul says in Galatians 2:20. The old self no longer lives, but instead Christ lives in us. But how did I die when I (my body) am still here?

The old sinful "you" died (crucified with Christ). And a new "you" has been risen with Christ (yet I live). You have already experienced the resurrection on the inside (Eph 2:7), even though you remain in your old body. The old body remains susceptible and temptable to sin as long as it is alive.

The new man or woman resides in the same old body, a body of death (Rom 7:24). And you will be in the old body until you die physically.

For now, the inner (new) person is being renewed daily (2 Cor 4:16), but you are in the same body that is being made alive and waiting to be made fully alive (Rom 8:11). So, we have this tension or overlap between the old and the new. We are fully new in Christ, but we are in process, anticipating our new body. The new redeemed body is given in glory after the old (this) body dies (Rom 8:23).

Now, our task is to be led by the Spirit and not our flesh. By the Spirit, we need to put to death the old body's desires to return to sin (Rom 8:13). We must walk in the Spirit and be spiritually minded or let the Spirit dominate our mind, will, and emotions, so we will not walk in the flesh and fulfill its lusts (Rom 8:5–6; Gal 5:16–17). This is a daily enterprise.

Ultimately, Christ's identification with our old life and our co-death with him are a mystery. Since sin is not a physical substance and neither is my old self, it is difficult to imagine that our sins and the sinner died with Christ. My old body is still here. As a theologian, I can attempt to speculate and explain our union with Christ, but in the end, it is a divine mystery that Scripture declares, and we accept by faith. Our co-death with Christ is a spiritual reality that we take by faith. But one day faith will be sight, if we are faithful and endure unto the end. One, day, we will physically die. One day, we will behold the redemption of our bodies (Rom 8:23).

As believers, we will *physically* die *in* Christ. This is the final realization of what we believed all along—that we died with Christ. What was once a spiritual reality received by faith will then become a reality by sight, the redemption of our bodies. Faith becomes sight! We will receive a new, glorified body, then it will be fully evident that we died with Christ and have been raised a new creation. However, until faith becomes sight, the Spirit leads us on the road to Calvary, where we daily realize what it means to die with Christ (Rom 6:11–18).

AN OBJECTIVE AND A SUBJECTIVE REALITY

The Holy Spirit is the agent of divine experience. What that simply means is that the Holy Spirit makes the Christian life real and true in us. He is the Spirit of truth and revelation. Salvation is not just something that occurred a long time ago on the pages of the Bible. What happened to the disciples in the Bible is now happening to me because of the Holy Spirit.

The work of the Spirit makes this objective truth (we died with Christ) a subjective reality in our life. We experience a real separation from sin. And we experience a real separation from who we used to be (our old life). The Spirit calls and empowers us to surrender everything and to come and die with Christ on the cross. We acknowledge that we are already dead to sin (Rom 6:11). But even though we are dead to sin, we still live in a body that can be tempted. And we still have free will, which can go backwards and choose to sin again.

So, in acknowledging that we died to sin, we need to keep that commitment and position, resist temptation, and put to death the power of sin that tempts us. In this way, sin will not gain dominion over us again. And Satan will have no power over us. Romans 8:13 and Colossians 3:5 instruct us "to kill" the power of sin by the power of the Spirit, when sin tries to tempt us again. Remember that you already died to sin and are a new creation in Christ. Do not go back and roll in the mud of sin again. You are not what you used to be. Your identity has changed. You are a new creation in Christ.

You may be asking, what does it mean to die when you are still alive? "To die" in a practical sense means that we are no longer alive or receptive to the old life of sin. Our heart no longer beats, and our lungs no longer breathe for what used to tempt us. Like a body in a tomb, we are dead to the temptations around us. We are no longer alive to or moved by pride, lust, greed, jealousy, envy, selfishness, image, anger, deception, and the rest. We are alive to Christ and moved by the Spirit. We surrender daily to the Spirit as he leads us to Christ and the cross.

When we fully surrender everything to Christ, then the Spirit joins us with Christ, and we are united in his death. Daily, the Spirit leads us to die more deeply and thoroughly into Christ's death. We participate in his suffering and become more like him in his death, so that we can know the power of his resurrection (Phil 3:10).

Not only does the Spirit lead us to die with Christ on the cross when we first come to Jesus, but he also leads us to deny ourselves daily, take up our cross, and follow Christ (Luke 9:23). Our minds and bodies must be subjected to the law and rule of the Spirit of Life. Where our will goes against God's will, we must say no to self and yes to God. We die daily to our own will. We are joined moment by moment to die a deeper death in order to rise moment by moment to a higher life in Christ.

We are called to put to death the sinful practices of the flesh and put on the new person in Christ (Rom 8:13; Eph 4:24–26; Col 3:5). Romans 6:5 indicates that "we have been united in his death." The verb is in the perfect tense, indicating completed action in the past with ongoing results. We died to sin, but the effect of that death has continuing results in our daily walk by "mortifying the flesh" and "walking in the Spirit." God wants to purify us in his refiner's fire (Mal 3:1–3; Rev 3:18).

The pattern of death and resurrection is a daily walk and part of a larger journey that will lead us not only to a victorious life in the Spirit here in this world but also to final victory in the world to come. One day we will witness the redemption of our bodies and the redemption of all things, which is the ultimate deliverance.

SIN AND SATAN ARE JUDGED AT THE CROSS

As we have reiterated, on the cross our sin is condemned in Christ's flesh (Rom 8:3). Jesus put sin to death in his body, and he also judged it. Sin has been condemned. Additionally, the power of the devil has been destroyed at the cross (Heb 2:14). When Jesus died, death could not hold him (Acts 2:24). He broke its grip. Jesus conquered death by death, as the Eastern Orthodox Easter liturgy proclaims. He defeated death at its own game, and thus stripped Satan of his power. John 16:11 declares that "the prince of darkness has been judged." Christ's death was a judgment of both sin and Satan (John 12:31). He "disarmed the spiritual rulers and authorities. He shamed them publicly by his victory over them on the cross" (Col 2:15 NLT).

Finally, after taking captivity captive, he took the keys of hell and death and is waiting for the end of time when he will administer Satan's eternal sentence in the lake of fire. Hell and death will be thrown in there as well (Rev 20:10, 14). Thus, the cross put an end to the power of sin, death, hell, and Satan. Good theology brings good results. Take a moment to fix it in your mind's eye that sin and the devil were judged and defeated on the cross. Remember saints, the devil is a defeated foe, awaiting his final sentencing.

THE CONNECTION BETWEEN SIN AND DEMONS

Some may ask, "I get the sin part, but I do not get why a person may need to be delivered from a demon. Why? What is the connection between sin and Satan? When I sin, why do I have to have Satan cast out?" Many teachers who do not believe in deliverance claim that sinning does not necessitate deliverance from a demon. Committing a sin does not mean that you have a demon. But if you continue to sin, then you may end up having a demon.

Most Christians know that a believer can have sin in their heart. Yet they struggle to comprehend that a believer can be under the influence of a demon to the point that they need deliverance. Not every sin committed calls for a demon to be cast out. But continual sinning in an area may require deliverance from the demonic.[9]

The premise we are establishing is that behind every sinful act is a demon that has tempted and/or influenced the person. We are temptable by nature because we are human. Our weak and susceptible nature is like a wick that catches the fire of temptation. But often it is the devil who lights the wick of temptation that sets off the bomb of sin. Satan is the tempter behind the sin (Gen 3:1; Job 1–2; Matt 4; Luke 22:3, 31; Rev 12:9).

The early church understood the connection between sin and demonic influence. That is why catechumens, or young believers in training, went through an exorcism rite prior to baptism. In that rite, they renounced sin and the powers of darkness. The priest would pray prayers of deliverance over them to set the catechumens free from the devil. The sacrament of baptism was connected to the forgiveness of sin. But the rite of exorcism dealt with the devil and his power over the person. Both sin and the demonic need to be addressed. A remnant of that exorcism rite remains in the baptismal liturgy of many Christian traditions.

Early on, the church made the connection between sin and the demonic. Simply, Satan is the author of temptation, and temptation can lead to sin. Continued sin can lead to demonic attachment. At that point, the devil is no longer resisted but stays attached to the flesh. The devil's assignment is to control you through sin, where sin is the chain that is attached to you on one end and the devil on the other. Satan is hunting for souls, and sin is his bait.

The work of the devil is the device behind all temptation and sin, linking sin with the demonic.[10] The two are connected. When you sin, you get

---

9. It is also important to note that the devil can be connected, at times, to sickness, though every sickness does not entail having a demon (Luke 8:2; Acts 10:38).

10. We can be tempted by our own fallen flesh as well as by the devil (James 1:14). However, I believe indirectly or directly at some point the flesh was tempted by the devil regarding that particular sin. Once the enemy gets in someone's mind, the flesh can be taught how to be tempted all on its own. The flesh learns to feed itself. So, Satan may not be directly involved in *every* temptation, but I believe that he is either directly or indirectly, and either immediately or remotely, connected to a particular temptation and sin.

Satan is the father of lies (John 8:44), and all temptation is a lie; therefore, the enemy is directly or indirectly and immediately or remotely connected with temptation and sin. 1 John 3:8 states, "The one who does what is sinful is of the devil, because the devil has been sinning from the beginning. The reason the Son of God appeared was to destroy the devil's work" (NIV). When we sin, it connects us to the enemy, directly or indirectly. So directly or indirectly all temptation and sin find is connected to the work of the enemy. Nonetheless, we are directly responsible for how we respond to temptation.

the devil too; it's a buy-one-get-one-free rip off, a two-for-one. This is the reason why a person who continues in sin will need deliverance from the demonic. Sin can open the door to the demonic that in turn creates the need for deliverance from the demonic. Put another way, when one submits to sin, one is submitting to the influence of the devil. Some are even worshiping the devil unaware.[11]

The devil is the tempter. The devil is the voice and power behind temptation. Temptation is the seductive bait that lures one to sin. The means of temptation or the bait of sin are "doors" that the devil crouches behind waiting to enter into the human soul. He enters in when someone opens the doors to sin (Gen 4:7). *The Doors* are not just a rock group from the 1960s. Through the doors of sin, Satan gains influence in people's lives. We need to be aware of the doors so that we do not open them. An unbridled and impulsive spirit of curiosity always wants to know what is behind door number one when the devil comes to play "Let's Make a Deal." Never deal with the devil. He always deals from the bottom of the deck!

Put to death carnal curiosity! It is imperative that we recognize when we are flirting with sin, then we are flirting with the devil. The sin is merely a door for the devil to step through and enter into one's life. Sin is how the devil influences our lives. His desire is to control us. If the person is no longer able to resist in that area of sin, then an attachment is formed. The attachment is both to the sin and to the influence of the demon that has tempted and seduced. The person needs deliverance at that point. The person can be an unbeliever or a believer in Christ. The devil does not care.

---

11. Examine 1 Corinthians 10:20. Paul told the Corinthians that when they were sacrificing to an idol, they were not only committing the sin of idolatry. He made it clear that they were making an offering to demons. They were partaking of the cup and table of demons (1 Cor 1:21). Further, they were fellowshipping with and worshiping demons through their sin. Some sin is not merely transgression against God, but also demon worship. Sin is actually submission to the demon behind the temptation and the sin.

When Jesus was tempted by the devil (Matt 4), Satan tempted Jesus to bow down and worship him. The temptation of idolatry was twofold, worship a false god and worship the devil, who is the false god. Of course, Jesus resisted the sin of idolatry on both counts. But it is evident that sin can lead not only to demonic influence but also to demon worship.

Many religious, occultic, and sexual practices today are nothing less than demon worship. Satan is the god of this world (2 Cor 4:4; 1 John 5:19; Rev 12:9); many worship him directly and fully aware, and many more worship him indirectly and unaware.

CAN A BELIEVER HAVE A DEMON?

"Can a believer *have* a demon?" is a tricky question. It depends on what we mean by "have?" Phrased the opposite way, "Can a demon *have* or own a Christian?" The answer is no. A Christian cannot be *possessed* by a demon. However, a Christian can be *influenced* by a demon beginning with temptation that leads to sin. Further, ongoing sin can lead to oppression and a stronghold or a demonic attachment in an area of one's life. A believer can *have* demonic influence over them, even an attachment to their flesh. We do not have to look far for two examples—the twelve disciples. They were called and chosen by Jesus. They preached and taught the gospel. They worked miracles, and they followed Christ. But Satan had an influence over Peter and Judas.

Peter told Christ he did not have to go to the cross. Jesus knew Satan was speaking through Peter (Matt 16:23, Mark 8:33, Luke 4:8). He was manifesting. This was the same guy who had just said, "You are the Christ, the Son of the living God" (Matt 16:16). Peter had a spirit of fear, and Satan spoke through him. He was not possessed, but the devil clearly had a degree of influence on him. He spoke through Peter, taking control of his thoughts and his mouth in that moment. Jesus had to rebuke the devil from Peter. Satan had an influence over Peter's tendency to fear and please people (Matt 16:23; Luke 16:15). The devil came through that weak area or crack in Peter's soul.

Consider Judas. He was one of the twelve. But he was a devil (John 6:70). Was he always a devil or was he predestined to be a devil, as has been interpreted by some (John 17:12)? Aside from the Calvinist vs. Wesleyan-Arminianism debate on predestination, it is not fully clear whether Judas chose to be a devil or God predestined him to be one. As a Wesleyan, I believe Judas chose that lot.[12] The Father did not predestine his decision. Christ did not control Judas' decision either. He had divine foreknowledge that Judas would choose to be the betrayer, who scripture had prophesied (Ps 41:9; 109:8; John 17:12). But foreknowledge is not predestination, nor does it prevent freedom of choice.

In any case, Judas was one of the twelve who preached Christ and worked miracles. Christ announced to the disciples that their names were written in heaven, indicating that the twelve disciples were believers (Luke 10:20). Nonetheless, Satan entered into Judas and used him to betray Christ (Luke 22:3; John 13:2, 27). The devil, the opportunist (Luke 4:13), saw an

---

12. I am assuming the Wesleyan-Arminian position after years of study on the subject. However, the debate continues. See Olson, *Against Calvinism*, and Walls and Dongell, *Why I Am Not a Calvinist*, among others.

opportunity to enter Judas through a crack in his soul, his weakness for greed and unfaithfulness. Satan attached his will to Judas' flesh and used him as an instrument to accomplish his purposes.

Jesus even told the religious leaders of his day that they were the children of the devil (John 8:44). It is noteworthy that many of the demons Christ cast out were in God's house (Mark 1:23, 39; Luke 4:33). Randy Clark cites two other cases in which believers needed deliverance: the woman disabled for eighteen years (Luke 13:10–17) and the Syrophoenician woman's daughter (Mark 7:24–30).[13] Further, my countless experiences and those of other deliverance ministers confirm that believers can have demonic attachments that require deliverance.

THE CROSS IS THE STANDARD WAY

So, we know that a believer can be influenced by a demon. How do we deal with demons that influence believers? There are two ways for believers to deal with the demonic in their life: the cross and casting out demons. The first is the cross; live the crucified life. Walk as dead people to sin. *Dead people do not sin.* We deny ourselves and carry our cross. The cross is a symbol of sacrifice and death. It is the place where we die. Where our will crosses God's will, that is where we need to die and say, "Not my will, but your will be done" (Luke 22:42). Die in the fires of sanctification (Mal 3:1–3; Rev 3:18). Romans 12:1–2 calls us to be "living sacrifices," meaning we die as we live, and we live as we die. Walk as the living dead. Of course, dying is not pleasant. But for Christians, there are only two real choices: die quick and easy or die slow and hard.

The way of the cross is the *normative* means of sanctification. Our union with the death, burial, and resurrection of Christ is the means of our salvation. It is the scriptural method for dealing with sin and the devil. When we die to sin, Satan has no power over us. Like Christ, in John 14:30, we can say that the prince of this world "has no hold over me."

Satan's curse is to crawl on the ground and eat dust (Gen 3:14). Our flesh is made of dust (Gen 3:19). So, Satan feeds off our flesh, the dust. Don't feed the snakes. Crucify the flesh and starve the devil. Thus, the way of the cross is the standard means of dealing with the devil. This is the Law of Deliverance #1—The Law of the Cross.

13. Clark, *Biblical Guidebook to Deliverance*, 53–55, and Clinton *Three Crucial Questions*, 73–142.

DELIVERANCE ONLY IF NECESSARY

The second way we deal with the devil is through deliverance, which is to cast out the devil. It is not the normative or preferred way. God prefers that we defeat the devil at the door of temptation, denying him a foothold. However, there may be unsanctified areas in a believer that they have not conquered yet. Someone may be struggling with an addiction or an old habit that brings them into sin. Remember, behind every sin is a devil that offers the sin through temptation. The individual is submitting his/her will to the power of sin and the tempter. This is the Law of Deliverance #2—The Law of the Will. *To the degree one submits to sin and the voice of the devil, to that degree sin and the devil have authority over them.*

If a person continues to practice that sin with intensity (passion and strength), frequency (how often), and duration (the period of time), he or she is opening up the door for the devil to establish a stronghold. If someone continues to sin in an area, eventually this becomes an open door for the devil. By submitting to sin and Satan, one has willfully given permission (legal access) by the law of the will to sin and Satan to have an influence over them (John 8:34; Rom 6:16; 2 Pet 2:19). Soon, the believer will not be able to resist the temptation. The person is bound. It is usually at this point that they need deliverance. We are our brother's/sister's keeper (Gen 4:9). They need intercessors to stand in the gap and pray deliverance over that bound area because the person is no longer able to resist the sin and break the stronghold of the devil. Advanced and progressive stages of transgression often require intercession and deliverance.

POSSESSION IS RARE

Yes, believers can be bound by sin and under the influence of a demon(s) and need deliverance. Demons can attach themselves to an area of the flesh that will influence the soul (the mind, will, and emotions) and the flesh in that unsanctified area. The believer is *not* possessed, which is actually a rare state.[14] The devil does not fully control them, but there may be a dimension

---

14. The word "possession" is often used erroneously to translate the Greek verb "*echo*" or "to have" (a demon) or the verb *daimonizoma*, which means literally to be demonized. I think "demonize" is a better translation than "to possess" or "possession." "Demonization" implies degrees of demonic influence and does not necessarily involve possession or full loss of control or agency. The penultimate goal of demons is to seek to inhabit and manifest their work through an abode or vessel (human souls and bodies). Their ultimate goal is to then operate through that vessel to steal, kill, and destroy.

of their life where they are no longer in control. Instead, sin and Satan have a grip on that area. In that one area, Satan is pulling the strings.

Under the direction of trained deliverance ministers, the person needs to pray, fast, and seek repentance and be open to the conviction of the Holy Spirit. And when the time is right and the person is repentant and ripe for deliverance, the team can minister liberation on his/her behalf. *Both* sin and Satan need to be dealt with in deliverance. Both were defeated and judged objectively at the cross. Both need to be defeated and judged subjectively in the person's heart. The cross needs to be applied in deliverance. There, sin is defeated, and Satan is defeated. There, sin and Satan are judged (John 12:31).

With true repentance and faith in Christ's sacrificial death, the legal right of sin is broken. The judgment and punishment for sin has been met in Christ. Also, sin received its judgment of death in the body of Christ (Rom 8:3). This is the Law of Deliverance #3—the Law of True Repentance. When sin is legally broken, Satan has no legal right to remain. As the will has submitted to sin, now it needs to submit to the Lordship of Jesus Christ. The will needs to be recovered and submitted. This happens through true repentance and the intercession and deliverance administered by the saints. This is the Law of Deliverance #2—The Law of the Will.

CASTING OUT THE DEVIL

After sin is broken, Satan cannot remain. He has to go. He has no right to stay. Evict him! True repentance and faith in the work of the cross break Satan's legal right to accuse or attach. Furthermore, the cross deals a death blow to Satan's power. His works are destroyed, and he is judged (John 12:31; 16:11). His legal right and his power are eradicated. His works are also condemned. We then bind and evict him in Jesus' name because Christ defeated him on the cross.

Believers are given divine authority (*exousia*) in the name of Jesus to cast out demons (Mark 16:17; Luke 10:18–20). We are given authority and a power of attorney in his name to carry out and enforce Christ's finished work on the cross. There is power in the name of Jesus, and it has been given to us! A power of attorney gives one the legal right to act on another's behalf. We are given power of attorney in ministry to act on Christ's behalf and do what he did, and even greater works (John 14:12). Deliverance is *intercession* on behalf of the captive.

We are given the power and authority to apply the work of the cross and declare to Satan that he is defeated and judged, and that he must leave. We enforce what Christ has already accomplished. Now, we can bind the strongman and plunder the house (Mark 3:27). We are given power of attorney by Jesus to act on his behalf and use his name to do his works, set the captives free. In fact, it is not we who are casting out the demons. It is Christ the mighty warrior rising up within us, by the Spirit, that casts out demons and heals the soul (Matt 12:28). Without Christ, we are no match for the enemy. But the true art of spiritual war is wielded by the Master and not the devil! This is the Law of Deliverance #4, the Law of Authority.

Thus, God gives the sinner mercy by taking their sin, but he takes sin's judgment onto himself. He exchanges his righteousness for the condemnation of sin. The Wall Street stock exchange does not make exchanges like that! God destroys the power of the devil and judges his evil works by condemning and destroying sin and death. That's Good News!!!!!!! And bad news for the devil!

FOLLOWING DELIVERANCE

Following deliverance, the person needs to continue to walk in the way of repentance and consistently turn away from their past sin and yield completely to God. Don't walk backwards! The door that the person opened needs to remain closed, regardless of how strong the temptation that awaits on the other side. Remember, *past* sin and brokenness can open the door to *future* demons unless there is *present* repentance and healing. Further, the broken and cracked area of the soul that allowed the temptation to leak through needs to be repaired. The breach is repaired through the renewing of the mind with the Word of God. We need the mind of Christ, to think as God thinks.

The freshly delivered person needs to replace the lies they once believed with the truth of God's Word. Lies bind, but truth sets free (John 8:32). Lies destroy. Truth transforms. The believer needs to learn more deeply who they are in Christ, and what Christ did for them on the cross. He/she must learn the way of the cross as a daily discipline (see chapter 7).

TAKE UP OUR CROSS DAILY (LUKE 9:23)

The cross is not only for our deliverance, but its daily power enables us to stay free. We experience deliverance and fullness of life when we surrender to the work of Christ on the cross. Yielding is a daily, even moment-by-moment, discipline (Rom 6:19, 8:13; 1 Cor 15:31). We die to old temptations. Go to a cemetery! It's full of dead people! Did you ever notice something? They do not sin. No matter how hard you tempt them. Dead people do not sin.

Drop a million dollars on their grave. No greed. Drop a mountain of pizza on their plot. No gluttony. Show hours of inappropriate internet content over their headstone. No lust. Curse them up and down. No anger. Romans 6:7, "Anyone who has died with Christ has been set free from sin." *Dead people don't sin.* In Colossians 3:5, Paul tells us to "mortify" the deeds of the flesh. To "mortify" means to "kill" or to "put to death." It is quite a violent verb. Overcomers must show no mercy to their flesh but do violence to it with every temptation.

The cross for the believer signifies the death and burial of the old life and resurrection of the new life. Walking in the way of the cross (*via crucis*) is the normative method of deliverance from temptation and sin. As our mind is renewed by the Word of God, we learn that we are a new creation in Christ. The Spirit transforms our life by first transforming our mind (Rom 12:2). We have a new identity. Afterwards, our practices will change as we walk daily in the Spirit. The sins we committed prior, we commit no longer. We resist the devil, and he flees.

This rhythm is the normative way a person is kept by or delivered from the power of sin and Satan, and it is the normative way that a believer stays free and does not become entangled again in the bondage of sin (Gal 5:1). The way of the cross is the New Testament method for salvation and sanctification and *not* the deliverance session.

Everything is not a demon. Everything does not need to be cast out. Don't be a hammer! When you are a hammer, everything looks like a nail. Repentance and faith in Christ are the standard way unbelievers come to Christ. Taking up our cross daily and crucifying the flesh in the power of the Spirit are the standard ways that believers resist sin and stay free in Christ.

We Spirit-filled Christians desperately need this teaching of the cross and dying to sin. We rarely hear it in our pulpits, which is why I am driving it home so frequently in this text. It is a pitiful deficit in our churches. We charismatics are known for teaching and demonstrating the power of the Spirit, but we gravely lack a robust teaching and practice of the sanctification of the Spirit. Positive confession, self-actualization, and health and wealth have replaced our doctrine of sanctification.[15] We have cut off our holiness roots and have paid dearly for it.

15. I do not blame the people in the pews. The problem in the pews points to a problem in the pulpit. Some of our leaders have not been officially and properly trained in historic Christianity, orthodox Christian doctrine, and proper biblical exegetical methods. They may have five doctorates from Three-Clicks-and-You-are-an-Apostle-Seminary.com or some other unaccredited diploma mill, or even a Bible Institute or School of Ministry that is accredited by an unaccredited accreditation body.

But they have never received proper, accredited theological training, which can help prevent exegetical and theological errors in their teaching. We need to invest more in

I have worshipped in all types of churches and denominations. In my experience, our so-called Spirit-filled churches frequently have the lowest or weakest doctrine of sanctification among the various evangelical denominations. We rarely talk about sin, suffering, sacrifice, self-denial, the cross, holiness, sanctification, crucifying the flesh, and the like. Because of bygone legalism, we have replaced holiness with positive confession and prosperity; we have entered denial about our sin and do not expect to suffer. Sin and suffering are negative, and we do not want to confess anything negative.

Thus, we preach and teach very little about the cross, especially our subjective experience of the cross. There is so much sugar in our sermons that I get a cavity listening to them. Many Spirit-filled congregations think that church is about grabbing the Holy Spirit at the altar and filling our mouths with Reddi-Wip every week. We can't live off dessert. We need meat and fiber (Heb 5:12). The cross is meat and fiber, although the enemy is content with our current spiritual diet.

Satan loves a cross-less spiritual diet. He has taken away our main weapon to defeat him! When Peter told Christ he did not have to die at the cross, Jesus rebuked Satan, who was talking through Peter. Satan created a cross-less gospel and was the first to preach it. Satan tempted Peter with a cross-less gospel. And Satan did not want Christ to go to the cross. Remember, a cross-less gospel is Satanic!

BALANCE IS ESSENTIAL

The cross or casting out demons—which is it? A balanced approach recognizes that every encounter with sin does not entail the need to cast out a demon from someone. A sound theology of sanctification stresses that the normative or regular method of deliverance is resisting temptation and sin through the power of the Spirit (Rom 8:13; Col 3:5). The Spirit leads us to resist sin and submit to the death and resurrection of Christ. When we are in Christ, we become a new creation. It is our new standing (2 Cor, 5:17).

---

a rigorous Spirit-filled education than in names and titles. Just a note: if the diploma, institute, college, or school of ministry is not accredited by the Association of Theological Schools (ATS), then usually the diploma is sawdust.

As a Spirit-filled leader, it makes no sense to say that education is of the devil and worldly, and then we pursue an unaccredited or a mail order degree that is not worth the paper it is written on, because we want everyone to call us doctor. On the other hand, those of us who have earned degrees and titles, may we be humble, fear the Lord, and obey his commandments. We know that knowledge can puff us up with pride (1 Cor 8:1), and knowledge without the Spirit will give us a mere form or appearance of godliness without the power of God backing us (2 Tim 3:5).

Further, we experience the new creation through the daily renewal of the Spirit (2 Cor 4:16). As a new creation in Christ, we are also called to know who we are in Christ by having our minds renewed with the Word of God (Rom 12:1–2). The truth, the Word of God, sets us free from the lies that bind us (John 8:31–32). When God renews our minds with the truth, then our beliefs change. When our beliefs change, then our sinful practices will change. Dying to the old life, walking as a new creation, and renewing our minds with the Word is the normative way we find deliverance from sin and evil.

Nevertheless, there are occasions in which a bound person needs intervention. Advanced and progressive stages of transgression often require deliverance. In deliverance ministry, we pray and minister the power of the cross in Christ's name on behalf of the oppressed. We minister Christ's authority as intercessors on behalf of another to liberate the captive and lead that person into new life.

DELIVERANCE, INNER HEALING, AND SANCTIFICATION

Deliverance, inner healing, and sanctification are all related. These are all types of healing, healing of the image of God within. God wants to restore his image within us, so that we look like Christ and experience wholeness. God does not want us beat up and bound. Wholeness is the goal of deliverance, inner healing, and sanctification. Wholeness means a new creation crafted in the holy image of Christ (Col 3:10). Deliverance, inner healing, and sanctification are means that achieve this end. Deliverance initiates the healing ministry.

Although believers may at times need deliverance from demonic strongholds, this is not the norm, as we have reiterated. The norm is sanctification through the way of the cross. I am repeating this teaching throughout the book because we do not hear it enough—making up for lost time! We need to get this teaching deep into our spirits and digest it. Our union with Christ in his death, burial, and resurrection provides our deliverance and victory over the body of sin and the power of darkness. The old is gone and the new is here. We are new creations.

In 2 Cor 5:17, the passing away of the old refers to the old creation. The verse speaks specifically to the believer, but the implications are extended to all creation. God's desire is a new heaven and a new earth (Rev 21:1). Christ came to transfigure the entire cosmos in his image. Christoformity, which is ultimately cruciformity, is God's plan. Are you cross-fit?[16]

As a believer, this transformation involves spirit, soul and body, a whole new being, and a new people. God's work of salvation is restoring all things to the image of Christ (Eph 1:10, 4:22–24; Col 3:10). The Spirit restores the image of God daily by renewing our minds with the Word of God, as we learn who we are in Christ.

In Luke 20:19–26, when the religious leaders tried to trip up and accuse Christ, they asked him if they should pay taxes to Caesar. Jesus, always light years ahead of these dullards, returns with a question: "Whose image is on the coin?" They replied, "Caesar's!" "Well then give unto Caesar what is Caesar's but give unto God what is God's." What is being implied here? Jesus is calling us to give to God what belongs to God in relation to the coin. What belongs to God? The coin has Caesar's image inscribed on it, so it belongs to Caesar. You have God's image inscribed on you, so you belong to God. The coin was made in Caesar's image; thus, it is his. You are made in God's image; thus, you are his. Give Caesar his money but give God yourself!

Who are we? We are the image of God. God's image is righteousness and true holiness unmarred by the disease of sin. Salvation is the healing and curative work of the Spirit that restores that image. Eastern Christianity has understood salvation therapeutically as God's cure for sin sickness. Salvation is holistic healing of all things leading to Christlikeness. God wants us healed and whole in spirit, soul, and body!

Thus, the heart and goal of salvation is sanctification (holiness, *theosis*). Sanctification is attained through the healing work of Christ and the Spirit beginning with our deliverance from the power of sin, death, and Satan. Salvation involves sanctification that involves healing that involves deliverance. These divine works are all intertwined and given by God's amazing grace. So, we learn that deliverance is a type of healing, and it is situated in the larger worker of salvation and sanctification.

DELIVERANCE, A TYPE OF HEALING

Deliverance is a type of healing. It heals the sin-sick soul from the toxic works of the devil. Deliverance is a function within the healing ministry, and healing is part of the larger work of sanctification, which is part of the whole work of salvation. Deliverance brings healing, both inner and outer healing. In Acts 10:38, Jesus "healed all of those who were oppressed of the

---

16. Cruciformity means allowing the cross, self-denial, sacrifice, and even suffering to shape our Christian life. We are to be formed by the cross.

devil." Jesus *healed* people of demonic oppression (Luke 8:2). Deliverance involves healing the damage inflicted by the devil to the human soul. People who have been oppressed by Satan have been deeply wounded and need to be healed, set free, and restored.

Often the work of inner healing and deliverance go hand in hand, liberating from captivity *and* mending brokenness. Deliverance is a vital component of the healing ministry. The healing ministry, in restoring the human person to wholeness and to God's original image of righteousness and true holiness, is a part of the sanctifying ministry of the Holy Spirit. Finally, sanctification is the heart of salvation. God wants us holy as he is holy (Lev 11:44; 1 Pet 1:16). Sanctification means to have God's heart, a circumcised heart of obedience (Ezek 36:26; Heb 8:10;10:16). Sanctification cleanses and renews us completely, spirit, soul, and body. The vital work of sanctification is not optional because "without holiness no one will see the Lord (Heb 12:14)."

The breadth and depth of salvation, and all that it comprises in terms of sanctification, healing, and deliverance, are fully realized in the work of the cross, which is shorthand for the death, burial, and resurrection of Christ. We are baptized into this cross and participate daily in its fellowship of suffering, death, and resurrection (Phil 3:10). Death is the front end of the cross, but resurrection is the back end of the cross and a further source of our healing. Resurrection is the beginning and end, the source and goal, and the measure and capacity of our deliverance and healing. In resurrection we are delivered and healed from sin and death and born to eternal life (John 11:25–26).

The work of Christ on the cross co-working with the power of the Holy Spirit is God's ministry of deliverance. The church is now invited to participate in the ministry of deliverance in the name of Jesus on behalf of others. Those called to deliverance ministry serve as priestly ministers and intercessors of this finished work of Christ on the cross on behalf of those who are held captive and desire freedom but cannot free themselves. Deliverance ministry is a priestly intercessory ministry that involves prayer, fasting, anointing, healing, and implementing the authority that Christ has given the church over sin, death, evil, Satan, and all the hosts of hell.

Lesson 3

The Four Laws of Deliverance

THE FOUR LAWS OF Deliverance are our foundation for deliverance work. Learn these laws first. Many ministers and ministries are ineffective in deliverance because they do not know or apply these laws. The four laws are as basic and essential to deliverance as Isaac Newton's three laws are to motion in physics. They control the dynamics for deliverance in the spirit world and in the natural world. Like our visible universe, the invisible realm of the spirit operates by laws, rules, and regularities.

As the natural world operates by the laws of physics, so the supernatural world operates by the laws of the Spirit. Our God is a God of law and order and not chaos (1 Cor 14:33). The Lord created the laws of the Spirit, and even Satan and his demons must abide by them. Demons cannot do whatever they please. They are forced to work within the boundaries and laws that God has established, even while they rebel.

Demonic rebellion has boundaries and limits (Job 1). Satan is merely a pawn for God, as he uses the devil for his purposes (Rev 20:1–3, 7). It is good to know that Satan must abide by these four laws. He cannot violate them. These laws are scriptural truths, and God rules and reigns by his Word. His Word is eternal. It does not change.

Psalm 119:89 says, "Forever O Lord, your word is settled in Heaven." God's Word cannot be broken. The evil one must submit to God's laws that limit his reach. Here are how the Four Laws of Deliverance impact demons. *First,* demons must submit to their defeat at the cross (Heb 2:14). *Second,* demons can only access a person as God permits and as the human will allows (Job 1:8–12). *Third,* they cannot hold a person in sin who truly repents (John 8:36; Acts 3:20; Rom 8:1–3; 2 Cor 7:10). *Finally,* demons cannot defeat a believer who knows and operates in the authority that Christ has given them (Luke 10:19–20). Learn, believe, and meditate on these four laws, if you want to be an effective deliverance minister (X Men and X Women). Let us unpack once again the Four Laws of Deliverance as we delve deeper into the mechanics of deliverance.

THE FOUR LAWS OF DELIVERANCE

The First Law of Deliverance: The Law of the Cross

We have already discussed in depth the profound truth of the cross. I really want you to grasp the cross until you get splinters. Let us briefly review it again. According to Romans 8:3 and Hebrews 2:14, sin and Satan were defeated at the cross. It is finished. Sin and Satan are defeated and judged when Christ died. The power of sin, death, and the devil were *broken* at the cross. We start here.

The finished work of the cross becomes our ground and basis for deliverance. Satan is already defeated. We are merely enforcing Christ's victory with the authority he has given us in his name. Both sin and Satan have also been *judged* at the cross (John 12:31; 16:11). Once the person who is bound truly repents of their sin, the devil has no legal right to remain. Christ has condemned sin and the devil with one momentous act on the cross. Satan is defeated. So, in the name of Jesus, we can evict the devil from his abode and cast him into outer darkness.

It is imperative when casting out demons that you do not trust in your own do-it-yourself strategies, methods, spiritual experience, thoughts, or feelings. Your faith and confidence must be in the finished work of the cross alone. It is a completed fact. Sin and Satan are already defeated and judged. You are not "defeating" Satan in the deliverance ministry. If you think victory depends on you, then Satan has already won the battle. He will convince you to look at yourself, your lack of faith, your fear, evil manifestations, or any intimidating or distracting tactic that will keep you from ministering in Christ's authority based on the work of the cross. The grounds for an effective deliverance ministry begin at the cross. Do not lose sight of the first law.

The Second Law of Deliverance: The Law of the Will (Agency)

The law of the will is simple. Authority is proportional to submission. Whatever you submit to has a degree of authority or control over you (John 8:34; Rom 6:16–18; 2 Peter 2:19). You can submit to sin and Satan, or you can submit to the Lordship of Christ. To the degree one submits to sin/the demonic or Christ, to that degree sin/the demonic or Christ has authority over that person. Neither God nor the devil will violate your will. Rather, God will not violate your will. He honors your freedom and personhood. And the devil *cannot* violate your will. God will not permit it. It's a law of the Spirit.

In the beginning of creation in Genesis three, God gave humanity a choice that neither he nor the devil violates. Temptation comes. A person begins with a choice. They give in to sin. Submitting to sin over time weakens the will to the point that the will is bound (Rom 7), and the window of choice closes.[1] After consent is given, the devil comes in like a flood and takes over until one cries out for deliverance (Rom 7:21–25).

God, through his love, grace, and truth, seeks to lead our will to submission. Satan, through deception, seduction, cunning, and fear, seeks to trap our will into submission (Gen 3:1; 2 Cor 11:3). But the decision is ours. Neither will override our will. The will is the heart of the person, and the key to controlling the soul. Both God and Satan want the will of each person's soul. The agency and choice are ours to give.

To the degree one submits to sin/the demonic or Christ, to that degree sin/the demonic or Christ has authority over that person. By degree, I am referring to the duration, frequency, and intensity of submission. These three variables are standard in measuring behavior in Applied Behavior Analysis (ABA). These variables determine how strong the behavior is and the difficulty of breaking it. I also add a fourth variable to the equation, the generations or the generational factor (generational sin and curses and generational blessing).[2]

---

1. According to John Wesley and early Methodist theology, and I concur, Christ's universal atonement restores a measure of grace in us to respond to God's early promptings and call. It is called *prevenient grace*. Prevenient grace means God's grace goes before and ahead of us through various means like our conscience to empower us to come to him. No one is at first in a natural state without some measure of grace.

We have inherited original sin. Inbred or birth sin seeks to thwart our every move toward God. Without God, our will is in bondage. Yet, God gives us a measure of grace to come to him and receive more grace, which results in more grace upon grace for repentance, justification, regeneration, sanctification, and glorification (John 1:16).

Though, we must *receive* his grace and turn to him. We cannot resist sin in our own strength. Inbred sin naturally has bound our will. But God's grace works preveniently in everyone. It is our prime mover. God moves first. Grace goes ahead of us to lead and empower us to repent, believe, and serve God. When we walk in the Spirit, the flesh opposes our will. There is then a war between the flesh and the Spirit. We are called to walk in the Spirit and not follow the impulses of the flesh. God's grace is his enabling power over sin (Rom 6:14). Amazing Grace indeed!!!

See Phil 2:12–13 and Collins and Vickers, "On Working out Your own Salvation," *Sermons of John Wesley.*

2. Francis MacNutt gives seven signs one is under a curse: mental breakdown,

The law of the will (agency) works both ways, toward sin and toward Christ. The authority of sin and Satan over a person's will increases with the practice of generational sin over a duration of time with frequency and intensity. Likewise, the manifest authority of Christ will increase in one's life with the practice of faith and obedience, across generations, over a duration of time, with frequency and intensity. In terms of deliverance, this law gives us insight into what has bound a person and how strong the authority is over that person. Not all bound people are bound to the same degree. Some strongholds are greater than others. Likewise, some who are in greater submission to the Lordship of Christ walk in greater manifest authority than others.

An Example of Degrees of Demonization

Consider the bondage of alcoholism. Consider our four variables: *generational, duration, frequency, and intensity.* We have two people who are addicted. We have been asked to minister deliverance to both. Person One does not have a family history of alcoholism (*generational*). This person has been binge drinking (*intensity*) on the weekends (*frequency*) for the last five months (*duration*). They have been drinking a twelve pack a night (*intensity*). They want to quit, but they cannot. Defeat is my primary indicator of addiction. You cannot quit, even if you want to. *If you cannot quit, you are addicted.*

On the other hand, Person Two does have a family history of alcoholism going back many generations (*generational*). This person has been drinking nightly (*frequency*) for the last twenty years (*duration*). They have been drinking close to a fifth of whiskey (*intensity*) nearly every night They want to quit, but they cannot. Both people are in bondage. But based on our four variables, *generational, duration, frequency,* and *intensity,* Person Two is in *more* bondage. The alcohol has greater authority over the will of Person Two than the will of Person One.

If we assigned a numerical value to each of the four variables and combined them, we could compute a numerical value (a bondage quotient) that could measure their degree of bondage. Someone with a lower degree of bondage may be able to pray for themselves, fast, and break the grip. Others with a greater degree of bondage may have allowed an attachment to form between their will and the sin and the demonic influence behind the sin.

---

chronic sickness, barrenness (tendency to miscarry), breakdown of family, financial insufficiency, being accident prone, family history of unnatural or untimely deaths. Some are debatable. Consult a medical professional as well. MacNutt, *Deliverance from Evil Spirit*, 107–108.

Over a duration of time, along with frequency and intensity of practice, an attachment has become a stronghold. They cannot break the attachment. They need deliverance.

Attachments

Let us look at how attachments work. We have all sent emails with and without attachments. The attachment is an add-on to the email. One receives an email and an attachment when sent. In the case of demonization, one receives Satan's message of sin (an email) and a demonic attachment that comes with sin. An attachment is a bond between a person, their sin, and the demon tempting the person to sin. When the sin becomes a stronghold, then there are degrees of demonic influence over the person, or attachments. The attachment attaches itself to that area of the person's life, for example alcohol addiction. The temptation and submission are at first occasional, then habitual, and then an addiction.

The desire and seduction, which are attached to the devil, have now attached themselves to the flesh that, in turn, controls the person's thought life, passion, and will. They think about and crave alcohol all the time. The attachment latches on to the brain's gratification and reward center as well as to the memory and learning center of the brain, creating a negative feedback loop to ensure addiction. These are the dynamics of an attachment.

So, there is a seducing spirit on one end of the attachment and a person on the other end of the attachment, with the alcohol addiction in the middle. The demon, at this point, has a strong influence over the person and is attached to their mind, will, and emotions through alcohol addiction.

Of course, the addiction involves more than just demonic influences, as mentioned above. Surely this attachment also involves the neuroscience of addiction, as well as demonic influence. The neural circuits related to the reward and pleasure center of the brain in the *nucleus accumbens* have been hacked and hijacked. We can explain the secondary causes through neuroscience and behavioral psychology. There can be multiple levels of causation that work together at spiritual, psychological, neurological, and physical levels. One level does not explain away the other. The neurochemical cause does not explain away the spiritual cause or vice versa. Multiple causes are at work; in fact, they are working together.

The problem is not merely neurological. As Christians we know that the created order is not merely matter or physical, as in neurons and biological neural networks. God created all things visible and invisible (Col 1:16). There is an invisible world with invisible beings. There are also spiritual dynamics at work here. We are not unaware of the schemes of the devil (2 Cor 2:11).

Why is measuring bondage so important? Because both Person One and Person Two are facing a formidable opponent (alcohol addiction) who has bettered them for some time. But the second person is fighting a much more powerful foe. Repentance and deliverance may end up being much more of a challenge for Person Two than for Person One. Repentance and deliverance may require more time, prayer, fasting, meditation in the Word, etc.

Granted, this calculation to arrive at a bondage quotient is a human effort to ascertain spiritual bondage. It has a margin of error. Additionally, God can do whatever he chooses. Obviously, he can deliver the person instantly with very little repentance and no prayer for deliverance. Sometimes the moment arises when deliverance presents itself, and there is no time for the extensive protocol that I am proposing. Like a baby ready to be delivered when there is no time for an epidural or to get to the hospital—the car will have to do. When I was converted, there was no one present. I was by myself. God gave me three candid, convicting visions. As a response, I got on my knees and cried out, "Jesus is Lord," and was instantly saved and delivered of all my issues. God is sovereign. We always need to allow the Spirit freedom to do as he pleases.

But in my experience, I found that God usually works with our will, our repentance, and our prayer. And often we do not overcome the sin and bondage overnight, just as we didn't get into the sin and bondage overnight. Even in my case, where I was instantly delivered, God later brought those issues back into my life and lead me to repent and struggle with each one. He knew I was so weak at the time of my conversion and that I needed a powerful deliverance to provide me with the escape-velocity to break the strong gravitational pull of sin on my life, or I was not going to make it. In his mercy he knew that.

But in his wisdom, he also knew that one day I would have to face the struggle with those sins. And what God initially gave me as a gift, I would later have to own with my repentance, faith, and whole heart. I always said that one can only ultimately be delivered from generational sin or any sin when one practices righteousness or lives a life in opposition to that sin (Ezek 18). Mere deliverance without a change of life will not stick. We want a *sticky* deliverance.

God wants to minister a deliverance to us that will stick to our ribs, that we can own for a lifetime. And this usually happens through deep repentance and a subsequent renewing of the mind with the Word of God. We will go through times of repentance, deliverance, and renewal at some point proportionate to and greater than our bondage quotient of sin. We reverse the curse. Our obedience is then practiced generationally, over a duration of time, with frequency and intensity greater than our previous disobedience.

Recovering the Will

A key in deliverance is that the will (agency) needs to be recovered. The will is bound, and it needs to be loosed through the work of the cross and the prayer of the saints. The Lord gives special grace for this task. Even if the will is chained, the person can still express a willingness to be free. They can say yes to deliverance, even when bound. The Gadarene man was bound with a legion of demons, and yet he came to Christ (Mark 5:6) and did not hide or resist. This is God's prevenient grace at work.

So, when I am ministering deliverance, even if the person is bound, I ask them to resist the devil. During the session, I ask them to confess Jesus is Lord. I ask them to renounce the powers of darkness, etc. God will give them grace to resist. Atrophy sets in on the will, and it needs to be jump-started and exercised. This practice coaches the person to exercise and re-cover agency, which had been made captive. We encourage them to respond to and cooperate with God's grace (Phil 2:13).

Once their will (agency) is recovered and they turn from their sin toward God, Satan begins to lose his grip. His legal access to their soul dwindles. At that point the devil often gets desperate during the session and may try some vocal or demonstrative manifestation to intimidate or distract the deliverance team. But we do not fear Satan. We have the authority, not him. He is defeated, not us.

Deliverance is a battle for the will. If the shackled person truly wants freedom, wants to renounce the devil, and wants to repent, and there is a trained and seasoned team interceding, that person will eventually be set free. If the deliverance team and the person in bondage know the four laws and are heeding them, then victory cannot be avoided. God's grace abounds and is greater than all our sin.

The Third Law of Deliverance: The Law of True Repentance

Preach and Teach Repentance

"Repentance" along with faith in Christ for the forgiveness of sins is the core of the gospel message. These are the elementary teachings of Hebrews 6:1. Today with our modern, microwave, highspeed, broadband, ATM, scratch-off, drive-thru, download, health and wealth, name it and claim it, blab it and grab it gospel, we often do not hear sin-preaching in our churches. It displeases people. It makes people uncomfortable. If they are uncomfortable, they will leave our church. If they leave our church, our offerings will go down. If our offerings go down, we will not stay in business. If we cannot stay in business, then we cannot own four houses and five cars. Solution: stop preaching on sin and repentance. It is bad for business. And it makes some of our big givers in the church uncomfortable. Keep the customers happy! Give them what they want!

Well, my friend, dying can be uncomfortable. Let us be about the Father's business and teach repentance. Why would we people-please, only to watch them die in their sins? Wake them up and speak the truth in love. Teach and preach repentance. True repentance breaks the legal authority that sin and Satan have over an individual. Once legal authority is broken, then Satan has no legitimate right to remain. There can be no deliverance if the bound person continues in their sin.

There also can be no deliverance if the bound person does not want to be free from that sin. There can be no deliverance if the bound person does not receive conviction and go through true repentance. And there cannot be true repentance if we do not preach on repentance. It is that simple. We need to build people's appetite for righteousness. The will has the power to give legal or rightful permission and access. Satan will not leave when you have invited him to stay. When a person submits to sin, their will has given rightful access to Satan to enter and do his work. He is lounging on the easy chair of your soul at this point. Satan will not leave until he is legally evicted. Ignorance of the first law of deliverance is no excuse.

Jesus has defeated Satan, but if a person keeps giving the devil power by submitting to him, they make the cross of no effect in their life. They are turning from God's provision and protection. God allows them to will what they want, and he will turn them over to the desire of their hearts. Don't give the devil permission, then cry that you are oppressed. No permission! No compromise! So, even though Satan is defeated, that victory needs to be enforced personally in each one of our lives, or we do not receive the benefit of what Christ has done. In essence, we are rejecting his gift. Many are still defeated despite the victory Christ has won. Many in the world and in the church are hypnotized and mesmerized in Satan's prison camp, even though Christ has broken the prison bars wide open. They are being held behind bars of air.

In boxing, awesome Iron Mike Tyson was an uncanny force of speed, power, technique, and demolition like the world had never seen before. He was as fast on the inside of a fighter as Ali was on the outside. And Tyson could hit as hard as Rocky Marciano or George Foreman. He was built and trained by the immortal Cus D'Amato who invented the explosive peek-a-boo style of fighting and taught it to Tyson with rigor, regimentation, and discipline. Tyson became an invincible machine of destruction in the ring. Well, almost.

One key quality that Tyson wielded was indomitable intimidation. Intimidation was the fuel that drove the Tyson wrecking machine. Many of his fights were won before he even stepped in the ring, e.g., Michael Spinks. His opponents were drained by fear of all their skill and courage before the fight began. Fights were over before they started. Tyson fed off primitive, raw fear.[3] It was only when fighters like Buster Douglass and Evander Holyfield overcame their fear and intimidation of Tyson that they had a fighting chance to win and did. Overcome your fear of the enemy. Do not let the devil feed on your fear. He is already defeated! Satan fears Christ (Mark 1:24) in you even more than Tyson's opponents feared him. The devil is defeated before you even enter the ring of the deliverance session.

It has been said that after the Civil War officially ended, there were soldiers in the South who did not realize the war was over. The South had lost. Satan wants us to be like the South. He hopes that Christians do not realize the war is over, because, in this case, he has lost. In fact, Satan is like the South, defeated but still fighting. Satan knows he is defeated. He hopes that you don't know. He is banking on your ignorance of the four laws of deliverance. He is betting that you do not know your identity in Christ and what occurred on the cross. He knows that he is defeated. He knows his time is short (Rev 12:12). He has been defeated and judged, but he has not been sentenced to the lake of fire yet. That comes at the end of time.

For now, he is permitted to comb the earth back and forth and seek to devour souls through the power of deception (1 Peter 5:8). Deception is all that he has. And if we do not know the truth, then we will be defeated and captured. Know the four laws of deliverance.

Repentance: The Message of John the Baptist

The Law of Repentance is instrumental to deliverance. It was John the Baptist's and Christ's central message (Matt 3). It should be ours too. "Repent and believe" (Mark 1:15). Contrition may be bad for church business, but it's great for the Father's business, which is Kingdom business. Coupled with faith, repentance rids us of sin and positions us for righteousness.

---

3. I am not condemning Tyson. All fighters need to be intimidating to get the winning edge. Tyson just did it better than anyone else.

Repentance and faith birth new souls into the Kingdom and cause it to expand and advance. They are great for the Father's business, which involves putting the devil out of business.

What are you doing to put the devil out of business? Stop competing with the church down the street that has more people in attendance. Pastor, stop trying to put other churches out of business. They are not your competitors. Some churches in that sense are doing the devil's business. *We are not salesmen and women in the church business. We are the church in the Kingdom business.* Stop marking down Jesus and putting him on the discount and clearance table. Stopping marking down repentance, the blood, sacrifice, the cross, self-denial, the resurrection, and the rest of the stumbling blocks of the gospel.

We mark down salvation until it has no cost, and people still discard it. They reject the discount Jesus. If they are going to reject Christ, at least make sure they are rejecting the real Jesus and not the discount Jesus. We have unjustly lowered the price on the gospel to where it is being given away, and they still do not want him. But it's not the real Christ they are rejecting. It's our culture-driven, over-marketed discount Jesus that they see right through and refuse to buy.

The discount, ChurchMart-Jesus is the attraction model Jesus. He is the Jesus that lets you keep your sin because he "loves" you. He is what's left of Jesus after we cut out all his hard sayings, tough teachings, and countercultural ways. He is the deflationary Jesus that has been deflated of the truth and inflated with the values of the prevailing culture. He is the Jesus that comes with accessories so you can dress him up in any clothes you desire. He is the Jesus of your own making. He is the Jesus that you can create in your own image. He is the Jesus of your political and moral persuasion. He is the Christ who supports your favorite sin. All this blasphemy is worse than any other form of idolatry.

No more cost cutting, price slashing, and marking down the gospel. In fact, raise the price to its true eternal value. The gospel's true cost is your life and everything in it (Matt 13:46; Luke 9:25; 14:26, 33; 18:22). And in the end, it will be the best deal you ever made (Mark 10:30). No more bait-and-switch in our mile-wide and inch-deep churches. Make it plain! Put the cost out there so it can be counted (Luke 14:28).

"Well, Dr. Bellini," you may say, "you don't know how to grow a church." Well, Jesus didn't either then. Jesus was not very good at church growth. He did not know what we know today in the American church. When his churches grew large due to their outreach feeding program, Jesus failed to follow up (John 6:26–27). Instead of attracting the new believers, he drove them away. "Come on Jesus, they are not ready for your hard teaching. Be positive! Let them continue to attend church and be blessed by our social ministry. Don't chase them away by preaching about yourself."

No, Jesus did not know how to retain visitors. He preached that hard teaching of eating his body and drinking his blood (John 6:47–51) right when the visitors were flocking to him. Suddenly, his church was down to only a handful (John 6:66). And he didn't even try to retain them. He poured gasoline on the fire and showed them the door, too, if they couldn't accept the cost (John 6:67–69). "Now they will leave our church and go to another church. Come on Jesus, you got the deacon board upset with you." By the time he got to the cross, he had only a handful of followers left. Jesus must have missed that conference on how to grow your church past a thousand and retain visitors.

Repentance Means to Make the Crooked Way Straight!

Why don't we preach and teach the full counsels of God? Why do we act like certain teachings in scripture are not there? Fear! We fear people. We fear being unpopular and unliked on social media. We will lose influence and cred. Such fear is fueled by the spirit of Jezebel.

The church and our culture are under attack from Jezebel. She has intimidated and frightened them both into silence, while the radicals have no problem speaking their mind and pushing their agenda. Cowardice has become the order of the day. Where are the John the Baptists? Be strong and of good courage, church! Let us stop following the lead of the culture and the market and get back to preaching repentance and faith.

The days of the attractional model are over. Following the CV-19 pandemic, God is putting ChurchMart out of business. The church is no longer front and center in the culture. She is despised and marginalized. Perfect, now we can't people please or please the culture anymore. We are free! Many already loathe the church. We are free to allow the gospel to offend because the world is already offended.[4] Preach a rugged repentance like John the Baptist!

The word "repentance" in the Greek is *metanoia*. It means a radical change of mind that involves a radical change of life. It implies turning from a life led by self and turning to God and a God-centered life. Turn from sin and turn to obedience. John the Baptist informs us that it means to straighten out our crooked ways. Our ways are measured by the standard of God's holy Word. We need to align with God's Word. The Word is God's

---

4. Of course, we do not intentionally seek to offend, which is a sin. But if one is faithful to the gospel, it has its own built-in, naturally occurring offense mechanism or stumbling block (*scandalon*) (1 Pet 2:8).

ruler that measures whether our life is straight or in line (Matt 3:3, 7:13). The high places of pride need to be leveled. The low places of brokenness need to be built up (Luke 3:5).

John instructed us to prepare the way of Christ's coming by making a straight road, and that road is repentance. In other words, John was letting us know that repentance is the only way or road that Christ will walk on to get to us. He will not walk on a crooked road of an unrepentant heart. Christ will only come to the one who repents. Repentance prepares the way.

John warned the Pharisees not to make excuses and point to their own credentials or righteousness. "Wait Jesus, you don't know who I am. I am bishop, apostle, doctor, prophet, pastor Pharisee. I have ten thousand in my church and have my own TV station." Somehow this didn't seem to matter to John the Baptist or Jesus. We have all sinned and fallen short. The axe of the Spirit is being laid at the root of sin and self-sufficiency. John went on basically to preach "turn or burn." (Read the rest of Matthew 3.)

He was letting God's people, the Israelites, know that if they did not repent and show fruit or evidence of their repentance through practical works that they would soon be facing unquenchable fire (Matt 3:10–12). John the Baptist would not have been a successful preacher today. He didn't understand how to live a happy and successful life. Today he would be cancelled. Nevertheless, the truth was never popular. He was also cancelled in his day and lost his head for it. Jesus and his disciples were cancelled as well. Cancel culture is nothing new. Nonetheless, we cannot leave out repentance, an essential component of the gospel and deliverance, or sin will not be cancelled. We must return to preaching and teaching true repentance. "What is true repentance?" you may ask.

What Is True Repentance?

I knew a person in church who was bound in witchcraft, drugs, and promiscuity. Their method of sanctification was not the cross and dying to sin. They did not seek true repentance to break their addictions. This person originally came from a church where they practiced deliverance as a *regular* means of finding victory.

What that meant was that, after he sinned, he wanted our deliverance team to pray deliverance over him. Then he would eventually go out and commit the same sins and want us to pray deliverance over him again. Repent and repeat. He went out and got dirty, then came back to the church for a shower again and again. We soon broke that chain, encouraging him to learn what repentance really means (John 7:24).

Deliverance became his false method of sanctification because he never truly was delivered or cleansed. Why? He did not seem committed to his repentance. He is not the first. Sure, he told God and us he was sorry and made vows to never do it again. Yet, he never truly turned from his sin and surrendered those areas to God. He would go out every weekend and blatantly do the same things. While we want to refrain from judgment, as pastors we are called to inspect the fruit and bring correction and help if needed.

He had to step down from the praise team. Leadership found it difficult to identify in our brother godly sorrow for his sin. He had what the Apostle Paul called "worldly sorrow" (2 Cor 7). He was sorry he got caught. He did not like feeling guilty. Who does? It was uncomfortable. But he did not hate sin. He hated feeling uncomfortable, which is good. God uses conviction to wake us up. So, he wanted to be rid of his guilt and shame which is right. But it does not go far enough. We need to be rid of *the sin* or the guilt and shame will come right back again.

Once we say what God's Word says about the sin and see sin the way God sees it, then the Spirit works mourning in our hearts (Matt 5:4).[5] We are saddened by the sin as God is saddened. We need to see that sinning against God makes us an enemy of God (Rom 5:10; James 4:4). We need to be open to conviction to the point of hating sin and seeing why sin deserved eternal damnation (Ps 45:7; 97:10; Prov 15:9; Isa 61:8; Rom 6:23; Heb 1:9). If not, then we will find it easy to fall into a self-serving false repentance that amounts to *repent and repeat*. We have all fallen into self-serving repentance.

I know this may seem harsh or over-the-top for some who are not used to hearing such a no-compromise approach to sin. But we need to realize that sin and Satan have a no-compromise, no-tolerance policy against God and his righteousness. It took me years to learn this lesson. There are *three events* that are certain for all, no matter who you are: *death, judgment,* and *eternity.* We better get ready and repent! Lord have mercy on us all!

---

5. 1 John 1:9 directs us to confess our sins. The word "confess" in that verse is the Greek word *homologeo*. It means "to say the same thing as" or "agree with." Confession is to say the same things and agree with God about the nature of the sin. Do not whitewash it, sugar coat it, make excuses for it, or be in denial. Say the same thing God says about the sin.

In order to say the same thing, one needs to know what God's Word says about the sin. Meditate on the scriptures that speak to that sin and its punishment. Then meditate on the only sacrifice he sent to atone for sin. His only Son Jesus Christ came into the world to die on our behalf for that sin. It is the goodness of God that leads us to repentance (Rom 2:4). Those who mourn for their sin will be comforted with repentance and forgiveness (Matt 5:4). Pray earnestly for the gift of repentance.

Imagine if you just ran several miles as part of your exercise on a hot summer's day. And you came to my house, and I offered you a glass of cold water. You then ask me if it was bottled water or from a filter. I said not to worry, the water was 99.99 percent pure. It only has .01 percent strychnine in it. Would you drink it? Why not? It is mostly pure. I mean it is just .01 percent impure. That is not much. We can see why God rejects sin and desires true purity. It takes .002 ounces of strychnine to kill a human. Because of the potency, even a tiny percentage of poison would make the water unacceptable for you to drink." God and sin do not mix either.

Even the sanctified and set apart prophet Isaiah cried out, "Woe is me. I am undone. I am a man of unclean lips," in the holy presence of God (Isa 6:1–8). Why did he say that his lips were unclean? He spoke the holy Word of God. He was a prophet. His lips were pure. He learned that God alone makes us holy. The prophet saw himself as he truly was in light of God's ineffable shekinah and recognized that no flesh can glory in this presence (1 Cor 1:29). We truly need grace and the blood of Jesus as our constant covering and sanctification to wash us white as snow (Heb 10:10).

We, like our unrepentant friend, often do not show adequate disdain for sin to want to part with it. We do not pray and seek *the gift of repentance* with all our heart. If our friend would have sought the gift, God would have surely granted it: "A broken heart and a contrite spirit, you will not deny" (Ps 51:17). But he is not the only one to repent and repeat. *We have all been there.* God gives us mercy, but we cannot give sin or the devil any mercy. Repentance is God's gift, but our part is to want it and to seek it with all we have. Without true repentance, we are like a dog returning to its own vomit, experiencing the dreadful, tormenting cycle of repent and repeat, repent and repeat . . . (2 Pet 2:13–22)

Repent and Repeat

Repent and repeat without much resistance is a sure sign of a false or inadequate repentance. Repent and repeat means that we have not broken our tie with sin. We are still trying to *manage* our sin—sin management. Jesus is not in the sin management business. He is in the sin exterminating business. The cross kills sin on contact. We cannot manage sin. Sin manages us. We cannot negotiate with the truth! It is not like we are basically good, and all we really need is a few modifications here and there. No, nothing is sufficient but death to the old creation and the birth of a new creation (Gal 6:15). Nothing of the flesh is salvageable. The only good sinner is a dead sinner (in Christ). If you are in the sin management business, you will soon be out of business. Worse yet, stay out of the God management business; that is even more risky! Managing God is more impossible than managing sin. We turn to God when we need him, and then put him back in our pocket until the next crisis.

The flesh is crafty and a master at bargaining and negotiating to control God and to get permission for sin. The object is to bargain to keep both Jesus *and* sin. Sin management. We give ourselves permission to allow just a whiff of sin without getting rid of it. Of course, this is self-deception, but our flesh does not care. Our repentance needs to be ruthless with the flesh and its sin management tactics. Be truly convicted of sin! Be intentional in repentance to not grant permission for sin, even a faint aroma or trace.[6] And get rid of every idol that exalts itself over God.

True repentance and co-death with Christ on the cross means that we have *ceased* sinning. We no longer permit even a whiff of sin. No sin whiffing! No, the cross is not a joystick. You get splinters. Your flesh will suffer. But when we suffer in the flesh, then we cease sinning (Rom 6:14, Heb12:4, 1 Peter 4:1). If Jesus had to learn obedience through the things he suffered (Heb 5:8), how much more do we need to learn it? True repentance involves ceasing from sin. It means we no longer give ourselves permission to have Christ *and* that besetting sin (Heb 12:1). Or think, I can sin, and God will *always* forgive me (Rom 6:1; Heb 6:4–6; 10:29). I realize that the devil and the flesh will fight us, but Christ has defeated both. He has overcome the world (John 16:33). By faith, his victory is ours. 1 John 5:4, "Faith is the victory that overcomes the world." Pray for a holy hatred of sin. Pray to see sin the way God sees it. Pray earnestly for the gift of repentance. Ask and it will be given. Seek and you will find (Matt 7:7).

Granted, some may sincerely turn from sin and put their faith in Christ and still occasionally fall, not as the norm, though, but the exception. The hope is that they are falling forward, and the power and practice of sin are diminishing, and righteousness and victory are increasing. God gives *true* grace so that we can gain dominion over sin (Rom 6:14). *Greasy* grace

---

6. Go back and read the Church Fathers and Mothers, the monastics (east and west), the Puritans, the Catholic mystics, the Wesleyan Holiness revivalists, and the Keswick writers for a real taste of meticulous and powerful teaching on repentance and overcoming sin. So many in our day have been raised on pablum and sawdust and need real meat. No more petting our sin.

We Spirit-filled Christians think because we have the gifts of the Spirit that we are more advanced than those saints from yesterday, that we can't learn anything from them. I invite you to give the following a try: Evagrius, Maximus the Confessor, Thomas A Kempis, Bishop Fenelon, Teresa of Avila, John Owen, John Wesley, Charles Finney, St. John of Kronstadt, Theophan the Recluse, S.A. Keen, Martin Wells Knapp, Andrew Murray and Jessie Penn-Lewis, among others.

allows you to continue in sin, and slide by, so that you can obtain more grace (Rom 6:1–2). 1 John 3:3–10 enlightens us that true believers do not continue to practice sin. At some point they stop. The bottom line is true repentance (ceasing from sin) with zero tolerance. There can be no other strategy when facing sin, however long or whatever it may take. Jesus came to save us from sin. If not, then what are we saved from?

The Fourth Law of Deliverance: The Law of Authority

Christ gives us power of attorney to use his authority and name to defeat and cast out devils (Mark 16:17; Luke 10:19). Jesus cast out demons. His disciples cast out demons, and we are to cast out demons. No excuses! Preaching and teaching the Kingdom, healing the sick and casting out devils (Matt 10:7–8) is a literary and missional formula that one finds in some form throughout the synoptic gospels (Matthew, Mark, and Luke). It defines Jesus' ministry. These core practices were identified with fully preaching the gospel (Rom 15:19; Heb 2:3) not just in word but in demonstration of the Spirit and power (1 Cor 2:4, 4:20). If we are not casting out devils, then we are not fully preaching the gospel.

Casting out demons was central to the core *non-verbal practices* of ministering the Kingdom (power evangelism). It is a sign and demonstration displaying that the Kingdom has come (Luke 11:20). With the "finger of God" Yahweh judged Pharaoh by sending plagues to deliver the Hebrews (Ex 8:19). Jesus came with the same "finger of God" to point out and judge the devil and deliver his people. "The finger of God" represents God's hand of judgment against evil. Allow the finger of God to work through you to judge Satan and cast him out. God is so great that he can defeat the devil with just one finger, as if that were even needed.

Deliverance is a sign that the Kingdom has come! Light has overcome darkness. Without deliverance and exorcism so many would still be bound in sin by the devil. And because so many do not understand or practice the healing of deliverance and because the church operates in unbelief and fear, many suffer needlessly. We do not know our authority in Christ and the mandate to cast out demons.

Remember Matthew 10:7–8 and Mark 16:17 are commandments for all of Christ's disciples. Those Christian ministers and authors who claim we are not called to cast out demons are simply unbiblical. They have turned a blind eye to these and other scriptures, as well as the standard practice of Christ and his disciples. Do they think demons died out with disco? No, they are still alive and well. Casting out demons, along with healing the sick, signs and wonders, teaching, and preaching are fundamental, standard evangelistic practices for proclaiming the Good News. Christ has given us authority and commissioned us to proclaim the Gospel in word and deed, including casting out demons: "I give you authority."

Understanding our authority in Christ is not too complicated. Jesus defeated the devil. He has authority over him, and he holds the keys of hell and death. His ministry was to defeat the devil. He accomplished that in *his* time. Now, he wants us to participate in his ministry by enforcing his victory over the devil in *our* time. Now he gives us the keys of authority to bind and loose (Matt 16:18–19). We have been given such authority that even the gates of hell cannot prevail against the church. We can bind the devil and loose righteousness. We can unlock any door where Satan resides in a person and banish him because we have the keys. We have the authority (*exousia*), or the X-factor, given by Christ, to set captives free.

On my key ring, I have the keys to my house and my car. You do not have those keys. Why? Because you do not own my house or my car. I do. I am authorized because I own them both. I turn the key and the car starts or the door opens. I have authority. All the keys of the Kingdom and all authority belong to Jesus (Matt 28:18). He owns everything. I also have my office key on my ring. You do not. Why? Because you do not own the seminary, nor did they delegate authority to you and give you a key to my office. But they did delegate authority to me and give me a key to my office, even though I do not own the office or the seminary. I hold delegated authority through the key to my office. The same goes with your keys. You have authority over what you own, and I do not.

Jesus delegates authority to us and gives us power of attorney. *He gives us his keys to bind hell and loose heaven.* He has every key to every prison in the spirit, and he has given them to us. Time for a jailbreak (Acts 15:19, 16:27)! He allows us to act on his behalf and use his name to enforce his authority over the devil (Mark 16:17). In Christ's name we shall cast out devils. Our key verses are Luke 10:19–20:

> I saw Satan fall like lightning from heaven. I have given you authority to trample on snakes and scorpions and to overcome all the power of the enemy; nothing will harm you. However, do not rejoice that the spirits submit to you, but rejoice that your names are written in heaven.

There are several facts to note here. First, Satan, formerly known as the angel Lucifer, has already been cast out of heaven by Michael the Archangel (Rev 12). Jesus watched him drop from heaven as fast as a lightning bolt falls from the sky to the earth. He is not in hell yet. That comes at the end (Rev 20).

Satan was cast out of heaven and is on the earth, deceiving and devouring. Yet, Jesus has authority over the devil on *earth* as well. He must because he is giving us his authority to trample on devils. Thus, he must have authority to trample on all the power of darkness as well, and he does. We see this demonstrated throughout the gospels culminating with the cross. Now, though, *we* have this authority. Satan is under Christ's feet (Eph 1:22; Heb 10:13), and now he is under our feet (Rom 16:20).

Other weapons that we possess, along with the name of Jesus, are the *blood, the cross, and the Word of God (the sword of the Spirit).*[7] *We also have worship (all forms: music, dance, art, etc.), prayer, fasting, speaking in tongues, humility, the keys to bind and loose, our testimony, the gifts of the Spirit, the full armor of God, and thanksgiving.*[8] Our weapons are mighty (2 Cor 10:3–5)!

There is not one demon or demonic manifestation that can defeat us. We have been equipped to "overcome all the power of the enemy." So, we cannot lose unless we defeat ourselves by sin or unbelief. Another fact is that, in the process of spiritual warfare or deliverance, we will *not* be hurt by the devil. Satan cannot hurt you! Jesus is clear: "Nothing will harm you." So, friends, we have no reason to fear the devil, evil spirits, demons, or demonic manifestations. Those who fear these things have not truly digested Luke 10:19. Christ is candid. Demons must obey us. They are subject to us. Or put another way, they are our subjects, and we humbly rule over them as kings and princes (Rev 1:6).

The only way we can be defeated is if we do not know our authority in Christ or are living in sin (Mark 3:24; Acts 19:14–16, the sons of Sceva). This is Satan's only hope. Why give the merciless devil any hope? Receive and walk in the authority Christ has given you to cast out demons in his name. At the name of Jesus, every knee must bow, and every tongue confess that Jesus Christ is Lord. Make the devil kneel and confess. Unlike the sons of Sceva, make sure the devil knows who you are!

---

7. In the wilderness, Jesus fought the devil and defeated him with the Word of God (Matt 4). We overcome the devil by the blood of the lamb and the word of our testimony. Our testimony is our agreement with the Word of God in our lives (Rev 12:11).

8. We recount how David's worship drove out the demons of rage and torment from Saul (1 Sam 16:14, 23; 18:10; Ps 18:1), and how the armies of God routed the enemy through the praise of Judah (2 Chr 13:14–15; 20:20–24). Worship is a weapon of war.

Other Wisdom

Deliverance from Abuse and Trauma

While some may resort to deliverance frequently or as a first resort to deal with sin and the devil, I believe real, trained, strategic, formal deliverance should often, but not strictly, be a last resort, unless it is an emergency situation. Sanctification and carrying our cross, as mentioned, are the normative scriptural ways to deal with evil. All sin does not necessarily lead to a deliverance session or intercessory deliverance. In most cases, a person can resist temptation and cast the voice and power of temptation and deception out of his or her own mind and submit to God. James 4:7 sums up deliverance from evil like this: "Submit to God and resist the devil." James 4:7 is an entire theology of spiritual warfare in one verse. This type of general deliverance is the lowest level of spiritual warfare and involves daily personal resistance of temptation and sin by saying no to the devil and the will of the flesh, and yes to God and the way of the cross, which is death to sin.

When the practice and power of sin increase to the point that the believer's will is broken and captured, and the believer can no longer defeat sin and the devil in that area, that person may consider help from the body of Christ. We need each other. There is a variety of assistance that can be offered. One way to help is to have a believer(s) stand in the gap and fight as an intercessor on one's behalf in prayer and specialized deliverance.

Another point of discernment is that not all deliverance is due to sin that one commits. Many who have been sinned against, for example in abusive and traumatic situations, may be attacked, tormented, and bound by the devil. In these cases, such people did not commit a sin but were sinned against. Sin committed against them became the open door. This does not seem fair, but Satan does not fight fair.

Doors to the demonic not only include sins we commit but sins committed against us.[9] The devil uses tragic experiences like abuse and trauma and the emotional damage connected to such experiences as a doorway into one's life.[10] Demons transfer from the victimizer to the victim. We know

9. These sins specifically do not need repentance but inner healing. Pray for Christ to transform the person's thoughts and self-talk regarding the traumatic event. Override the lies with the truth. If sins committed against someone subsequently led to the person committing willful sins, then one needs to repent of those sins.

10. Demons can also harass and even attach to a child or youth through generational sins. The child did not sin. They do not need to repent, and yet they can be attacked by the devil through generational sin that is transferred to them. Often a child is not aware of the nature of the attacks or how to defend themselves, and so the demon is able to get a foothold and tempt the child into sin at some point. In such a case, the

Satan cannot act against their will. But the victimizer, by nature, violates the will of the victim. The abusive victimizer breaks the law of the will in order to violate the victim. The victimizer has broken the law of the will and the devil rides the coattails in. These traumatic experiences that expose our vulnerability provide opportunities for the devil to further take advantage of our tragedies. Deliverance and inner healing are needed.

One of the most common psychospiritual wounds I found in ministry is the *father wound*.[11] This is simply the wound inflicted and left on the soul due to an abusive or absentee father who did not fulfill his role in his child's life the way God intended. The father relationship is the initial and primary

---

child will eventually need deliverance due to the attachment. And if they yield to the temptation, they will need to find repentance at some point and seek deliverance and healing. This footnote stems from a conversation I had with Mark Sandford, 1/12/2022.

11. Our first human relationship is our biological relationship with our mother in the womb. It is a natural, physical, and emotional bond formed between mother and child in which she conceives and nurtures the child through the initial and crucial stages of development. Our connection with our mother is involuntary and dependent. We did not choose it, and yet it is vital and necessary. Due to biological dependence, the relationship is internal and natural at first.

On the other hand, our relationship with our father is the exact opposite. In the early stages of development, it is not a relationship with such strict biological dependence. Mom has that covered. It is more a sociological relationship. The relationship is not internal and biological but is formed from a psychosocial dependence between the child and the father, who is "the other" and the "first" other. Our encounter with "the other" initiates us into society, if you will, and social relations. Thus, the father is the first other the baby encounters.

As a result, the father is the paradigm or model for all other relationships the child will form. The father-child relationship is one that needs to be intentionally formed, at first by the father and later reciprocated by the child. The baby is born into the world already knowing the mother but has yet to encounter the other. That first encounter with "the other" begins with the father relationship, which will be the first and often most powerful influence to shape all other relationships.

The father relationship is also key to molding and modeling our first concept of God, as parents are intended to be the first and primary reflection of God's nature in the child's life. Often a skewed concept of God comes from a skewed relationship with the parents, especially the father who is the first other and the mold for all others. The image of God as abuser, dysfunctional, condemning, permissive, tyrant, enabler, pushover etc. are distorted concepts of God that can come from a father wound.

Thus, the father plays a key role in a child's identity and development, and when the father is abusive or absent and does not fulfill their God-given role, a father wound is inflicted on the soul of the child. This wound is devastating and will have an adverse and damaging impact on the child's biological and psychosocial development that in turn will detrimentally impact overall health and wholeness, future relationships, and the person's attempt at achieving a good, successful life.

Nevertheless, our Father in heaven is a father to the fatherless and desires to heal the brokenhearted and mend the father wound with his unconditional healing love (Ps 68:5; 147:3). He reverses the curse (Gal 3:13).

lens for viewing God, ourselves, and others. Thus, the father wound will adversely impact how we view and interact with God, ourselves, and others.

Case in point, a church that I planted was located in the largest sexually oriented business district in Ohio and the fourth largest in the country. Many of these strip clubs were run by small-time organized crime that used the clubs to traffic women and drugs. As a response, our church launched a Women's Center, The Oasis House, to minister to those trapped in the sex industry.[12]

Over time we learned that most of these women were sexually abused as children, often by fathers, and were later tempted by the devil into a life of promiscuity, drug use, and the sex industry. Others were kidnapped and trafficked. Father wounds and early childhood trauma opened the door to further demonic attack and bondage. Their early father wound shaped how they interacted with others. Some needed deliverance and inner healing not only because of their sins, but also because of sins committed against them.

As a sidenote, the women of our church led many women to the Lord who were working in those strip clubs along what was called the Dixie Strip. The Oasis House also equipped the women to leave the sex industry and get jobs in the mainstream work world. After several years of prayer and "cursing the fig tree" for not producing good fruit, we witnessed the Lord tear down *every* sex club—over a dozen—on the Dixie Strip; it was a modern-day miracle. The last one came down with a tornado (see footnote for news article).[13]

Many of the women we ministered to were bound because of sins committed against them long before they entered the sex industry. Those early wounds resulted in ACEs (Adverse Childhood Experiences) that produced trauma and mental health issues. In my book *Unleashed!* I also make a clear distinction between mental disorders and demons. *They are not synonymous.* Granted, mental disorder may weaken an individual and open them up to demonic attack. Demons are opportunists. They can take advantage of a mental disorder. They smell weakness and attack. They look for brokenness and cracks in the walls of our soul and direct their efforts at those weak points. When we are vulnerable, they sense the advantage and strategically attack.

So, mental disorders and demonization may be comorbid (work together), but they are not synonymous. On the other hand, the opposite can occur. At times the church tries to counsel what needs to be cast out. We cannot counsel out demons. They are not compliant patients. So, spiritual discernment and use of the C1–13 can be helpful in making the distinction.

---

12. Refer to oasisforwomen.org/ for information.

13. Sweigart, "No Strip Clubs," para. 1.

In the next chapter, we will examine the C1–13 instrument that I created to ascertain whether someone needs deliverance. The instrument walks you through a checklist to make sure other measures are tried first before resorting to deliverance. We want an accurate diagnosis that means eliminating all other possibilities. Depending on the case, there may be a need for a physician, a psychiatrist, medication, social work, an accountability partner, a small group, a recovery group, a mentor, or other assistance that can help the person before deliverance is administered. Our approach is integrative using all the resources from faith and the sciences that God offers through his prevenient grace and his saving and sanctifying grace.

The same God who heals us through Christ created the universe and all its healing properties. Satan cannot create anything but deception. But the same God who created the universe also created doctors and gifts us with medical science and other sciences to help improve our quality of life. And that same God created the human body with its own immune system and neurological resilience to fight off disease and overcome trauma. God causes the sun to shine and the rain to fall on the just and on the unjust because God is good (Matt 5:45).

Spiritual Bonds and Chains

A final point is that each deliverance case is unique and different, even though the same four laws apply. Remember, our gauging of deliverance is not black and white, all or nothing, possessed or not possessed. We identified that the New Testament word *daimonizomai* means "demonized" or "degrees of demonic influence." Some people are afflicted to a greater degree than others. Thus, sessions of repentance and deliverance may look different from person to person. Only a caring heart can discern the differences.

The unique brokenness of each person uniquely attracts certain chains and clusters of sin, which are attached to certain chains and clusters of demons, that influence regular patterns and cycles of behavior. The dynamics of sin and the demonic are like chemistry and chemical bonds. Certain elements bond to other elements better than others. People find themselves attracted to the same types of sin and sin patterns along with certain demonic attachments. One common chain I find is unbelief/fear/deception chained to pride/idolatry/Leviathan/narcissism linked to anger/murder/control/Jezebel connected to covetousness/lust/sexual sins.[14]

---

14. For one person's explanation of a Leviathan spirit, see Eckhardt, *Deliverance and Spiritual Warfare Manual*, 144–155. He sees this spirit as a fire-breathing dragon representing pride and stubbornness that cannot be bound by anyone but God. Its defense

Demonic dynamics sometimes parallel family systems and personality traits in psychology. Spiritual bonds or ties also attract people with similar personality types and traits, sin patterns, and demonic attachments that are compatible and work together. The laws of attraction. Many people get connected in a physical tie or a soul tie to the same person repeatedly.[15] They just have a different name each time. Same character and sins with a different name and face. Same bull, different rodeo. Thus, one can often calculate which sins go with which demonic attachments.

Demons operate in typologies or typological traits that work together. For example, Jezebels will always find an Ahab. Ahabs are looking to submit to a controlling Jezebel. They need each other to survive. They feed off each other. The Samson type will always find a Delilah type. And the Delilahs will always seek out the Samsons. When Davids are weak, they seek out a Bathsheba. Murmurers will always look for a Korah or Dathan to lead them, and the Korahs will find the murmurers. Saul types will be jealous of the Davids and seek to kill them. The Cains are jealous of the Abels and will try to murder them. The Judases are looking for corrupt religious leaders, who in turn are looking for Judases to do their bidding. We notice that the soul-sin-demon triadic connection is unique from person to person. But once you crack the code, you understand what sins, demons, and behavior patterns have been in operation in one's life. They work together as a chain and often as a cluster (a family system).

Strategies will look differently as well. One person may need one demon cast out. Others may need more than one expelled. More often, demons work in teams, and more specifically, like a chain, a cluster, or a network. When one enters in, it holds the door for the others. They link to each other as sins are linked to each other (like a family system). The chain becomes a cluster and the cluster a network. We may find that after we cast out one demon, another appears, and so on. They are linked. In fact, that is their strategy; they work as a team, a group, or a cluster. One may enter in and hold the door for two, three, or four more to enter in. And the specific

---

is its armor like scales, a protective coat of impenetrable pride, ego, and unteachableness. Leviathan is boastful, arrogant, defensive, stiff-necked, hard hearted, unbending, unyielding, unchangeable, untamable, will not serve, cannot enter covenant, lawless, and rebellious. See Job 41.

15. A soul tie is an unhealthy connection between people that is not a connection of the Holy Spirit but of the soul-mind, will, emotions, and personalities. Between sexes, the soul tie can be suggestive but not necessarily consummated. It remains an emotional affair, though it can involve a physical tie, which binds the people together spirit, soul, and body (1 Cor 6:15–18). A soul tie is not a normal, healthy friendship, but a connection that is out of order and sinful, often based on power, control, manipulation, and emotional satisfaction. It is an over-attached relationship that finds it difficult to detach.

demons that link together are related by their traits, powers, and assign-ments. This is how they are like a family system, or chemical structures and bonds in complex chemical compounds, for you chemistry majors.

In the C1–13, I organize sins and demons in clusters, so we are aware of their expanded influence on a person. Sin and the demonic work across clusters to form a network connecting certain types of people and traits with certain kinds of institutions or systems to create systemic evil. And the system of evil in turn works on the networks and cluster to recruit more in-dividuals. Systemic evil (like racism) is tough to bring down. You need war-fare and repentance on multiple levels: individual, institutional, spiritual, psychological, sociological, and political. And the battle is also against rul-ing spirits over a jurisdiction. Watch out though! New levels, new devils![16]

In terms of the individual, the strongman or the ruling sin may be unbelief/fear that manifests as false religion or witchcraft. This demon may open the door for the sin of pride/idolatry, which may open the door for a spirit of blasphemy, that may in turn let in a murder spirit, that manifests as anger and domestic abuse, that may open the door to lust and perver-sion, that manifest in sexual abuse and pornography, that may get a pastor removed from a local church, that may thwart a citywide revival.

We can see the chain and network here. One sin leads to another, and behind each sin is a demon which leads to another demon. There is a chain, a hierarchical chain of command. We may at first think the problem is sexual addiction, but then as the person is open, repents, and confesses, and we follow the Spirit's discernment, we discover that there are more players working behind the scenes.

And so, we work backwards until we get to the ruling sin and spirit that are often generational. Somehow, one of our ancestors committed an unrepented sin that has been passed down to the third and fourth genera-tion both genetically and spiritually (Deut 5:9). In that case, we trace the chain all the way back through the generations, and we declare that Christ became a curse for us. We enforce the cross and declare that Satan has no legal right to pass that curse on because Jesus broke it (Gal 3:13). We can proceed to cast the evil spirit out.

One can see how these chains can become quite complicated and in-tricate, like a family system or family tree, or a map of chemical compound structures. Sometimes one session finishes the job, but often it does not. It depends on the level of repentance, the willingness of the individual, and the X-ministers walking in a high level of the manifest authority of Christ

16. Regional and national repentance and deliverance are taking the work of this book to the next level and would require another book to unpack. See the *excursus* at the end of this book.

(the Four Laws). However, if the sessions are led by the Spirit, and the person is repentant, you should see progress even if there are bumps, hiccups, and an occasional roadblock.

One Strike and You Are Out

Also, it is significant to note that some sins do not need to be committed with the same duration, frequency, and intensity as other sins in order to open a door to a demon. Some sins practiced just once can serve as direct contact with the demonic. One and done. Some of these sins are Satanism, witchcraft, murder, pornography, the occult, and sexual perversion, among others (1 Cor 6:9–10; Gal 5:19–21; Rev 21:8, 27; 22:15).

Other sins may not involve a demonic attachment until practiced more frequently or intensely, e.g., telling a so-called little white lie, taking a pen from work, glancing for the first time at an attractive person, getting angry when you hit your finger with a hammer or stub your toe on the bed, and similar sins.

Though in one sense a sin is a sin, and all are equal in terms of breaking God's laws (James 2:10), some sins do not seem to be of the same magnitude as those mentioned above. In this sense, all sins are *not* equal. Sins express evil to various degrees. For example, as Paul mentioned, fornication, unlike all other sins, is with the body (1 Cor 6:6–20). Not all cases are the same. Not all cases will experience liberty in the same amount of time or number of sessions.

Lesson 4

Pre-Deliverance Preparation (Pre-Op)

HOW DO I KNOW WHEN SOMEONE NEEDS DELIVERANCE?

You may be working with a person who seems troubled and possibly bound by a demon. Do they have a demon? Do they need deliverance? How do I know? How can I be sure? Deliverance is not a simple "dirty deed done dirt cheap." Have them take the C1–13 assessment. In this chapter, we will introduce the C1–13 (Colossians 1:13) assessment instrument that determines whether an individual needs deliverance. It should be filled out by the leader of the deliverance team who asks the seeker questions. Prior to the assessment, there is a 10-point checklist to ensure the seeker is *ready* to take the assessment. Although an emergency deliverance session may be done on the spot, a formal deliverance session has a specific protocol (or proper diagnosis and procedure).

EMERGENCY AND FORMAL DELIVERANCE SESSIONS

Let me unpack what I mean by that last statement.[1] I am making a distinction between an *emergency situation* that is ministered to on-the-spot and a *formal deliverance session(s)* that involves a formal protocol (the C1–13) of preparation, prayer, fasting, testing, scheduling, and deliverance. An emergency situation either arises in the moment or can afford no time to waste

---

1. The following distinction and explanation of ER and formal deliverance services was inspired by a conversation I had with Candy Gunther Brown.

for various reasons. The situation demands immediate attention. On one hand, the ER session is like non-elective ER surgery. On the other hand, the formal deliverance session is like getting tested and if needed scheduling an elective surgery.

We have ER deliverance and scheduled, formal deliverance sessions. We need to be prepared for both. In the case of ER and formal deliverance sessions, both will at minimum still employ the Four Laws of Deliverance, the 5 Step Method of Deliverance, and post-deliverance follow-up with Truth Therapy and renewing the mind.

For example, if someone needs ER heart surgery, we do not schedule them for a visit in five months. If the situation is not an ER situation, we can run through much of the protocol (the $C1-13$) needed to make sure the person is receiving the proper informed, integrative healing that comes from multiple sources, lest we try to cast something out that can be treated medically, for example.

We need to make sure that what we think is the problem is really the problem. Treating a problem that is not the problem can result in malpractice and further harm done. The $C1-13$ protocol is an instrument that helps us ascertain what the real problem. We are dealing with people's lives and are liable before God and humanity and should take our work seriously, professionally, and carefully. The consequences can be spiritual, moral, psychological, sociological, and legal.

In light of such gravity, what I am attempting in much of our deliverance and healing work is to legitimize, standardize, and professionalize or certify what is often a hit or miss, shoot from the hip, anecdotally led ministry, which often leads to excesses and malpractice. If there is any field and practice that needs quality control, it is deliverance ministry. Since deliverance and divine healing are working with spiritual and medical categories, such as health and wholeness, we draw from a medical model as well as from the Spirit. We are seeking to integrate the best from the sciences and combine them with the best theological practices to establish effective, careful, tested, and credible integrated models and practices of deliverance and healing.

Thus, in "diagnosing" and treating spiritual problems like deliverance, we are attempting to develop thorough, sophisticated procedures and protocols that cover all the bases and incorporate the learning, methods, and approaches from all relevant fields. Hence, medical model diagnostic testing is simulated in our instruments and strategies. We are not medically treating people, but we are drawing from the medical model by testing, caring for, and practicing at the optimal level.

Thus, I created the $C1-13$ instrument as a protocol to address the problem thoroughly and spiritually as well as to integrate treatment from other fields. *The C1–13 is the first of its kind in the field.* Often in my ministry I have found that prior treatment in areas like mental health, followed up with deliverance and healing if needed, have been more effective than deliverance alone. Undergoing the C1–13 testing also helps the diagnostic (elimination) process in discerning etiology (causes) for more effective treatment. I have witnessed so much abuse in this area, especially around mental health. It is too easy to jump the gun, demonize, and attempt to cast out things that may be better treated elsewhere. I have seen too many people walk away more damaged after a deliverance session than they were before.

So, let me qualify a statement made that deliverance *often needs to be a last resort.* I believe in certain situations that deliverance needs to be immediate, and not initially go through the protocol that I prescribe. Sometimes a case may be urgent, and the person is ripe and ready. There is no time for a lengthy protocol. I have been in that situation as a pastor, revivalist, and deliverance minister countless times. I cite a few cases in this book.

A deliverance minister and team should be prepared to take on "ER" (emergency) situations which require immediate attention, treatment, and ministry. They should also be prepared to minister a formal deliverance session that goes through the C1–13 protocol. ER situations often but not always occur with unbelievers in evangelistic settings. Signs and wonders (including deliverance) are non-verbal proclamations and demonstrations of the Kingdom and the gospel and should be standard in ministering the gospel. Deliverance and healing happen as the Spirit leads and, at times when needed, can bypass protocols, i.e., happen spontaneously and not in a scheduled session with standardized practices.

In a worship service or prayer meeting, when sometimes demons manifest on the spot or a person is in dire need and should be taken to the deliverance room, we need to follow the Spirit's lead and minister to the person. But there should still be a follow up appointment for the more formal and standardized approach to deliverance. The protocol will help the deliverance team be more thorough and effective and catch anything that might have been missed. In my experience, most of the prerequisites have already been met prior to one filling out the C1–13. Having a person who goes through an emergency deliverance session later go through the protocol is more of a both/and rather than an either/or.

The standardization I created is to prevent abuse and excess, but I do not want the protocol to become the problem it was meant to solve. A deliverance team needs to use wisdom and prayerful discernment in making the call as to when to practice deliverance. In summary, I am making the distinction in deliverance situations between "ER non-elective surgery" situations and "scheduled elective tests and surgery." *There are both emergency and formal deliverance session(s).* The Holy Spirit, discernment, the case, and the circumstances will determine which is needed. All emergency sessions should still be followed up with a formal session and its protocol. The C1–13 is protocol for a formal deliverance session.

EVERYONE SHOULD KNOW HOW
TO CAST OUT DEMONS

In this chapter, we will also explore how to prepare for a deliverance session(s). Preparation is necessary and should be taken seriously. Groundwork involves planning and homework for both the deliverance team and the person in bondage, who we will call the seeker. We will examine essential items, such as qualifications for a deliverance team, repentance, prayer and fasting, scriptures related to deliverance, and other helpful wisdom.

Deliverance is a standard and historical practice of the Christian faith. The occasion may arise in which you have to minister to someone in need. Even if you do not have a call to deliverance ministry, you should be equipped to perform a deliverance session in an emergency situation or when needed. Let me plainly state that *every* pastor and minister should know how to cast out demons. And *every church* should have a deliverance ministry. Further, *every disciple* should know how to cast out demons (Matt 10:7–10; Mark 16:17; Luke 10:19–20), simply because you are a disciple of Christ. Jesus cast out demons. His disciples also did two thousand years ago, and his disciples should today as well. No excuses!

INTRODUCTION TO THE C1–13 INSTRUMENT

When does someone need a deliverance session? Many ministries approach this question differently. My approach is an integrative approach using the best resources that the Spirit and the sciences can afford. Thus, you need good discernment, the inner witness of the Holy Spirit, and an effective assessment instrument, as you pray about a particular case.[2] In addition, the testimony of the seeker concerning their own oppression is very helpful.

I developed the C1–13 (Colossians 1:13) assessment instrument several years ago for ministry use. My intent was to develop something more

2. The inner witness is when God's Spirit directly bears witness with our spirit about the truth (John 14–16, 15:26; Rom 8:14–16; Heb 10:15; 1 John 2:20, 27). Or simply, the Spirit tells us the truth about a matter. The witness is immediate, direct, and self-evident. It is often a still, small, knowing voice that leads the believer into truth. It is our sixth sense, or spiritual sense by which we know God and discern good and evil.

sophisticated and accurate beyond the usual inventory checklists offered at the back of many deliverance books. The C1–13 is modeled after instruments developed and used in the soft sciences, like psychology. The C1–13 probability assessment is a qualitative and quantitative research instrument that evaluates the *probability* of the need for deliverance. No instrument is 100 percent accurate. After the person takes the assessment, the results are not absolute but *probable*. Thus, discernment must be employed. Read over the C1–13 several times until you understand it before administering.

The C1–13 measures the degree of demonization and bondage to a sinful practice. The instrument also evaluates the need for deliverance, utilizing a score that will indicate whether deliverance is probably needed or not needed. This instrument seeks to identify areas of bondage and to ascertain the degree of bondage in a particular area. The instrument is based on the understanding that to the degree one submits to an area or practice, to that degree the sinful practice has authority or control over one's will. This proportional relationship between submission and control is, as you now know, the law of the will. Sin and the demonic have control over an individual to the degree he/she submits to them.

One of the main goals of deliverance is the liberation of the will. This goal is acheived by taking authority in the name of Jesus over the powers that hold one's will in captivity, resulting in a will that is liberated. At that juncture, a liberated will can respond to grace, believe in Christ, and choose righteousness. Satan may tempt us, but we have the responsibility and choice to resist him, and he will flee (James 4:7).

The C1–13 instrument is broken up into five sections: *Personal Information, Inventory of Prior Treatment of the Problem, 10 Point Checklist, the Assessment Inventory, and the Score Sheet.* The first three sections are intended to gather information to form a comprehensive picture of the problem and document prior treatment. Treatment from other fields may involve psychiatric care, clinical therapy, pastoral counseling, or even small group accountability. The premise is that a formal scheduled deliverance session is often a *last* resort to alleviating symptoms and solving the problem. Other prescribed spiritual measures and prescribed healthcare treatment need to be considered holistically and prior to a formal deliverance session.

These first three sections assist in locating missing pieces in a comprehensive plan of treatment and refer seekers to other types of treatment prior to participating in a deliverance session. If a seeker has any items unchecked on the 10 Point Checklist, they are to address those prior to continuing with the deliverance assessment process.

The final two sections of the C1–13 instrument are the actual assessment inventory and the score sheet, which is a worksheet for tallying up the composite score and evaluating the score for the need for deliverance. At the end of the C1–13, there is a key that evaluates the score. The key lets you know if the person probably needs deliverance or not.

The assessment inventory is divided into eight categories or clusters/ classes of sinful practices with an itemized list of practices under each category. The eight categories or clusters of sinful practices are: **occult, mental health-related, addictive, sexual, criminal, religious, family of origin, and other.**[3]

The person taking the assessment marks each practice that they or a family member is or has been involved with. Family member involvement (generational) may impact all members and can open the door to the demonic for the entire family, so it must be identified (Exod 20:5; Deut 5:9). The assessment scores each practice in relationship to four variables: *generational, frequency, duration, and intensity of practice.* From these four scores a composite score (**BQ—Bondage Quotient**) is derived. The BQ score is then evaluated in terms of the probable need for deliverance.

There are two notable distinctions made in this instrument. The first is that mental disorders are not demonic in themselves. The second is that deliverance is different from exorcism. These two points you have already learned. First, it is important to recognize that mental disorders are not demonic in themselves, but they can impair the person in a way that can open the door to demonic attack and demonization. There is an awareness inventory under section two of the assessment that helps the seeker to identify current mental health issues that may render one *susceptible* to certain sinful and demonic practices.

The awareness inventory does not contribute to the actual scoring of demonization but is used for critical self-awareness. The awareness inventory is not factored into the overall score for demonization, because demons and mental disorder are not synonymous. The inventory is to make one aware that a mental disorder can make them vulnerable to demonic attack.

---

3. Here are some of the spirits affiliated with each cluster or category of sin. The list is not exhaustive. Occult: spirits of divination, witchcraft, Jezebel, necromancing, prognostication, and others. Evil spirits can take advantage of Mental Health disorders—Spirits of murder, control, Python, lawlessness, deception, fear, and others. Addiction: rejection, reproach, Ahab, violation, fear, witchcraft, and others. Sexual: spirits of pride, idolatry, Leviathan, Jezebel, lawlessness, murder, Python, abuse, violation, confusion, perversion, rejection, reproach, Molech, and covetousness. Criminal: spirits of fear, murder, lawlessness, deception, rejection, abuse, confusion, and others. Religious: spirits of deception, idolatry, adultery, witchcraft in various local forms, Python, Jezebel, doctrines of devils, confusion, fear, among others. Family of Origin: spirits of rejection, reproach, guilt and shame, Python, Jezebel, Moloch, addiction, Leviathan, abuse, lawlessness, deception, idolatry, murder, and others.

Following this awareness inventory is an *actual* inventory of related sinful practices that are to be scored.

When deemed necessary, proper psychiatric treatment and counseling must precede any assessment of deliverance. Often many confuse mental disorders for the demonic.[4] I have watched too many people unsuccessfully try to cast out schizophrenia, rather than treat the disorder psychiatrically, minister inner healing, and then cast out spirits (if there are any) that attacked the individual due to the disorder. When mental healthcare professionals properly treat the mental disorder, it often becomes clearer what is a clinical issue and what is a demonic issue. If a mental health issue is detected and treatment has not been prescribed yet, then a person should be referred to a mental health professional.

Second, it is also significant to note that this assessment makes a distinction between deliverance and exorcism. The former involves degrees of demonic influence and can occur in believers. The latter is rare, involves demonic possession, and cannot occur in believers. The former involves degrees of demonization and control, while the latter involves total demonization and control. However, both deliverance and exorcism are handled in the same manner. The Four Laws of Deliverance apply to both. Exorcism is just a more intense and involved version of deliverance because it is dealing with possession.

Although this instrument seeks to assess areas and degrees of demonization, again, not every Christian challenge or trial involves a direct encounter with a demon or needs intercessory deliverance. As referenced above, the normative way to deal with sin and evil is through resisting temptation, sin, and the devil with the power God gives us. The Lord has thoroughly equipped the church with a variety of weapons for the battle. For instance, God gives us power in his name, the scriptures, humility, thanksgiving, prayer, the keys to bind and loose, fasting, the gifts of the Spirit, his armor, worship, his blood, the cross, and his presence to do battle with sin and evil. In our everyday struggles with evil, we are called to take up our cross daily and put to death our flesh and its passions and temptations (Gal 5:24). The cross is our basis for deliverance.

There are occasions, however, when we fall. If anyone does sin, we have an advocate in Jesus Christ (1 John 2:1). We are called to come to the throne of mercy (Heb 4:16), confess, and repent of our sins. If we turn away from our sin and toward God, God will forgive us, and the blood of Jesus Christ cleanses us from all unrighteousness (1 John 1:7–9). Yet, there are

---

4. For a rationale for differentiating between mental disorder and the demonic, see Bellini, *Unleashed!* and *The Cerulean Soul*.

instances following sin and repentance where one cannot break the cycle because a door to the demonic has been opened. In other cases of advanced and progressive transgression, one continues in a sin(s), opens the door to the demonic, is oppressed, and needs assistance through the ministry of deliverance in order to be liberated.

When ministering deliverance, it is important that deliverance is ministered by church leadership that has been trained, certified, installed, and recognized in this area. Deliverance needs to be ministered in teams of two or more. Also, there needs to be pre- and post-work that contributes to the overall deliverance and healing process. I recommend this book, of course, *Truth Therapy* (Peter Bellini, Wipf and Stock) or a similar work, like *Deliverance and Inner Healing* by John Loren Sandford and Mark Sandford. The pre- and post-work involves teaching, counseling, repentance, confession, faith and forgiveness, inner healing, renewing the mind with the Word of God, accountability, prayer, and discipleship.

It is also essential to approach deliverance and healing holistically. Utilize all necessary means and treatment available that can work together comprehensively. For example, a healthy diet, daily exercise, deep breathing, good and sufficient sleep, counseling, and medication when needed can work well together with prayer to minister healing to people struggling with depression and anxiety. If a person is on medication, do not counsel them to stop treatment. Let all doctor prescribed treatment be assessed by the doctor alone. Leave medical counsel, diagnosis, and prescribing to the medical professionals.

THE C1–13 INTEGRATIVE DELIVERANCE NEEDS ASSESSMENT

Can be filled out by the client, minister, or deliverance team leader in an interview

Personal Information

Name _____

Address _____ Ph # _____

Sex ( ) M ( ) F   Age _____

Marital Status:

( ) Single   ( ) Married   ( ) Divorced   ( ) Remarried   ( ) Widowed

Profession _____

Your parents' status:

( ) Single   ( ) Married   ( ) Divorced   ( ) Divorced and Remarried   ( ) Widowed

Number of children and ages _____

Currently in Counseling ( ) Y N ( )   For how long? _____

Currently taking meds ( ) Y N ( )   Names of med_____

How long on meds _____

How many hours of sleep do you get a night? _____

Have you gained ( ) or lost ( ) more than give pounds in the last month?

Have you experienced loss of appetite ( ) or increased appetite ( ) lately?

Do you have constipation ( ) or diarrhea ( ) in the last month?

Have you experienced lately loss of interest in things you once enjoyed ( )?

Have you experienced any of the following: a strange invisible presence ( ), hearing voices in your head ( ), strange sights or sounds in your house ( ), thoughts that someone or something is watching you ( ), moments of blanking or blacking out.

Have you had odd experiences lately, such as nightmares ( ), accidents ( ), sudden significant financial loss ( ), irregular fights with family members ( ), explosive fits of rage ( ), other _____?

Any other mental health issues in your family, past or present?_____

Faith Information

Do you currently attend a local church? ( ) Y ( ) N

Church Name_____

How long attended? _____

Do you profess saving faith in Jesus Christ? ( ) Y ( ) N

Salvation? Date _____

Have you been baptized in the Holy Spirit? ( ) Y ( ) N Date_____

Are you familiar with phenomena such as the work of the Spirit, angels, and even demons? ( ) Y ( ) N

Do you have a time of regular prayer and Bible Study? ( ) Y ( ) N

How much time? _____

Are you involved in any ministry? _____ For how long?_____

Reason for this Deliverance Appointment

Description of problem and symptoms _____

_____

_____

Is there a family history of this problem? ( ) Y ( ) N Explain _____

_____

Inventory of prior treatment of the problem

Since deliverance is a type of healing, it is often helpful to think of deliverance in terms of wholeness and health. Issues of health are often treated holistically and comprehensively from an integrated approach that affords the best resources from faith and science. Thus, it can be helpful and effective to approach certain problems and issues with multiple types of treatment that impact body, mind, emotions, and spirit. Indicate which types of treatment you have used or are currently using.

What other forms of treatment for the problem have you used? Mark (X) and fill in blanks.

__ Repentance.   How long ____   Results _____
   What type _____
__ Medical.   How long ____   Results _____
   What type _____
__ Counseling.   How long ____   Results _____
   What type _____
__ Support group.   How long ____   Results _____
   What type _____
__ Prison or jail.   How long ____   Results _____
   What type _____
__ Recovery group (AA, NA)   How long ____   Results _____
   What type _____
__ Medication.   How long ____   Results _____
   What type _____
__ Prayer group.   How long ____   Results _____
   What type _____
__ Prior deliverance.   How long ____   Results _____
   What type _____
__ Confession and forgiveness.   How long ____   Results _____
   What type _____
__ Diet.   How long ____   Results _____
   What type _____
__ Exercise.   How long ____   Results _____
   What type _____
__ Sleep therapy.   How long ____   Results _____
   What type _____
__ Other lifestyle changes.   How long ____   Results _____
   What type _____
__ Other: _____

10 POINT CHECKLIST

Check off each item, 1 through 10, that you have completed and still found no difference, relief, or change in your condition. If you mark a check by **all ten statements**, then you qualify for deliverance. If you have left any statements unchecked, you need to have those addressed with the proper professional (general physician, psychiatrist, therapist, or pastor) before continuing with the inventory assessment. Note you cannot continue with the assessment if you have any unchecked items on any of the 10 statements.

1. Confessing sin, repentance and faith, forgiveness, accountability, participation in worship, inner healing, prayer, and discipleship groups are not breaking the cycles of sin or oppression in an area. ( )

2. Attempts at prayer, fasting, and spiritual warfare, and those by other intercessors, are not breaking the cycles of sin or oppression in the area. ( )

3. You addressed your beliefs and practices, especially questionable ones, with your pastor or spiritual leadership in your church. ( )

4. Leadership discerns demonic presence and influence in your life. ( )

5. You sense demonic influence in your life. ( )

6. You visited a physician, therapist, or other mental health professional for evaluation. ( )

7. Treatment such as counseling, medication, diet, exercise, rehabilitation, recovery group, or other form of treatment is not working. ( )

8. You feel helpless in one or more area(s) and struggle at times to perform daily functions. ( )

9. You have been seen by professionals (medical, pastoral, or other) about your problem(s). ( )

10. After trying other means of help, deliverance is often seen as a last resort. ( )

Follow-up: Identify each numbered question that you did not check. Find that number below for follow-up instructions. For example, if you left numbers 6 and 9 unchecked, then go to numbers 6 and 9 below and follow the instructions for each. After you have followed through with the instructions on each question and can eventually check all 10 statements, then you can proceed with the assessment.

1. You need repentance and faith in that area of sin. Take time to follow up in this area. Participate in spiritual disciplines, the means of grace, confession of sin, repentance and faith, forgiveness, accountability with one or more people, worship service, inner healing, or a discipleship group.

2. You may need to pray, fast, and execute spiritual warfare, as well as approach intercessors on your behalf to do the same. Take the time to follow up in this area.

3. Take time to meet with your pastor or spiritual leadership to address your specific beliefs and practices and have them evaluated by scripture, especially any questionable ones. Transformation of beliefs can lead to transformation of life and practice. Christian catechesis, conversion, and discipleship are all necessary for right belief, worship, and practice.

4. You need to make an appointment with leadership for prayer, discernment, and inner healing. Intercessors, prophets, spiritual directors, and counselors, among other qualified leadership, can assist you in hearing the voice of God and discerning God's direction and will for your life.

5. Take time to discern in prayer if you are battling an evil spirit(s).

6. Schedule an appointment with a therapist or other mental health professional to be evaluated concerning the problem.

7. Receive proper treatment from the proper professional (medical, mental health, social worker, sponsor, nutritionist, trainer, recovery etc.).

8. You may not need deliverance. Confide with a counselor, spiritual director, confidant, or accountability group or partner to make sure you are being open and honest about personal struggles in your life.

9. Discuss your problem with the proper professional: pastor, medical doctor, specialist, or mental health professional.

10. Have the problem addressed according to the follow-up instructions given in 1–9.

If you have checked all ten statements, then proceed to take the Inventory Assessment to determine the probability for deliverance. If you have any unchecked statements, then you should *not* continue with the assessment. Those areas need professional follow-up prior to proceeding further with this assessment. Do not take the Inventory Assessment until you have had those areas addressed by a medical professional, psychiatrist, therapist, pastor, or other appropriate professional. Only proceed with the Inventory Assessment after checking off all ten statements.

THE INVENTORY ASSESSMENT

Inventory of Practices

There is no formula, metric, or scientific test to discern with absolute precision the presence of demonization. Detecting demonization is a spiritual process. One can discern from scripture, the Holy Spirit, and the fruit in one's life whether deliverance is needed. However, the spiritual process of discernment can be aided by a qualitative analysis of one's behavior as well as a cross-evaluation with other disciplines in the hard and soft sciences, such as general medical practice, psychiatry, or clinical therapy.

This inventory is a tool that assists the spiritual discernment process by working in concert with other professional fields while analyzing behavior that is considered sinful and possibly demonic according to the Christian scriptures. The C1–13 assumes cooperation with other professional fields and as a last resort assesses the probability and need for deliverance based on practices or fruit and the frequency, duration, and intensity of the practice. The inventory identifies doors of evil influence that may require deliverance. Not all the practices implicate demonization. The scoring following the inventory, along with the 10-point checklist above, can ascertain the probability of demonization.

*Practices indicated in the inventory by an asterisk can be highly traumatic and open doors to the demonic and may not need to occur frequently but sometimes just once. Scoring is determined by the experience of the person taking the assessment.

Check off any of the following influences or practices that involve you or your family. Only check a sinful practice once. Do not check the same sinful practice twice.

1. **Occult Practices** (spirits of divination, witchcraft, Jezebel, necromancing, prognostication, and others).

___ Witchcraft of any form

___ Curses—cursing or cursed

___ Inner vows, pacts, and covenants

__ Curses—history of inexplicable systemic accidents, tragedies, or misfortunes

__ Sacrifices

__ Ouija board

__ Crystals, charms, amulet use

__ Numerology

__ Fortune telling

__ Hypnotism—giver or receiver

__ Macumba, Santeria, Umbanda, Candomble

__ Tarot cards

__ Kabbalah

__ Trances

__ Evil eye or similar curses

__ Books, music, movies, or other forms depicting the occult

__ Freemasonry or secret societies

__ Levitation

__ ESP, telekinesis

__ Witchcraft medicine, witch doctoring, shamanism

__ Alchemy (modern type involving magic)

__ Mind reading

__ Automatic writing

__ Horror movies, violent and gore related movies

__ Astrology, zodiac

__ Séance

__ Satanism*

__ Wicca

__ Esotericism

__ Vampirism

__ Crystal ball use

__ Table lifting or other telekinesis

__ Black Magic or magic of any type

__ Divination

__ Gang vows or rituals

__ Astral projection or out of body experiences

__ Channeling

__ Spirit guides or mediums

__ Clairvoyance

__ Sacrifices*

__ Role playing games involving other gods' or spirits' demonic practices

__ Necrophilia, necromancy

__ Contacting the dead or use of mediums

__ Palm read or reading, palmistry

__ Reiki, energy healing or other types of healing

__ Covenants, vows, oaths, pacts to any spirit or deity

__ Psychics

__ Do you possess paraphernalia related to the occult:books, movies, games, music, or any objects that have been used for non-Christian religious purposes, like masks, idols, statues, fetish objects, etc., or for any of the above purposes? (Acts 19:18–19)

__ Gnostic type practices

__ Summoning spirits, demons, the dead, or any non-physical beings*

__ Role-play games involving any of the above

__ Other paraphernalia

__ Animal abuse

__ Other occult practices_____

List not exhaustive. See Christian Bible.

2. **Mental Disorders and Susceptibility to Destructive Practices**

   NOTE: *It is important to recognize that mental disorders are not demonic in themselves, but they can impair the person in a way that can open the door to demonic attack and demonization. When necessary, proper psychiatric treatment and counseling must precede any assessment of deliverance. Often many confuse mental disorder for the demonic. Once a mental disorder is properly treated by mental healthcare professionals, it often becomes clearer what is a clinical issue and what is a demonic issue. If a mental health issue is detected and treatment has not been prescribed yet, then seek help from a mental health professional.*

Check the following mental health issues to determine the susceptibility to unwanted or destructive practices. These items are not part of identifying and scoring practices used to assess the probability of the need for deliverance. Checked items create an awareness of vulnerability to certain practices. This list identifies mental health issues that may or may not be collaterally related to practices that need deliverance. Mental disorders alone are not necessarily demonic.

Awareness Inventory of Mental Disorders and Susceptibility

__ Minor Depression diagnosis from a professional

__ Major Depression diagnosis from a professional

__ DSM-5 on Major Depressive Disorder. If one has five of the following nine symptoms daily:

__ depressed mood or irritable most of the day, nearly every day, as indicated by either subjective report (e.g., feels sad or empty) or observation made by others (e.g., appears tearful)

__ decreased interest or pleasure in most activities, most of each day

__ significant weight change (5 percent) or change in appetite

__ change in sleep: insomnia or hypersomnia

__ change in activity: psychomotor agitation or retardation

__ fatigue or loss of energy

__ guilt/worthlessness: Feelings of worthlessness or excessive or inappropriate guilt

__ concentration: diminished ability to think or concentrate, or more indecisiveness

__ suicidality: Thoughts of death or suicide, or has suicide plan

__ Mood Disorder/Bipolar diagnosis from a professional

__ Schizophrenia diagnosis from a professional

__ Panic or panic attacks

__ Anxiety Disorder diagnosis from a professional

__ DSM 5—The presence of excessive anxiety and worry about a variety of topics, events, or activities. Worry occurs more often than not for at least six months and is clearly excessive. The individual experiences at least three characteristic symptoms including:

__ restlessness or feeling keyed up or on edge

__ being easily fatigued; always tired

__ difficulty concentrating or mind going blank

__ difficulty focusing

__ irritability; easily disturbed

__ muscle tension

__ and sleep disturbance

__ ADD diagnosis from a professional

__ ADHD diagnosis from a professional

__ OCD—compulsions or compulsive behavior—diagnosis from a professional

__ ODD—oppositional, defiant—diagnosis from a professional

__ Hearing voices

__ Trauma* (from any number of incidents of war, abuse, or other)

__ Racing thoughts

__ Very difficult to focus

Susceptible to Destructive Practices—These items are to be identified and scored to assess probability for the need of deliverance. Spirits of murder, control, Python, lawlessness, deception, fear, and others can be related to this category of sinful practices. Score the following items:

__ Suicidal (ideation, plans, or attempts)

__ Death wish (want to die)

__ Self-mutilation or cutting

__ Curses—cursing or cursed

__ Inner vows, pacts, alliances, and covenants

__ Compulsions or compulsive behavior

__ Thoughts and feelings of rejection or low self esteem

__ Hallucinations, irrational paranoia, or hearing voices not related to treated Schizophrenia. These symptoms should first be assessed by a mental health professional.

__ Feelings and thoughts of hopelessness, worthlessness, and helplessness

__Violent behavior toward self or others

___ Lying or stealing

___ Promiscuity

___ Criminal behavior (See section #5)

___ Vertigo, dizziness, or involuntary movement or manifestation not related to other somatic or mental health issues

___ Night terrors/violent nightmares

___ Fear (undifferentiated)

___ Fear of people, crowds, death, the opposite sex, the dark, future, sickness or disease, or any other specific type

___ Obsession(s)

___ Any addictive behaviors (See section 3)

___ Other unwanted or destructive practice. See Christian Bible 3.

3. **Addictions/Addictive Practices** (see chapter 4)—rejection, reproach, Ahab, violation, fear, witchcraft.

___ Alcohol, drunkenness

___ Prescription Drugs_____

___ Illegal drugs _____

___ Marijuana, hashish, opium

___ Heroin

___ LSD, hallucinogenics, N-Bombs

___ Krokodil

___ Methamphetamines, crystal meth

___ Opioids of any sort like Gray Death, Fentanyl, Pink AH-7921, and others

___ Flakka, bath salts

___ Ecstasy

___ Molly

___ Anabolic steroids

___ Crack cocaine, cocaine

___ Pornography

___ Cigarettes

__ Sexual addictions

__ Gambling

__ Excessive, compulsive or needless spending or spending sprees

__ Obsessive and compulsive internet use

__ Internet chatting, dating, sexting, or encounters for sexual or illicit purposes

__ Other_____

List not exhaustive. See Christian Bible 4.

4. **Sexual Practices** (often connected with spirits of pride, idolatry, Leviathan, Jezebel, lawlessness, murder, Python, abuse, violation, confusion, perversion, rejection, reproach, Molech, and covetousness)

__ Any sexual practice forbidden in Scripture (See Christian Bible.)

__ Gender dysphoria

__ Autoeroticism, masturbation

__ Polyamorous relationships

__ Pornography

__ Adultery*

__ Fornication*

__ Lust, covetousness

__ Incest—victim* or perpetrator*

__ Abuse of others*

__ Experienced sexual abuse* Being abused is not a sin.

__ Pedophilia*

__ Prostitution

__ Paraphilias

__ Necrophilia

__ SMBD

__ Soul tie(s)- connections between people that are not connections of the spirit but of the mind, will, emotions, and personalities. Between sexes they can be suggestive but not consummated, an emotional affair, though it can involve a physical tie, which binds the people together spirit, soul, and body (1 Cor 6:15–18). A soul tie is not a normal, healthy friendship, but a connection that is out of order and sinful, often based on power, control, manipulation, and emotional satisfaction. It is an over-attached relationship.

__ Incubus, succubus, or sexual experience with a presence in dreams or awake at night

__ Voyeurism, stripping or watching, or exhibitionism

__ Bestiality*

__ Rape* or was raped*

__ I molested* or I was molested*

__ Perverse forms of sex or sexuality

__ Confusion around one's gender or sex (may not be demonic itself but may invite demonic attack)

__ Sex paraphernalia, objects, files, books, videos, games, etc. related to pornography or sexual abuse

__ Other_____

List not exhaustive. See Christian Bible 5.

5. **Criminal Practices** (Often connected with spirits of fear, murder, lawlessness, deception, rejection, abuse, confusion, and others)

__ Theft, forcible entry

__ Murder*, homicide, manslaughter

__ False witness, perjury

__ Assault or battery of any kind

__ Racketeering

__ Extortion, conspiracy, or treason

__ Manslaughter*

__ Homicide*

__ Gang affiliation and activity

__ Abortion*

__ Fraud _____

__ Drug use, sales

__ Prostitution

__ Rape, Sexual assault, other forms of abuse

__ Incarcerated

__ Experienced physical, mental, verbal, or sexual abuse

__ Sex trafficking/trafficked* or working in the sex trafficking industry*

__ Other_____

List not exhaustive. See Christian Bible 6.

6. **Religious Practices**

Note: Religious affiliations do not always necessitate demonization and the need for deliverance. As a religious affiliation facilitates beliefs and practices contrary to scripture, it can open the door to sin that in turn can open the door to the demonic. However, it is significant to note that some religious affiliations' teachings about the nature and activity of God or moral conduct may parallel or be in line with the teaching of scripture, and not be sinful or demonic.

For example, a religion may teach that God created the universe, or that stealing, lying, and adultery are forbidden practices. Sinful practices and potential doors to the demonic are identified by Christian scripture. World and folk religions, beliefs, practices, and forms claiming to be "Christian," new religious movements, cults, and various spiritual movements that foster unbiblical beliefs and practices, can not only be sinful but can also open the door to the demonic.[1]

Sinful religious practices can be connected to spirits of deception, idolatry, adultery, witchcraft in various local forms, Python, Jezebel, doctrines of devils, confusion, and fear, among others. These items are to be identified and scored to assess probability for the need of deliverance. Score the following items:

__ Idolatry—Prayer, use of artifacts in magic or worship, communication, or a specific practice or devotion to any god besides the God of the Christian scriptures

__ Transcendental Meditation or other forms of meditation that involve other gods including self

---

1. According to sociologist William Bainbridge, "A cult movement is a deviant religious organization with novel beliefs and practices. Bainbridge, *The Sociology of Religious Movements*, 24. Due to pejorative examples and connotations of the word cult, this particular use of cult derived from sociology and anthropology of religion is not in current use as much as "new religious movements." However, this instrument is claiming that both new religious movements and the more limited, pejorative understanding of cult need to be examined for beliefs and practices and weighed out culturally through critical contextualization in light of scripture.

__ Doctrine of devils and seducing spirits: World religions, indigenous religions, or Christian syncretistic religions with unbiblical teachings and practices, for example Baha'ism, any polytheistic or animistic religions, and others. Can include false doctrines held within a Christian denomination or by an individual unrelated to any movement

__ Cultic manipulation, control, and abuse found in "Christian" cults, such as Mormonism, Jehovah's Witnesses, Unification Church (the Moonies), Boston Movement, Christadelphians, Rosicrucian, or others

__ Cultic manipulation, control, and abuse found in non-Christian cults, such as Scientology, Eckankar, Twelve Tribes, EST (the Forum), the Family, NXIVM, and others

__ Religions, syncretism, folk religions, or spirituality that uses sorcery, channeling, fetishes, spells, enchanted objects, or any other means to conjure, communicate, contact, gain power, or be influenced by spirits or the spirit realm, such as New Age, paganism, Wicca, shamanism, Satanism, Freemasonry, secret societies, paganism, Course in Miracles, Umbanda, Macumba, malocchio, distinu, Santeria, Yoruba, orichas, Voodoo or other similar forms and practices. Acts 19:18–19

__ Legalism of any sort, whether Christian or non-Christian religion

__ Doctrines and practices of racism and racial supremacy, regardless of race

__ Practices of witchcraft

__ Book of Urantia

__ Umbanda, Candomble

__ Freemasonry and secret societies

__ Necromancy

__ Trances

__ Reiki

__ Hearing voices not explained by mental disorder

__ Night terrors

__ Sleep paralysis (demons riding the person)

__ Curses: given or received

__ Inner vows or covenants

__ Conjuring spirits

__ Spirit possession (intentional or unintentional)

__ Talking to spirits

__ Sacrifices

__ Covenant or alliances made to any spirit or god besides the God of Christian scripture

__ See occult practices

__ Ancestor worship (beyond honoring) that involves devotion as unto God or covenants and alliances made

__ Paraphernalia related to religious practices

__ Other

List is not exhaustive. See Christian Bible 7.

7. **Family of Origin Practices** (See the other categories for related demonic activity.) Often connected with spirits of rejection, reproach, guilt and shame, Python, Jezebel, Moloch, addiction, Leviathan, abuse, lawlessness, deception, idolatry, murder, and others. In this section, if you marked a particular sinful practice in another previous category, then you may mark it here as well.

__ Occult_____

__ Addiction _____

__ Sinful or destructive practices related to mental disorder _____

__ Criminal acts _____

__ Unbiblical religious belief practice_____

__ Sexual sin _____

__ Divorce

__ Abortion or survivor of one*

__ Curses—cursing or cursed

__ Inner vows, pacts, and covenants

__ Rejection issues, orphaned, abandoned. Other rejection issues.

__ Trauma of any type

__ Prone to systemic accidents, injuries, sickness, miscarriage, financial crises, premature death etc.

__ Incest*

__ Rebellion

__ Disobedience to parents

__ Abuse(ed) (sexual, physical, mental, or verbal). Being abused is not a sin.

__ Other _____

List not exhaustive. See Christian Bible 8.

8. Other Sinful Practices

__ Pride

__ Jealousy

__ Lust

__ Laziness or sloth

__ Envy

__ Greed

__ Gossip, slander, backbiting

__ Condemnation

__ Judging, judgmental

__ Unforgiveness

__ Hatred

__ Spirit of fear of future, others, the opposite sex, heights, closed spaces, death, sin, insanity, water, going outside, and other objects of fear

__ Competition

__ Rebellion

__ Idolatry

__ Anger or rage

__ Swearing/cursing

__ Drunkenness

__ Gluttony

__ Malice

__ Blasphemy

__ Profanity

__ Taking God's name in vain

__ Lying, false witness, deceit

__ Heresy

__ Division, schism

__ Legalism

__ Bitterness

__ Experienced familial, marital, short or long-term abuse of any type

__ Books, movies, games, music, or other forms that depict sinful practices that have influenced your thoughts and behavior

__ Other _____

\# List not exhaustive. See Christian Bible 9.

Evaluation of each practice:
Score each practice that was flagged in the inventory of practices by assigning a numerical value (1 to 5) to each of the four areas of assessment (generational, duration, frequency, and intensity). The total added score represents the Bondage quotient. Note some practices need only occur once to open the door to the demonic and require deliverance.

Generational—Over how many generations has it been practiced?

1. First generation
2. 2 generations
3. 3 generations
4. 4 generations
5. 5 generations

Duration—How long has it been practiced?

1. Less than 3 months
2. 3 months to a year
3. At least a year
4. 1–5 years
5. More than 5 years

Frequency—*How frequently has it been practiced?*

1. A few times a year
2. Once a week to once a month
3. 3 times a week
4. Daily
5. More than 3 times a day

Intensity—*How intensely has it been practiced?*

1. Practice with little interest and passion
2. Practice with some interest and passion
3. Practice with moderate interest and passion
4. Practice with high interest and passion
5. Practice with intense commitment and passion

Scoresheet

Type of Practice	Generational +	Duration +	Frequency +	Intensity =	BQ Total
_____	_____	_____	_____	_____	_____
_____	_____	_____	_____	_____	_____
_____	_____	_____	_____	_____	_____
_____	_____	_____	_____	_____	_____
_____	_____	_____	_____	_____	_____
_____	_____	_____	_____	_____	_____
_____	_____	_____	_____	_____	_____
_____	_____	_____	_____	_____	_____

Evaluation of BQ Composite Score (the *Bondage Quotient*) for each practice and levels of demonization		
	0—	No deliverance needed 0%
Level 1:	1–5	Need for repentance and faith with very low probable need for deliverance 0–20%
Level 2:	6–10	Repentance and faith needed with low to moderate probable need for deliverance 20%–50%
Level 3:	11–15	Need for deliverance is moderate to likely probable 50%–70%*
Level 4:	16–20	Need for deliverance is highly probable 70%–100%*
*Asterisk indicates probable need for deliverance		

LEGAL WAIVER FOR MINISTRY

Legal protection from liability when ministering deliverance is wise counsel. Besides training workers in proper ministry conduct and boundaries that can prevent infractions of misconduct, harassment, abuse, and similar charges, ministries should require participants to sign a release of liability. Here is a sample waiver drawn up by my attorney Ronald Koch. This sample can be used as a template or guide for crafting one specific to your own context. I recommend your ministry or local church draw up its own that is approved by its board of trustees and is based on the laws of your state and the specific context of your ministry.

RELEASE AND WAIVER OF LIABILITY

DISCLAIMER: THIS FORM DOES NOT CONSTITUE LEGAL ADVICE. ANYONE USING THIS FORM SHOULD DO SO ONLY WTH THE ADVICE OF THEIR OWN LEGAL COUNSEL.
Read before signing
IMPORTANT. READ CAREFULLY. This document affects your legal rights. You, the "Participant," must sign it whether you are an adult or minor, if you are participating in "Activities" (generally referred to as "Deliverance Ministry") facilitated by [CHURCH use actual legal entity] ("Facilitator").

Your parent or legal guardian must sign it also if you are a minor Participant (under 18 years of age.) The parent or guardian agrees to these terms individually and on behalf of the minor. Only a parent or legally appointed guardian may sign for a minor Participant. References in this agreement to "I" or "We" include all who sign below unless otherwise clearly indicated.

PARTICIPANT AGREEMENT (Including Acknowledgement and assumption of Risks, Agreements of Release and Indemnity, and Additional Provisions)

In consideration of the opportunity to participate in activities offered by Facilitator,

I, _____   the Participant (adult or minor), and,
(Please print name)

_____,   the parent or legal guardian of a
(Please print name)   minor Participant, understand,
acknowledge and agree as follows:

ACTIVITIES, HAZARDS AND RISKS
The various activities may include [LIST ACTIVITIES].

The hazards and risks (together referred to as "risks") associated with the various activities may include [LIST], as well as associated reasonably foreseeable risks.

Participant, and the parent or guardian of a minor Participant, acknowledge and understand that the description of the activities and risks described herein is not complete and that all activities, whether or not described, may be dangerous and may include risks which are inherent and cannot be reasonably avoided without changing the nature of the activity.

Facilitator has made no effort to determine, and accepts no responsibility for, medical, physical, or other qualifications or the suitability of Participant, or other participants, for the activities. [MAY NEED TO CHANGE THIS IF YOU DO BACKGROUND CHECKS, ETC]

Participant, and the parent or guardian of a minor Participant, accepts full responsibility for determining Participant's medical, physical, or other qualifications or suitability for participating in the activities.

Participant, and the parent or guardian of a minor Participant, HEREBY CERTIFIES that the Participant, and the parent or guardian of a minor Participant has personal health insurance. Insurance company is

_____

Alcohol will, and other substances may, impair judgment and reduce a Participant's ability to effectively manage the various risks described herein, and are therefore strictly prohibited by Facilitator except for necessary prescribed or over the counter medications, and if applicable, approved by the Parent or legal guardian of a minor participant.
Failure to adhere to instructions, should they be provided, may result in serious injury or death.

ACKNOWLEDGMENT AND ASSUMPTION OF RISKS
I, the Participant (adult or minor) and the parent or guardian of a minor Participant, understand the nature of the services of Facilitator and other associated activities which may occur, and their risks. I acknowledge and expressly assume all risks of the activities, whether or not described above, known or unknown, and inherent or otherwise. I take full responsibility for any injury or loss, including death, which I, or the minor child for whom I sign, may suffer, arising in whole or part out of such activities.

AGREEMENT OF RELEASE AND INDEMNIFICATION, AND ADDITIONAL PROVISIONS

If I am an adult participant, or the parent or guardian of a minor Participant, I agree, for myself and on behalf of the minor Participant for whom I am signing, as follows:

I release Facilitator, its employees, contractors, volunteers, and directors ("Released Parties") from any and all claims of injury or loss which I, or the minor child for whom I sign, may suffer arising out of or in any way related to my, or the minor's, enrollment in or participation in the activities of Facilitator. Neither I, the minor child, nor anyone acting on our behalf, will bring suit or otherwise assert any such claims against a Released Party. I will indemnify (that is, defend and satisfy by payment or reimbursement including costs and attorney's fees) each Released Party from any claim of liability, including one brought by or for a minor child whom I sign, a co-participant in any of the activities of Facilitator, a rescuer, a member of my, or the minor's family, or anyone else asserting a loss arising out of or on any way related to my, or the minor's enrollment in or participation in the activities of Facilitator.

ADDITIONAL PROVISIONS

I authorize Facilitator to provide or obtain for me, or the minor child for whom I sign such medical care as it considers necessary and appropriate, and I agree to pay all costs associated with such care and related transportation.

Any dispute between Facilitator and me or the minor child for whom I sign will be governed by the substantive laws of the State of Ohio [VERIFY STATE] (not including the laws which might apply the laws of another jurisdiction).

This agreement is entered into voluntarily and after careful consideration. Its terms cannot be amended except in writing. I understand that it is binding, to the fullest extent allowed by law, upon all people signing below, our respective heirs, executors, administrators, wards, minor children (whether or not they are Participants) and other family members.

If any part of this agreement is found by a court or other appropriate authority to be invalid, the remainder of the agreement nevertheless shall be in full force and effect.

I, and the minor child for whom I may sign for, read and understand the English language.

I or the minor child for whom I sign shall be responsible for the return of all equipment supplied by the Facilitator or independent contractor in the same condition that existed at the time of taking possession of said equipment and that no alcohol, intoxicating liquor or illegal drugs shall be taken or consumed during or in the course of any activity described herein.

Participant: _____   Age: ____   Date: _____
(Signature)
Parent or Legal Guardian: _____   Date: _____
(Signature)

QUALIFICATIONS FOR DELIVERANCE

It goes without saying that people called to minister in the church of Jesus Christ, including deliverance ministry, need to meet appropriate biblical qualifications. I advise the reader to study thoroughly the Scriptures, especially the pastoral epistles (1 and 2 Timothy and Titus). 1 Timothy 4:16 is key: a mature Christian leader pays attention to how they live their life and to their doctrine. This will ensure salvation for both the leader and those who follow their teaching.

In Scripture, you will find the moral and spiritual qualifications needed for leadership in the body of Christ. Some of the qualities and characteristics highlighted in Scripture are: the fruit of the Spirit; the gifts of the Spirit; the call of the Spirit; the character of Christ; sound doctrine; handles conflict well; maturity; seasoned, not a new Christian; integrity; reputable; submits to authority; accepts proper correction; accountable; wise problem solver; a spiritual son or daughter to a mentor; teachable and able to teach; not argumentative; not seeking glory or attention; works well with others; a servant; balanced; humble; available; faithful; financially content with little or much; not greedy; conduct above accusation in family, ministry, and public life; sharp discernment; people-wise; full of faith and the Holy Spirit; wise; committed; quick to hear and slow to speak; an encourager; a good steward; and more.

Proper Leadership Selection

We have listed some general qualifications and traits of a high-quality Christian leader. Let us add a few more related specifically to deliverance ministry. I cannot stress enough the gravity of proper and prayerful leadership selection. Keep in mind that Jesus prayed all night prior to selecting the twelve apostles (Luke 6:12). How much more consideration should we give for this vital process?

In my long tenure of ministry, I have discovered that proper and prayerful leadership selection prevents a host of potential problems in the future and is crucial to building an effective ministry. Proper and prayerful leadership selection is worth its weight in gold. We need to understand why and how God chooses leadership.

God builds people, and people build the Kingdom. People over programs. We do not build programs and grow churches. We cannot. That is
God's business. We merely participate. God makes disciples. Disciples are
the church. And though we plant and water, only God can give the increase
and grow disciples (1 Cor 3:6–8). The seed, the water, and the increase are
his! Like Jesus, we focus on building people, as he did with the twelve. It is
the order of Elijah and the order that Christ followed. This method goes
counter to the ways of the world and the business model of the church to
select leaders to build programs and churches for profit.

Throughout my ministry, I noticed that many church leaders select
new leaders for all the wrong reasons: competence, money, fear, friend-
ships, yes-people, protection, nepotism, cronyism, sycophancy, popularity,
ego, and others. Later, the sycophants whom they selected will only follow
them so far. Plus, the in-crowd, us-and-them culture that they create alien-
ate the rest of the workers. Or they find that the highly competent person
they selected for ministry was not faithful, teachable, humble, or at times
not even saved.

Because they were the most competent in that area of ministry, the
adept person felt they were beyond teaching or correction. They could not
work well with others on a team. It was their way or the highway. They
became controlling over the ministry and would not line up with the vision
of the leadership. They offered a different vision. Anything with double vision will stumble and fall, including a leader or a church. Trying to take the
ministry away from such a person would be like trying to take a bone away
from a hungry, wounded dog.

Soon this type of person begins to attract followers who are immature,
broken, and susceptible to authoritarian, dysfunctional leadership because
perhaps they were raised in a dysfunctional family of origin. Now the
church leadership cannot correct or remove this person because it would
cause a rift in the church, since the person's following has grown.

Our friend begins to give power to his/her proteges. They reproduce
the same chaos that their mentor is spreading. They agree with him/her that
he/she is more anointed than the pastor. And the church needs to follow
him/her. Conflict increases in the church. Suddenly there are too many fires
to put out. Confusion and discord are spreading rapidly, along with gossip
and evil speaking against church leadership. Many pastors in these situations have thrown their hands up in frustration and cried out, "What can I
do?" I want to say, "Who gave the monkey the gun?" It is on us, the leaders.

We equip people and give them the keys of responsibility and ministry.
Do not be surprised when you pick ill-prepared servants, and they start
swinging from the chandeliers and shooting randomly at people. Trust me.

I know. I made this mistake early in my ministry. Don't give a badge to Barney (Fife), and don't create a Frankenstein that becomes too powerful to stop. The answer is prayerful and proper leadership selection from a crop of spiritual sons and daughters, not a hireling (John 10:12–13; 1 Cor 4:17; 1 Tim 1:2).

Train, Certify, and Install Deliverance Ministers

Be wise. Apply scriptural standards. Make sure mentees are faithful with little before you give more (Luke 16:10). And make sure that the little that you give them is behind-the-scenes and not a glorious job. Attention seeking is one of the primary signs of immature or dysfunctional leadership. Give them spiritual latrine duty. That is what my spiritual father gave me when I got started. If they do menial tasks wholeheartedly unto the Lord, as if they were preaching to a thousand people, then they earn responsibility, respect, and authority. God will promote them. Promotion comes from the Lord (Ps 75:6–7).

Let leaders in training grow in responsibility relative to their growth in character. Do not be tempted to violate scriptural qualification and put a person in power for all the wrong reasons (1 Tim 3:6). You will pay dearly. I had to learn early. And I have been in many organizations where I have watched these principles violated to the detriment of the organization. Hiring yes-people, cronies, and sycophants is a recipe for disaster. Nip it in the bud early. Select properly and prayerfully.

In the churches that I pastored, we had classes to train and certify altar workers and X-ministers. Then we publicly installed them as certified ministers in a special worship service. In this manner, church people know those who labor among them (1 Thess 5:12). They know that these ministers have been trained, approved, and certified by church leadership, and they can trust receiving ministry from them. Give every minister, paid or unpaid, a ministry description-covenant and evaluate them at least annually for quality control. This method prevents dysfunctional people from holding office or ministries.

Too many times in Spirit-filled churches we place charisma over character, power over holiness, and gifts over fruit and allow anyone with an anointing to minister to our people. Too many times in Spirit-filled churches, I watched someone walk into a church for the first or second time and begin to prophesy and take control of the service. It becomes the wild, wild west.

Some are even what I call "spiritual terrorists." They come into a church and start prophesying against the church or the pastor. They call out some sin that they claim the church or leadership is guilty of, saying that the church needs to follow the new vision or revelation that they have. If they do not follow, God will judge the church. They are trying to build on another's foundation (Rom 15:20).

They will say the church is not spiritual enough and does not walk in the level of revelation and anointing that they do. They start to gain young, impressionable followers who are led by their charisma. Why not? They are anointed and have prophesied amazing things. They have all the spiritual bells and whistles. They are brother or sister glow-in-the-dark. Wooooo. Choirs of angels sing every time brother or sister glow-in-the-dark speaks. And everything they say is prophetic, as they bat their eyes and glitter falls from heaven. They can instantly conjure up a word for anyone. They get revelation about everything they do; what car they buy; what cereal they eat; what clothes they wear; and every number in their life has prophetic significance: phone numbers, addresses, bills, prices etc. Like some kind of Christian Kabbalism. At times, it has been said that their feet don't even touch the ground. (I am facetiously drawing a caricature to make a point.).

It seems those with their nose in the charismatic catnip also have "led poisoning" too. They will not do anything unless they are *led*. They will not love their neighbor, submit to authority, get a job, pay their taxes, or change their undergarments, unless they feel led. They will not do things that the Bible already commands us to do, unless they feel led. "Led poisoning," charismatic drama at its finest. The Bible gives us enough revelation to work on for a while. We really do not need any *new* revelation until we obey the *old* revelation and get this "love thing" down, mastered, and perfected (1 John 2:7). I know I have a way to go. How about you?

However, anyone with any degree of maturity can see that this type of glow-in-the-dark spirituality is more of what I call "spooky spiritual." Something is not quite right. If you look with the Spirit's eyes and listen with his ears, you will pick up on the glitches. Usually, their family and vocational life are in disarray. They may be in considerable debt. They are rarely planted in a church for a long period of time. And at times they are using the church to gain attention, power, money, and/or converts. Unless they are in leadership, they cannot work well with anyone. And they rarely submit to authority.

In the churches where I pastored, we would never let anyone give a word unless they were trained and certified in our church. Even then, all revelation was tested by me and the local church elders. I know this may sound strict, but I have been in those situations and tried being "nice" and working with such people. First, we would apply Galatians 6:1–12.[1] This passage speaks to the proper way to restore someone with gentleness who had been caught in sin. In the case of the Galatians, they were dealing with the Judaizers and their false teaching and practice around circumcision. Paul encourages leaders to be careful and cautious when helping people who have fallen that one does not make the situation worse. I soon found out those were prophesying out of line did not speak that language of gentleness or correction nor were they receptive to it. They usually take it as a sign of weakness or permission and continue to do what they were doing, even taking it to the next level. Things would get worse.

Early in my ministry I was fearful of conflict and would do anything to avoid it. I would kick into my default mode of people-pleasing, which was easier. Needless to say, that did not work; it made things even worse. If you think you can placate Jezebel to get her to fall in line, you are gravely mistaken. You are actually feeding and enabling her. I finally learned to confront prayerfully and humbly with grace and truth. Simply, don't give Barney a badge.

Spiritual Sons and Daughters

One way to prevent spooky spiritual people from taking over is to raise and use exclusively spiritual sons and daughters in your ministry. You have invested your life in them. They share your spiritual DNA and vision, for it is part of their spiritual, genetic makeup. Intentional discipleship is essential to training leaders. It has been my practice as a pastor and professor to work closely with spiritual sons and daughters and invest in their lives with one-on-one mentoring that involves modeling, prayer, study, accountability, and ministry training (the order of Elijah and the 2 Tim 2:2 principle).[2]

At the core of intentional one-to-one discipleship is modeling that results in life-to-life transference. My spiritual children know not only my doctrine but my life (1 Tim 4:16). Exemplify and embody the person of God that you want your spiritual sons and daughters to become. Invest trust and

1. Galatians 6:1–2 is a powerful scripture for leaders attempting to restore leadership and others who have fallen or erred. However, it can also be used improperly by conflict avoidant people, or taken advantage of by non-compliant, unrepentant people.

2. No method is fool proof against selecting unfaithful leaders. At times even our spiritual children can betray us. Jesus chose twelve and one was a devil. Be humble. Love them. Pray for them. Seek to restore them. Do not pursue or seek vengeance against a Judas. An old friend once told me that if they resist redemption, to shake the dust off your feet and give them just enough rope, and they will hang themselves. Though I prefer they get restored.

deep commitment into the teaching relationship. And they will respond. The growth is supernatural. I recommend it over every other form of leadership development.

As a spiritual son, I have seen it work with me. As a spiritual father, I have seen it work with my students. The fruit is abundant and long-lasting. We move beyond superficial relationships between pastor and congregant or merely information-based relationships between teacher and student. Paul said to the chaotic Corinthian church, which did not lack gifts of the Spirit or information, "You have ten thousand teachers but not many fathers." Young leaders are looking for the growth that can only come from the one-on-one commitment and care of seasoned spiritual parenting.

Apprenticeship

Deliverance ministry training occurs most effectively under an apprenticeship, which is a type of one-to-one intentional discipleship model, like Elijah and Elisha and the School of the Prophets.[3] The apprenticeship is modeling and shadowing and hands-on experiential training in an area and skill that cannot be learned merely from a book. Yes, an apprenticeship involves theory, abstract reasoning, and studying books, but more importantly, it involves learning from a mentor who models the skills and invites one into the process for hands-on training that can be directly supervised.

The mentor takes the apprentice to a ministry event, like a home or prison visitation, or in our case a deliverance session. The apprentice observes and studies what is being modeled. Then they shadow and participate in the background. They are supervised and evaluated. As they advance, they move to the foreground of ministry, while the mentor moves to the background. Eventually, they are mature enough to be released without the mentor's direct supervision (see the classic by Robert Coleman, *The Master Plan of Evangelism*).[4]

Early on, I learned that raising spiritual sons and daughters is not a means to the end of making yourself look or feel good. People should never

---

3. The spiritual parenting model seems to be prevalent in scripture and throughout church history. Moses raised up the seventy elders (Num 11:25) and Joshua (Deut 34:9). Eli raised up Samuel (1 Sam 3). Elijah raised up the school of the prophets (1 Kings 19—2 Kings 2). Jeremiah trained Baruch (Jer 36—45). Christ and the twelve (Mark 3:16). Barnabas discipled Paul (Acts 13–16). Paul trained Silas (Acts 15–18). Paul raised up Timothy (1 Tim 1:2). There are many more biblical examples. We see the model of spiritual parenting throughout the eastern and western monastic traditions as well.

4. Coleman, *Master Plan of Evangelism*.

be a means to our own ends. Spiritual parenting is for the glory of God and the disciples' edification. I recommend that people with control issues refrain from spiritual parenting. Or at least be a penitent control freak in recovery.[5]

Desirable Traits and Practices in an X-Minister

When I am apprenticing leaders in deliverance ministry, I expect them to be certified in my deliverance course, saved, baptized with the Spirit, humble, willing to enter into a one-to-one discipleship relationship, and demonstrating all the scriptural traits of a candidate for Christian leadership, as mentioned earlier in the chapter. I look for someone who has a hunger to see people set free. They have heard a specific call to this type of healing ministry. The call is confirmed by church leadership because they have witnessed the fruit that has been produced early in their ministry. God has providentially already sent them deliverance assignments.

They seem to attract broken people and are attracted to them, but not in a dysfunctional way. They usually are intercessors with a high level of compassion and empathy. And they have a compatible gift set that includes discerning of spirits, the gift of healing (since deliverance is a type of healing), the gift of faith, and some combination of revelatory gifts, such as word of knowledge and prophecy. Frankly, I would have been helpless in most deliverance cases that I faced without the Spirit's toolbelt of gifts, especially word of knowledge, word of wisdom, and discerning of spirits. These gifts revealed to me the demons and schemes that I was confronting in each session as well as God's strategy for victory. I went into deliverance expecting to hear God. And he did not disappoint. We need "superpowers" to fight a supernatural war (2 Cor 10:3–4).

Expect God to speak to your heart. Expect God to give direction and fill you with his yoke-breaking anointing, even a breaker anointing, which is needed to break through the gates of a bound and chained soul (Mic 2:13). The gate is the stronghold of the city and the soul. It is the most heavily fortified ground because the gate is the entrance and the exit. The manifest authority empowers the prayer warrior with a breaker anointing to bring the gates down (Prov 21:22; Is. 43:14; 45:2; Matt 16:18). Expect for God to send his Word, the right Word at the right time, to break the stronghold,

---

5. I think that is where I am at, penitent and in recovery. It took some time to recognize the subtle control, but the Spirit points it out for our growth, so we do not inhibit the growth of others. I began to observe control first in my natural parenting with my own children. God dealt with it early in my ministry.

heal, and deliver (Ps 107:16–20). The rhema sword of the Spirit (Eph 6:17) will proceed from Christ's mouth on the inside of you and be released from your lips to slay the enemy.

Seek the weapons of warfare that are spiritual and not physical. Our battle is not a battle with flesh and blood (people) but with demonic powers. Although deliverance is clearly spiritual warfare, it is not physical warfare fought with physical and natural prowess. Christ the warrior within will crush the head of the enemy, but he rules in our hearts as the Prince of Peace. Though we are bold and confident in battle, we must walk in the fruit of the Spirit and Christlikeness when fighting on behalf of the captive. Christ won the battle over sin, Satan, and death through *humility* on the cross.

While many think of exorcists as radical, intense spiritual warriors with type-A personalities, I prefer the personality type, traits, temperament, and strengths that parallel someone in the medical health field, like a nurse. Deliverance and exorcism are more like performing open heart surgery or delivering a baby than destroying a building (demolition) or taking out the enemy in a crossfire during battle (Prov 16:32).

In deliverance, we are ministering to broken and wounded souls. We need people who are not fearful of the devil and who walk in power and authority, but they need to be filled with Christ's love, care, and compassion above all else. Bold but humble. Ruthless with Satan and sin but caring and gentle with people. Look for a high compassion quotient in potential X-ministers.

To extend the nurse metaphor, in some cases a nurse in a mental health unit or a prison may be more appropriate. In such facilities, there are often patients or inmates who become violent and need restraint. It does not happen often, but it does happen (Matt 17:15; Mark 1:26). So be prepared. One Sunday Service at an altar call, we had a young woman come forward for prayer for healing. As soon as the altar workers began to pray for her, she began to manifest in a rage. She began to pick up altar workers and ushers and toss them around like ragdolls.[6] Her voice changed, as she growled with a deep male voice, shouting expletives at various leaders in the church. She then bolted to the stage and began to heave the altar flowers and plants at the ushers.

I was at the other side of the altar praying for someone when this storm hit. It all happened quite suddenly before I was able to restrain the young

---

6. A demonically influenced person can acquire supernatural strength that they never possessed before. They can turn into spiritual Hulks in an instant. I have seen this numerous times. Be aware and be careful. Try not to instigate or exacerbate a volatile situation. Teach your deliverance team de-escalation strategies and tactics.

woman and eventually minister deliverance and watch her be set free. We do all we can to protect the safety of the seeker, but also, we need to be aware to protect the safety of the deliverance ministers. They need to be aware that incidents like this one, though rare, can occur.

Training needs to include safe restraining techniques. Teach communication skills that focus on de-escalation, though demons usually do not abide by de-escalation tactics. Some ministries' aggressive tactics can actually *instigate* such scenarios. Other times such things occur for no apparent reason, as in the incident mentioned above.

In any case, have no fear. Fear attracts and intensifies demonic activity. Satan, like a wild animal, feeds on fear. In a situation where someone is manifesting anger and is looking to become violent, it is imperative not to be afraid. Yes, be gentle, caring, and attempt to deescalate their aggression, but do not be afraid or show fear. The devil will sense this, manifest more intensely, and may even cause the person to strike at you. I had this happen recently with a young man. He was a good-sized fella. I am, too. I could see the rage in his eyes when I began to pray. He glared at me with eyes that could kill. He began to growl.

He was clearly trying to intimidate me. I even heard the demon in the spirit say, "If you come any closer, I will kill you through this man." The devil wanted me to back off and abort the session. No way! Nothing by any means will hurt me (Luke 10:19–20)! And in the natural, I am not going to back down from anyone either. I bound the spirit of violence. And then I went right past that demon and bolted at the man with a bold, fearless love that pursued his soul until we found victory. I would not be intimidated. Jesus would not be intimidated. We won the victory! He was delivered from drug addiction, rage, sexual promiscuity, and rebellion and gave his life to Christ!

Humility as a Weapon

Often in some of our Spirit-filled circles our priorities are out of order. We fervently pursue gifts. We go to conferences for impartation and activation of gifts. We love to manifest the gifts. We spend time and money to get better equipped to utilize those gifts. These pursuits are all admirable. But the greatest virtue to pursue is not a gift at all. 1 Corinthians 13 admonishes us to pursue love above all. Love is a fruit and arguably the summation of all the fruit of the Spirit (Gal: 5:22–23). I believe our priorities are out of order when we place gifts ahead of fruit. When was the last time you attended a conference on humility and self-denial? When was the last time you even heard of such a conference? Imagine going back to your friends and saying,

"I waited in the altar line for an hour, and I finally received this awesome anointing for suffering. It was worth the wait. Do you want me to lay hands and impart it unto you?"

Now, I do not believe we have to choose between gifts or fruit. This is a false dichotomy, a false choice. Fruit and gifts are both from God, and Scripture encourages us to pursue both. But we need to prioritize. Charisma without character, power without holiness, and gifts without fruit is a recipe for disaster. We become too top-heavy without the proper foundation and substructure to uphold and properly employ all that firepower. It is like giving an AK-47 to a five-year-old. And yet, we seem to be teaching this very thing to young believers, pursue gifts and power above all else. For many Spirit-filled believers, charismatic gifting *is* their Christianity. Charismatic operation *is* the goal of the Christian life. This is a dangerous reduction to make. To the contrary, love is the essence and goal of the Christian life, not the gifts.

As a result, we mistake gifts for fruit. God judges our tree based on fruit and not gifts (Matt 12:33). Fruit is cultivated in faithfulness and obedience. On the other hand, gifts are freely given and do not fully reflect our faithfulness. (Rom 11:29). We can be outside of the will of God and still operate in the gifts. We can operate in the gifts of the Spirit, become a false prophet, and even go to hell (Matt 7:22–23). God does not take back the gifts that he gives us, even if we are no longer in his will (Rom 11:29). They are not a gauge for holiness. Many people have operated in their gifts, even though they were outside of the will of God, such as Saul, Samson, Judas, and others.[7]

Many mistake the anointing for God's approval of a minister's life. Let us be clear that the anointing is a sign of God's goodness and holiness and not yours. Charisma is not the fruit. It is not a marker of your faithfulness or holiness. Do not confuse being an instrument of the gifts with being an instrument of righteousness. Don't confuse gifts for fruit or obedience. Charisma is not character. The gifts are a sign of God's faithfulness and not yours.

One way to balance our teaching on the gifts is to prioritize the fruit of the Spirit over the power of the Spirit.[8] One way to make this move is to prioritize humility. Why humility first? All that we receive from God, including our salvation and the gifts of the Spirit, comes from God's grace. Without grace, we have nothing. Grace comes first. So, grace is essential and a

---

7. Unfortunately, recent Christian history is replete with ministers that operated powerfully in the gifts of the Holy Spirit but were in known for sin, false, doctrine, or false prophecy, such as B.H. Irwin, Charles Parham, William Branham, A.A. Allen, Leroy Jenkins, Lonnie Frisbee, and Paul Cain among others.

8. But do not exclude the gifts. The fruit are not in opposition to the gifts as many cessationists and groups that oppose the gifts would claim.

priority. However, scripture claims that God only gives grace to the humble but resists the prideful (James 4:6; 1 Pet 5:5). Humility is a prerequisite or qualifier for grace. So, if grace is paramount, and you cannot receive grace without humility, then how significant and precious is humility? Regarding how to stay faithful to the truth, St. Augustine was claimed to have said:

> This way is first humility, second humility, third humility, and however often you should ask me I would say the same, not because there are not other precepts to be explained, but, if humility does not precede and accompany and follow every good work we do, and if it is not set before us to look upon, and beside us to lean upon, and behind us to fence us in, pride will wrest from our hand any good deed we do while we are in the very act of taking pleasure in it.[9]

Humility, Humility, and Humility! As we pursue Christ and excellence in deliverance ministry, let us be clothed in humility (1 Pet 5:5). When we are clothed in humility, it functions as armor against Satan, whose nature is prideful. Humility strengthens our immunity to Satan's nature and his attack. Humility fortifies us to resist the devil. Remember, God resists the prideful but gives grace to the humble. Pride attracts the devil but repels God. However, humility attracts God's grace but repels pride and Satan (James 4:6). Humility empowers us to submit to God and resist the devil (James 4:7). It is therefore indispensable.

Simply, humility is demon repellant, especially against witchcraft. On the contrary, pride is an aphrodisiac for Satan. He is attracted to our pride like flies to manure. Satanic attack, and specifically witchcraft and leviathan, feed off the stench of human pride. The antidote is humility. Pride cannot cast out humility. But humility is an invincible weapon against pride and the enemy. Be baptized and clothed in humility prior to entering into battle.

Prayer and Fasting

Call a solemn time of prayer and fasting to prepare for a deliverance session (Joel 2:12–27). Preparation for both the deliverance or X-Team and the seeker should be three to four weeks prior to the deliverance session(s) unless an emergency requires a shorter preparation time. All participants should pray, repent, and fast daily for three to four weeks prior to deliverance. Make a list of each sin that the C1–13 has identified that needs

---

9. Defarrari, trans. Parsons, "Fathers of the Church," *Letters (83–130)*, 282.

deliverance. Both the deliverance team and the seeker need to pray and fast over each of these sins.

The team is praying also for their own cleansing, repentance, conse-cration, preparation, and manifest authority. When you think of manifest authority, think of the authority that Jesus carried as the Son of God. His authority was weighty upon him and evident to those around him. It was manifest. He taught with authority like no one they had ever heard before (Matt 7:29). Even the demons knew he was Lord. His very presence would manifest authority that lifted the demons to the surface of a sin-sick soul. They would cry out, "What do you want with us Son of God? Have you come to destroy us?" (Matt 8:28; Mark 1:24; Luke 8:28). Without speaking a word, the demons manifested from the Gadarene man crying for mercy. Believers are inheritors of that kind of spiritual authority if they are willing to submit every inch of their spirit, soul, and body to the Lordship of Jesus Christ.

The seeker is praying and seeking true repentance for each sin. Throughout this chapter, there will be repentance strategies to follow. In terms of fasting strategies, the team and the seeker can fast three days at a time on only water. Then take four days off. Or they can fast one or two meals a day for the entire three to four weeks with water only during the fasting portion. It is important to consult one's physician to craft a plan that fits your health profile and capacity.

Take at least one or two hours in the morning, one or two hours in the afternoon, and one or two hours in the evening during your fast for the next three to four weeks to go over this chapter and prepare. Remember that the Holy Spirit comes to convict, convince, correct, reprove, and point out sin, righteousness, and judgment (John 16:9–11). Pray for the Holy Spirit to freely convict sin and lead you to true repentance. Decide to follow the Spirit's leading no matter what. Be willing to die fully and completely to sin.

The X-Team should pray repentance and cleansing prayers for them-selves and the seeker before they go into a deliverance session. Like the priests in the Old Testament, they should cleanse themselves before min-istering in the Holy of Holies. Remember this biblical axiom: Satan cannot cast out Satan (Mark 3:23). A Kingdom divided cannot stand.

If a team member has unrepented lust or anger, then they will not be able to cast out lust or anger. If one is guilty of the same sin as the seeker, one has compromised their spiritual authority. The devil will laugh saying, "You come to cast out anger with anger in your heart. You are on my side. We are not divided. You are standing with me." Repent and be cleansed so you can overtake the strongman and plunder the house (Matt 12:29).

Get Equipped with Scripture

The deliverance team and seeker will take considerable time to pray and fast. They will also be feeding on the Word during their season of preparation. The Word is spiritual protein that builds spiritual muscle. We will need strength, power, and authority for the battle ahead. Hearing the Word also produces faith in the heart (Rom 10:17). All our work in Christ requires faith (Mark 11:22–24; John 6:29; Heb 11:6). Faith is paramount for casting out demons as well. In Matthew 17:20, Jesus rebuked the disciples for unbelief when they could not cast the demon out of the boy. Throughout this book, we have been examining scripture and scriptural principles to build faith in our heart. Just as we need the prayer of faith to heal the sick, we also need the prayer of faith to heal the sick and oppressed of demonic influence (James 5:15)

Meditate on these and other related scriptures to build your faith.

On Repentance:

Exod 20:2–17; Deut 5:6–21 Repent using the 10 Commandments.
Ps 32; 51
Ezek 18
Joel 2
Matt 3
Luke 3
Mark 1:15
Acts 2:38; 3:19; 5:31
2 Cor 7:9–12
1 John 1:7–9; 2:1
Rev 2–3

Casting out Demons:

1 Sam 16:14–16, 23; 18:10; 19:9
Matt 8:16, 31; 10:8; 12:43–45
Mark 1:34, 39; 6:13; 7:26; 9:38
Luke 7:21; 11:14, 13:32
Acts 19:12

On Authority:

Num 23:23
Ps 8:6; 47:3; 144:1
Prov 26:2
Matt 1:16,19; 7:29; 10:1; 12:22–30; 18:18
Mark 3:15; 16:17
Luke 8:2; 9:1; 10:18–20; 11:20
1 Cor 15:24–27
Heb 2:8,13–14
1 John 3:8
Jude 1:9
Rev 12

On Warfare:

Ezek 8:19
Josh 1:1–6
Ps 18; 28:7; 35; 46; 68; 91; 144
Prov 24:6
Dan 10, 11, 13
Matt 18:18
Luke 4
2 Cor 2:11; 10:4–6
Eph 6:10–18
Rev 12, 19

On Victory:

Ps 18:38; 20:5l; 44:4; 98:1
Prov 21:31
Mal 4:3
Matt 10:8; 16:9
Luke 11:14
John 19:30
Rom 6; 8:1–3, 35–39; 16:20
1 Cor 15:55–57
Eph 1:22
1 John 3:8; 5:4
Rev 19:15; 20:10

THE SEEKER'S PREPARATION

True Repentance: The Legal Access to Deliverance

A significant part of X-team's and the seeker's preparation is repentance. We discussed repentance at length in the last chapter when we analyzed the Third Law of Deliverance: The Law of True Repentance. However, this spiritual practice is so vital that it is helpful if we revisit it and go deeper, looking at a specific scriptural passage (2 Cor 7:9–11).

Repentance is a foundational practice of the Christian life. Without repentance there can be no salvation. Central to the Gospel is the call to repent and believe (Mark 1:15; Acts 2:38). Repent and turn from ourselves and our sin and turn in faith to God. Repentance is not a popular term or practice because it is premised on the unpopular notions that there is a right and wrong and that we can be wrong. No one likes to be wrong, let alone told that they are wrong, even if it is Almighty God who is telling us that we are wrong. It is said that the truth hurts and that we cannot handle the truth. Both are often true.

To experience transformation and renewal, it is vital that we turn from our sinful and wrong ways of thinking and living and turn to Christ with a broken, humble, yielded, and fully sincere heart (Ps 51). Repentance is our heart's response to the revelation of the truth. The renowned nineteenth-century revivalist Charles Finney wrote a classic work on the subject entitled *True and False Repentance,* which was originally a revival sermon he had preached. Finney witnessed many people respond to altar calls, but he noticed that not all would be converted, and fewer still would continue their walk with Christ years later. One of the reasons he discerned was that the seekers did not find true repentance. They were looking for a shortcut, and as a result, their repentance did not go deep enough. They turned back to their sin.

Finney realized that repentance begins with a change in one's thinking toward sin and God, and that a change of feeling toward sin and God would follow. The sinner needed to see and think about sin the way God does. When people were convicted about how God sees and feels about their sin, then they could have the mind of God or God's thoughts on the matter.

They will hate the sin as God hates the sin. With a change in thought comes a change in feeling and a change in life. When truth is deeply planted in the heart, then the feelings toward sin begin to change from passion to disdain. He felt that hating wickedness and loving righteousness were key to repentance (Ps 45:7, 97:10, 119:163, Heb 1:9). Charles Finney, a leader of the second Great Awakening, knew a little something about revival. It was said that he would walk through town and pass by bars, and people inside the bars would get convicted, repent, and convert to Christianity without a word spoken to them!

Let us briefly look at a foundational text for repentance found in 2 Corinthians 7. In this passage, Paul sets forth some of the essential qualities and actions that constitute true repentance.

2 Corinthians 7:9–11 (NIV)

> Yet now I am happy, not because you were made sorry, but because your sorrow led you to repentance. For you became sorrowful as God intended and so were not harmed in any way by us. Godly sorrow brings repentance that leads to salvation and leaves no regret, but worldly sorrow brings death. See what this godly sorrow has produced in you: what earnestness, what eagerness to clear yourselves, what indignation, what alarm, what longing, what concern, what readiness to see justice done. At every point you have proved yourselves to be innocent in this matter.

Let's break this passage down and reflect on the qualities and actions of repentance.

7:9

Paul rejoices that the Corinthians experienced real sorrow for their sins. They saw sin as God sees it, and they were grieved to the point of wanting to flee from it and to return to God. The truth made them see their sin in the light of God's judgment and assessment and not human opinion on the issue. God's will be that they would be exposed to the truth so that holy grief and sorrow would be produced in their hearts to the point that they would seek conversion and salvation. In salvation, they would recover what they would have lost without salvation, and that is their souls. They repented so that they would not suffer loss.

7:10

Paul sets forth two types of remorse, "true and false repentance," as the great nineteenth-century revivalist Charles Finney wrote, or in other words repentance and regret. False repentance and worldly sorrow or the sorrow of unbelievers is one in which people are convicted of the truth and the wrong of their actions, but instead of turning to God in repentance and salvation, they have a regret that they have been caught or exposed. They even know God punishes them for their sin, but inside they still relish the sin and enjoy it.[1] They continue to like the sin, but they just do not like the feeling of guilt and shame related to the sin.

However, in their sorrow for exposure, they have no intention of stopping and fully turning to God. They may just find better ways to hide the sin, cover it up, and commit it again later and in another more hidden or safe way. **Repent and Repeat.** This is false, inadequate, insufficient, or underdeveloped repentance based on worldly sorrow. Worldly sorrow produces a repentance that leaves regret. This suggests that we have repented and then we take our repentance back and go back to the sin, i.e., we repent that we have repented.

Thus, our false or inadequate repentance still needs true repentance. On the other hand, true repentance is a repentance that we do not regret, and we do not take back but follow through by not turning back to our sin but continually turning to God. We make a resolute decision to cease from sin and seek God for the gift of repentance. We do not cease from seeking until we find it.

7:11

After Paul wrote his stern letter of correction to the Corinthians, they responded with true repentance in Paul's estimation. Paul highlights some of the attitudes and actions that they displayed; "what earnestness, what eagerness to clear yourselves, what indignation, what alarm, what longing, what concern, what readiness to see justice done." The Corinthians were alarmed, concerned, and even angered by their sin and were ready, sincere, and eager to turn from it and be forgiven.

---

1. Charles, *True and False Repentance*, 13. Finney's term "false repentance" may sound severe for readers today, but it is a reality. However, I nuance the term and include descriptors such as, inadequate, insufficient, and underdeveloped along with "false" to characterize repentance that falls short of arriving at the goal of true repentance, which I am defining as "ceasing from sin."

In Matthew 3:8, Jesus preached that if we are truly repentant then we need to show fruit that demonstrates that we have repented, a changed life specifically in the area in question. If a man were a thief and stole, then repentance showing fruit would mean that the man would stop stealing, and more so, start working for a living, a real and practical repentance. He would even give back what he had stolen, restitution.

However, like forgiveness, sometimes true repentance can be a process. A person may sincerely exemplify all the criteria that Paul listed in verse 11, and yet find that they still struggle with an issue and may at times fall and not overcome so readily. Repentance is grace upon grace and grace from beginning to end, as our entire walk in Christ is by grace from beginning to end. We seek until we find.

Five Characteristics of True Repentance According to 2 Cor 7:9–11

6. God's Perspective: Seeing the sin as God sees it and feeling how God feels about it is Godly sorrow. Hatred toward wickedness. Deep, true, conviction of sin.

7. Cease from Sinning: Godly sorrow that leads to repentance and salvation. Truly turn from the sin and never go back to it. Turn to Christ for forgiveness and salvation. Cease from sinning. Not repent and repeat. Not a worldly sorrow, a repentance that leaves regret. True repentance is a repentance that we do not regret that we have repented, and then we take it back, i.e., repent that we repented.

8. A Longing for Righteousness: Alarmed by one's sin and its depravity and guilt and awakened to righteousness. A concern, longing, desire, and zeal for deliverance, forgiveness, and righteousness.

9. A Holy Hatred of Sin: Shows a righteous anger toward sin and hates the sin and evil but loves God and righteousness. Aware and agrees that sin should be punished with eternal damnation.

10. Restitution: A desire to right what was made wrong. Make restitution when needed. A desire to repent, obey, and walk in righteousness in that area of sin. Avenge unrighteousness. Shows the fruit of repentance. Concrete actions that break ties with the sin, including cutting off people, places, and things related to the sinful practice. It may mean abandoning books, movies, paraphernalia, images, so-called friends, clubs, etc. that function as open doors to the sin. Also, concrete actions that demonstrate forgiveness, deliverance, and righteousness in that area, like restitution, apologies, reconciliation, etc. (Matt 3). [/NL 1–5]

Repent Over Each Sin Individually

It is essential that the seeker reviews the results of the C1–13 and lists all the sins that the instrument has identified that need deliverance. The seeker needs to take each one of these sins individually to the Lord in prayer and fasting and seek true repentance for each prior to the deliverance session(s). You may say this seems over the top. Yes, much is required, but if you want an effective deliverance ministry with a high percentage of results, radical and sold out are what I found work best after decades of ghostbusting. Keep in mind the definition and parameters we established above for true repentance. An effective practice is to go over the Ten Commandments (Ex 20:2–17; Deut 5:6–21) and Christ's interpretation of the law (Matt 5). The law reveals our sin (Rom 3:20). Let the Spirit of Truth convict you.

Christ's interpretation goes deep to the spirit of the law. If you put anything before God, then you are an idolater, breaking the first commandment. If you use Jesus' name or speak of the things of God flippantly or without faith, then you have taken the name of the Lord in vain. If you look at someone lustfully, then you are adulterer. If you have ever been angry with someone, then you are a murderer. Ouch! Jesus was not playing. Use the law to bring conviction in your heart, which is one of its functions (Rom 3:20). Let the law be the light under which you examine your heart (2 Cor 13:5). Give the Spirit free reign. Ask the Spirit to use the commandments to convict you. Read each one and listen to God's voice.

True repentance can be an arduous and exhausting spiritual exercise. It often does not come easy. It is a spiritual workout (1 Tim 4:8). The reason is that our flesh is deceitful and desperately wicked (Jer 17:9). The flesh does not want to be exposed. And the flesh does not want to die. It will fight, lie, resist, hide, disguise, and use every trick in the book to defy the light of the truth. The flesh will bargain, manipulate, and twist the truth to repel conviction. And Satan will use the flesh's weakness to his advantage to distort and deceive.

The one who seeks to repent truly of outward and especially inward sins is in for a battle. It can take a considerable amount of time, depending on one's willingness. That is why fasting is so essential. It weakens the flesh and allows for the Spirit to arise (Matt 17:21; 26:41 KJV).[2] The Spirit sup-

2. A boy was tormented by demons. The demons tried to get him to kill himself. The father brought the boy to the disciples who failed to "heal" him. The text uses the word "heal" because deliverance from demons is a type of healing. Jesus healed the boy. After the disciples asked why they could not cast out the demon, Jesus rebuked them for their unbelief. It takes faith to cast out demons. Jesus also informed the disciples that this type of demon is expelled with the manifest authority that comes only from praying *and* fasting. Jesus clearly walked in authority over demons, and everyone witnessed his

plies the willingness to put to death the misdeeds of the body and part with our sin (Rom 8:13).

Repentance is a gift. The struggle is not a matter of prying it from God's hand. God is more than willing to give it once *his terms* (not our terms) are met. We must be willing to let go of our sin and die to it. Cease from sinning. Further, we must be willing to *receive* repentance and walk in it. Those are God's terms. Willingness is our part. God cannot do it for us, though he will help us get there. Therein lies the battle.

Many do not hate their sin, and so do not truly want to part with it. I have been there as well. They do not like to feel the unease of conviction, guilt, shame, and condemnation. None of us do. Conviction and guilt can be from God, but not shame and condemnation. These are from the devil. Despite promptings from God to repent, some may still relish and coddle their sin. So, repentance becomes a bargaining process. Many, in their heart of hearts, want to be rid of the ill effects of sin, like guilt and shame, but want to keep the pleasure or comfort of sin. Bargaining. But God's terms will not permit such a compromise. God wants us free. He will deliver us. He will even grant us the gift of repentance, but we must be willing to turn and receive it. It is often easier said than done.

"Rend your hearts," the prophet Joel cried out (Joel 2:13). The seeker needs to have an open heart and be willing to receive the conviction of the Spirit and the testimony of the conscience that may point out sin. He/she needs to be willing to be pierced and laid open to reveal the depths of the heart, especially blind spots. Our natural response to this grueling process is defensiveness and denial. We think that we cannot really be that bad. I have been there. The deflation and crucifixion of pride is never pleasant, but we must see sin as God sees it.

I liken true repentance, especially of inner character sin, as spiritual surgery, often without anesthesia. It cuts. It can be excruciating. But it removes the spiritual cancer of sin. When the terms of repentance (willingness) are met, God releases repentance to us. And the Spirit will bear witness that the work is done. True repentance will bring true deliverance and freedom.

Four Truths from Truth Therapy

At this point, we will look at repentance through the lens of *Truth Therapy*, a book and a method of renewing the mind that I developed years ago. The basic premises of *Truth Therapy* are that the lies we believe bring us into

authority (Mark 1:27).

bondage and destruction. However, the truth we believe will set us free. Lies bind. Truth delivers. Throughout our lifetime, we have swallowed hook, line, and sinker many lies. It's time to cast out those lies and be set free by the truth found in the Word of God. Unlearn lies. Relearn the truth.

We are transformed by renewing our mind with the Word of God (Rom 12:1–2). When we receive, believe, and act on the Word, it will revolutionize our life. This section will assist the seeker in walking through the process of repentance for each sin that has been identified. We will go through four foundational truths in scripture that will help the seeker find repentance and build faith in preparation for the deliverance session(s). The truths are: all have sinned, Jesus Christ is Lord, the Cross (it is finished), and repentance.

The seeker is encouraged to go through these four truths in times of prayer and fasting daily (as outlined above).

Sin

"I have sinned and fallen short of the glory of God." Scripture:

- Psalm 38:18 (NIV): "I confess my iniquity; I am troubled by my sin."

- Jeremiah 17:9 (NLT): "The human heart is the most deceitful of all things, and desperately wicked. Who really knows how bad it is?"

- Luke 5:8 (NLT): "When Simon Peter realized what had happened, he fell to his knees before Jesus and said, 'Oh, Lord, please leave me—I'm too much of a sinner to be around you.'"

- Romans 3:10 (NIV): "As it is written: 'There is no one righteous, not even one.'"

- Romans 3:23 (NIV): " . . . for all have sinned and fall short of the glory of God."

REFLECTION

Ralph Venning, Puritan pastor:

> Sin is the transgression of a law, yea of a good law, yea of God's law. Sin presupposes that there is a law in being, for where is no law there is no transgression (Romans 4.15). But where there is sin, there is a law, and a transgression of the law. Whoever committeth sin transgresseth also the law, for sin is a transgression

of the law (1 John 3.4). That this is the sin intended in our text is apparent from Romans 7.7.

Now the law not only forbids the doing of evil, whether by thought, word, or deed, but also commands the doing of good. So, to omit the good commanded is sin, as well (or ill) as is the doing of the evil that is forbidden. Against the fruit of the Spirit there is no law, but against the works of the flesh (for the antithesis holds) there is law, for they are all against the law, as the Apostle tells us (Galatians 5.19–24). Whatever, then, transgresses the law of God—in whole or in part (James 2.10)—is therefore and therein a sin, whether it break an affirmative or a negative precept i.e., whether it is the omission of good or the commission of evil.[3]

John Wesley, founder of Methodism:

Universal Misery is at once a consequence and a proof of this universal corruption. Men are unhappy (how very few are the exceptions!) because they are unholy. "Pain accompanies and follows sin." Why is the earth so full of complicated distress? Because it is full of complicated wickedness.[4]

The New Hampshire Confession, Article III (Baptist):

(We believe) that man was created in a state of holiness, under the law of his Maker; but by voluntary transgression fell from that holy and happy state; in consequence of which all mankind are now sinners, not by constraint but choice, being by nature utterly void of that holiness required by the law of God, wholly given to the gratification of the world, of Satan, and of their own sinful passions, therefore under just condemnation to eternal ruin, without defense or excuse.[5]

The doctrine of universal human sinfulness is not a popular truth to teach today or in any day. We do not like to be told that we are wrong, let alone that we are sinful or even compliant with evil. Postmodern thinking has relativized morality and moral standards in public judgment. We feel that no one stands on any privileged ground to make moral evaluations or pronouncements on anything or anyone. Everything is permissible. Even in a court of law it becomes more and more challenging to prove guilt beyond a reasonable doubt in cases that seem straightforward.

3. Venning, *Sinfulness of Sin*, 25.

4. Wesley, *Wesley's Works*, 9:235.

5. Leith, ed. *Creeds of the Church*, 35.

From the beginning of time, humanity has wrestled with the problem of evil. Why does evil exist? Why does evil exist if there is a good, all-powerful God? Today, we have a new and different type of "problem of evil." Identifying the *existence* of evil has become a problem. The postmodern problem of evil is a problem *with* evil, evil's existence. Does evil exist at all? The postmodern problem of evil is the problem of identifying evil in a specific location and instance. Identifying evil is not morally or politically correct.

If we can identify evil in terms of an agreed standard, it is usually as a vanishing point on the extreme periphery of social and moral action. The standard for evil always gets moved away from us and to the furthest edge of human behavior. Evil is always something outside of ourselves. Rarely does it involve me. And it is usually only identified in its extreme forms.

For example, when asked to identify what we mean by evil, we can without hesitation point to Hitler or slavery or some comparable figure or event. Outside of such extremes, however, we rarely can agree on what is sin or evil, if anything is sin at all. Evil is only something extreme and far removed from us. Or worse, there is no evil except to say that there is evil.

The real test would be to identify sin or evil in our own lives if asked. For the most part, it would seem like we all would admit that we are basically "good people." We never killed anyone. We do not steal. We pay our taxes. We have never cheated on our spouses. We believe in God and try to do good by our neighbor. We are basically good people, if we are making the call.

The problem is that we are not called to judge. We are not making the call. God is. We are basically good people . . . in our own eyes, but in God's eyes there is no one good or righteous. Even Jesus gave us the example when called "Good Master." He replied, "there is only One who is good," (Matt 19:17) meaning his Heavenly Father. Surely, Jesus was good, but he was humbly identifying with humanity in this exchange about keeping the commandments and salvation. Humanity should realize that only God is good. Besides Christ, no one perfectly obeys the commands to obtain salvation. When God is judging and making the call, we all sin and fall short of God's glory (Rom 3:23).

Really, who can attain the glory of God? Who can even claim to attain the glory of God? Even the most righteous, such as the Apostles Peter and Paul, sinned in God's eyes, even after their salvation experiences. In fact, as long as we remain human in this world, and in these bodies, we will be tempted and susceptible to sin. Salvation means salvation from sin. We need to be saved from sin every moment, and so we cling to Christ, who was given "the name Jesus, because he will save his people from their sins."

We all have equal and infinite value, and we are all morally equal as sinners in need of God's salvation. No one is more righteous than the other when God is the judge and the standard. No one is innocent, even in our readiness to polarize people into "us and them" binaries.[6] Thus, our response to each other should not be judgment but mercy, and our cry to God is also for mercy (James 2:13).

NAMES OF GOD:

Study and meditate on the names of God that relate to our teaching on sin. The names of God reveal God's nature and attributes. He is his name. And he extends the attribute represented by his name to us in covenant. For example, *Yahweh Shalom,* "the Lord God is peace." His name is peace. He is peace. His peace he extends to us becomes our peace.

Lord, Yahweh

Yahweh or Jehovah (transliteration of Yahweh; used by English and German speaking people) comes from Exodus 3:14. Attribute: Covenant. *Yahweh* (YHWH) is God's covenant name. It is a personal name reflecting God's intimacy and faithfulness to God's people. The root comes from the verb "to be." Many see this name as referring to God's being or essence, meaning "the one who is self-existent." God is the great I AM. God is the "I AM THAT I AM." God is who God is. Others interpret the name in the sense of becoming, i.e., "God will be who God will be." God is Lord over all history, past, present, and future. In *Yahweh* all things live, and move, and have their being. This name for God means that God is absolute in presence, power, and knowledge. He alone is Lord and King. He alone reveals what is true, right, and good. Because he is supreme, we need to submit to his Word. We need to submit to his truth and not our own. Yahweh is also God's covenant

---

6. In our current culture, it is common to divide and polarize groups into binaries of oppressed and oppressor, rich and poor, cis and non-cis genders, gay and straight, black and white, right and left among others. The presupposition is that one group is purely right, and the other is purely wrong in the binary tension. There may be degrees of truth in such an evaluation, but overall, no one is innocent. The binary may have a *degree* of truth, but both sides are not perfect, pure, or innocent. The conclusion is an oversimplification of complex issues. None of these so-called binaries are pure categories. At times, we all have been on both sides of the offender and offended equation. The binary of oppressed and oppressor is not absolute and too easily drawn. Human relations are much more complicated than simplistic caricatures, stereotypes, demonizing, and overgeneralizing.

name to God's covenant people. Through Christ, God is in covenant with us. God is our God, and we are God's people. Yahweh is faithful to minister the fullness of God's covenant blessings to us in every area of life.

The Lord our Righteousness, Adonai Tsidkenu

Attribute: Righteousness. This compound name means "the Lord our righteousness." Righteousness means right or good standing, right relationship, of excellent moral quality of character. Righteousness as an attribute is distinct from human righteousness. Even the most righteous of people falls short of the righteousness that belongs to God. Our most righteous deeds are like filthy rags compared to the righteousness of God. The Lord's righteousness is a perfect standard. It demands a perfection that we cannot produce. Thus, God offers it to us as a free gift, and we accept it by repentance and faith. Jesus is our righteousness. He makes us acceptable in God's sight. By his blood we are forgiven, accepted, and made new. As we walk the Christian life, we are to stand in his righteousness and allow the Spirit to work Christ's righteousness through us in right action, action that reflects the character of God.

Law-Giver, Isaiah 33:22

Attribute: Just. Scripture tells us that all things hold together in Christ. By his word and power, the universe was made, expands, and yet coheres. Through the various sciences we learn how God establishes laws in the natural order to facilitate God's will that the universe gives and sustains life. God also gives us laws, his Word, so that our hearts may be ordered to experience abundant life. God has given us the perfect law of love. Love God and neighbor with all our whole being. It was the Lord's intention that all of creation be governed by the law of love that we see demonstrated in Christ. The problem is that we have all sinned and fall short of God's law. According to Jesus' interpretation of the law, if we lust, then we are adulterers. If we are angry, then we are murderers. If we put anything ahead of God, then we are idolaters. Romans 3:20 states that "the law lets us know we are sinners." Indeed, it does.

List the sin(s) that the C1–13 has identified and that need repentance:

1. _____

2. _____

3. _____

4. _____

5. _____

Pray and repent over these sins. Confess and ask for forgiveness. Ask God for the gift of repentance. Pray that you will say, see, think, and feel the way God does about these sins. Believe, receive, and confess the following truths we learned about sin:

- I have sinned and fall short of God's glory.

- All have sinned and fallen short of God's glory.

- I do not trust my own heart for it does not know itself, but I trust fully in the Lord.

- Yes and Amen. I believe and receive these truths.

- My trust and righteousness are not in myself but in Christ.

AFFIRMATION

Say aloud: The heart of humanity is deceitful and desperately wicked. Who can understand it? The good I want to do; I find that I do not do. The evil that I do not want to do, I find myself doing. There is a war inside of me between the good I want to do, and the sin that I do not want to do. Who can help me, but the Lord Almighty my Deliverer? I do not put my trust in my own understanding, my own goodness, or in my own ability, but I fully trust in the Lord who is my salvation and my strength. In Christ I find mercy for me and for others. I seek to not judge anyone but offer them the same mercy that I seek from Christ my Savior.

MORNING REFLECTION

The M.E.E.T. Method—In the morning, purpose in your heart to:

M—Monitor your thoughts during the day and

E—Evaluate them. Do they align with God's word? Are they distortions of what is real?

E—Expel any thoughts that are contrary to the truth and replace them with the

T—Truth of God's word, created in the image of God.

EVENING REFLECTION—THE 7RS METHOD

1. Rest and Receive

Rest and receive God's truth. I entrust myself and others to God's grace and care.

- Receive the truth in your heart. We have all sinned and need God's grace and mercy. Rest in this fact.

- Sit and relax in a quiet place. Calm and quiet your mind as you think on this truth.

- Breathe deeply through the nose and out the mouth repetitively, as you rest in what God has done for you. As thoughts of the day come into your mind let them go. Give each thought to God.

- Be mindful of God's goodness. Be mindful of the gift of this moment. Be mindful of the gift that you are.

- Imagine every care being taken into God's loving embrace. Let the cares, concerns, and details of the day unravel slowly, layer after layer. Give each thought to God. You are intentionally casting your cares on God. They belong to God and not to you.

- Give to Christ any thought that is contrary to the truth. Let him nail it to his cross.

- Pray that Jesus would come into your mind and shine the light on any area that he desires. Also ask Jesus to come and speak specifically to any situation that is on your mind.

- Listen to God speak through your conscience concerning your thought-life today. Do you need to repent, or offer thanksgiving or a praise? Do you need to resolve to do God's word?

- Write down what God is impressing upon you.

- Hear and receive the truth of God's voice as he speaks to your thought-life.

2. Repent

Turn away from the lies and turn toward the truth. Also repent of all acts that are contrary to the character of Christ.

- Identify any lies in your thought-life that would lead you away from God's mercy and grace or lies that tempt you to believe that you are better than others or others are better than you. Also identify lies that would say that your own goodness supplants the goodness of God.

- Uproot the lies by rejecting and casting them down.

- Renounce the lies by making a decision to renew your thoughts.

- Turn from believing the lies to believing the truth. Replace the lies with the truth.

3. Renew

Renew your mind with the truth. Plant the word of God in your heart and believe it personally for your life.

- Meditate on the Scriptures for this section.

- Read and declare those Scriptures several times.

- Agree with God's word by saying, "Yes" and "Amen" to what it affirms. "Yes, and Amen, we are all sinners in need of God's grace."

- Receive the truth. Own it. Personalize it and make it yours.

4. Recite

Confess and declare the word of God.

- Think God's thoughts. Say what God says in his word.

- Declare several times, "I have sinned and fallen short of God's glory and am in need of mercy and salvation. My neighbor has sinned and fallen short of God's glory and is in need of mercy and salvation."

- In the future, remember and confess boldly God's word.

5. Resolve

Resolve yourself to action. Be a doer of the word.

- Make a decision to put this truth into practice. Practice it daily in every area of your life. Make clear resolutions to manifest the truth in concrete actions that impact others and the world around you.

6. Repeat

Repeat the process.

- Repeat and strengthen your commitment to the previous five steps. Repetition and rehearsal strengthen the truth in you.

7. Reality

Repetition brings reality.

- After much repetition from thought → word → deed, the truth becomes experiential and a solid concrete reality in your life that will yield the fruit of wisdom and righteousness.

Jesus Christ Is Lord of All

Let us move on to the next truth about Jesus Christ. Jesus Christ—Jesus Christ is Lord of all. Scripture:

- Matthew 16:16 (NIV): "Simon Peter answered, 'You are the Messiah, the Son of the living God.'"
- John 20:28 (NIV): "Thomas said to him, 'My Lord and my God!'"
- Philippians 2:10–11 (NIV): " . . . that at the name of Jesus every knee should bow, in heaven and on earth and under the earth, and every tongue acknowledge that Jesus Christ is Lord, to the glory of God the Father."
- Jude 24–25 (NIV): "To him who is able to keep you from stumbling and to present you before his glorious presence without fault and with great joy, to the only God our Savior be glory, majesty, power, and authority, through Jesus Christ our Lord, before all ages, now and forevermore! Amen."

REFLECTION

The Definition of Chalcedon:

> Following then the holy fathers, we unite in teaching all men to confess the one and only Son, our Lord Jesus Christ. This selfsame one is perfect in both deity and in humanness; this selfsame one is also actually God and actually man . . .[7]

Catechism of the Catholic Church:

> From the beginning of Christian history, the assertion of Christ's Lordship over the world and over history has implicitly recognized that man should not submit his personal freedom in an absolute manner to any earthly power, but only to God the Father and the Lord Jesus Christ: Caesar is not "the Lord."[8]

In one way, Christianity seems to be an inversion of so many other religions. Where in most religions, we are presented with a way to get to Heaven or salvation, Christianity brings Heaven and salvation to us. Many of the world religions offer a model or pattern of living that serves as a moral ladder to attain the goal of salvation. In Christianity, God descends to humanity through Christ, the ladder, and offers us salvation through Christ's work and not our own. Instead of a method, a plan, a discipline, or a book as the vehicle for salvation, Christianity offers the world a person, the God-man Jesus Christ.

Jesus Christ is unique in so many ways. The Church teaches that Jesus is fully Divine and fully human. He is the second person of the Trinity made flesh for our salvation. Jesus Christ is the only Son of God and is eternally begotten of the Father. Scripture states that the Word is God, is eternal with the Father, became flesh, was born of a virgin, lived a sinless life, preached, and taught the Kingdom, ministered signs, wonders, and miracles, was crucified, died, and was buried, on the third day he rose again in a real body, ascended into Heaven, and will come again to judge the living and the dead.

Holy Scripture claims Christ is the Savior of the world, and that he is Lord of Heaven and earth. One of the earliest creeds and baptismal confessions of the church was "Jesus Christ is Lord." Later conciliar developments pronounced in consonance with Scripture that Jesus Christ is the Son of God who was the only begotten of the Father, is one being with the Father, and thus is God. The claims of Christ and about Christ are too grave to be ignored or dismissed.

7. Leith, *Creeds of the Church*, 35.
8. *Catechism of the Catholic Church*, 126.

In Matthew 16 Jesus asked Peter, "Who do you say that I am?" This is the key question for each of us that we all must answer and give account for our answer in this world and in the world to come. God has spoken God's Word of grace and truth to us all. God has come to us in Jesus Christ and has given his life for our salvation. He has sent us the Holy Spirit to invite us to meet Christ and allow him to dwell in our hearts by faith as Lord. How will the world respond? What will our response be? How will you respond?

NAMES OF GOD

Study and meditate on the names of God that relate to our teaching on Jesus Christ. The names of God reveal God's nature and attributes. He is his name. And he extends the attribute represented by his name to us in covenant. For example, *Yahweh Shalom*, "the Lord God is peace." His name is peace. He is peace. And his peace he extends to us, so it becomes our peace.

Jesus, Y'shua

Attribute: Savior. Jesus' name is a form of *Yoshua, Y'shua, Yehoshua* meaning savior. Jesus is the name given to us for salvation and all of God's covenant blessings. "*Whoever calls on the name of the Lord shall be saved*"—Acts 2:21. Jesus is the name above all names. Even outside of Christianity, it is perhaps the most widely recognized name in history. More books have been written about Jesus Christ than any other historical person. As a historical figure, few have had the influence that Jesus Christ has had on the world. For believers, Jesus is an influential historical figure and more. He is the Son of God and Savior of the world. The name of Jesus is the mightiest name in heaven or earth. Jesus is the name of salvation, redemption, healing, sanctification, authority, and victory. There is power and authority in the name of Jesus, so we are encouraged to meditate and think about Jesus Christ, who he is, and all that he has done for us. We give praise and glory to God for the gift of the name of Jesus. Through the name of Jesus comes salvation, answered prayer, and every spiritual blessing.

Christ, Christos, Anointed One, Messiah

Attribute: Messiah, King, Deliverer. "Christ" means anointed one and points to the claim that Jesus is the Messiah. Jesus is the Christ or God's Messiah (Savior and Deliverer) for the Hebrew people and for the world. St. Peter rightly testified that Jesus was the Christ, the Son of the living God, in Matthew 16:16. Jesus Christ is God's chosen and anointed one to bring salvation and the Kingdom of God. He is also Christ within us, the hope of glory. Jesus is the anointed one and the "greater one" inside the believer. Because Christ dwells in us, the Kingdom of God is within us. Because Christ dwells in us, we are children of the King, sons and daughters of the Most High God. The reign of God begins in the hearts of Christ's followers. We are called to spread his Kingdom as we are led by the anointing, the Spirit, that dwells within us that leads us to obey God's will.

Lord, Kurios

Attribute: Lordship. One of the earliest baptismal creeds of the church was "Jesus is Lord." The early church was making a radical and dangerous claim that Caesar was not their Lord, but Jesus alone was their Lord. Believers were making a confession and commitment to Christ, one of absolute allegiance. There would be no other lords or gods but Christ. Their confession was based on their testimony of their experience of the truth of the gospel. They experienced that Jesus had indeed defeated sin, death, and the devil. He was their Savior and their Lord. Our confession is also that Jesus is Lord. Our confession also reflects our own testimony that the Gospel is true. Jesus has taken away our sins and has defeated death. He is our Lord and Savior. He is also Lord over Heaven and earth. He sits on the throne over all the universe. In our daily Christian walk, Jesus wants to be Lord over every area of our lives. To the degree we yield to Christ's authority, to that degree Jesus and his Kingdom will reign in our lives. The invitation is also for everyone to make Jesus Lord over their lives. Make him Lord today and yield to his authority in every area of your life. He is either Lord of all, or he is not Lord at all. The Lord our God is one God. There is no other!

Savior, Soter, Savior/Salvation

Attribute: Savior/Salvation. Early in my ministry I was a university campus evangelist. I would preach regularly outdoors where the students would gather. Once when I was preaching salvation, a student fired back at me, "Salvation, salvation from what?" That student asked the right question. Many people who attend church do not know why they need salvation. I responded to the student, "Salvation from sin, and salvation from ourselves." The world may not admit it, but it is seeking salvation in its own way, an amelioration of the human condition. The world is constantly seeking betterment in every aspect of life: health care, education, civil rights, safety and security, and overall quality of life for all. Although the world seeks to ameliorate the human condition, it does not recognize that the problem that causes all other problems is itself. The problem is the human condition itself. We are forever bound and invested in our own selfishness. Our pride, lust, greed, and hatred are causal to the very problems we seek to solve. We need salvation from ourselves. We can improve many of the conditions mentioned above, like health care or poverty, but we cannot cure our own self-centered living, which is the root of our problems. We cannot solve this problem because we are the problem. Salvation needs to come from outside ourselves. God sent a Savior from Heaven to cure this problem. Jesus Christ came to save us from ourselves. Jesus Christ is the one who delivers us from sin and death and the power of evil. When we are baptized, we are baptized into Christ's death and resurrection. The old life dies, and a new life is born. We are delivered from ourselves and given a new start through a new life in Christ. There is no other name given to us that can save us but the name of Jesus. We trust him today with whatever we may be facing. He is more than enough to save us from all our trials and tribulations.

God, Theos

Attribute: Divinity. The early church made a radical and controversial claim that Jesus is God. The early church was primarily Jewish, and Jews were staunch monotheists. "The Lord God our God is one Lord," was their creed. However, if Jesus is God, then how is God still one. The issue of the oneness and eventually also the "threeness" of God would challenge the church's theology for the next four centuries. Even after much thought and debate during the early ecumenical church councils, the claim that Jesus is Divine did not change. Our church fathers and mothers discerned that the divinity of Christ was evident in Scripture, witnessed by the Spirit and confirmed by the testimony and experience of the Church. We also note that Scripture provides evidence that Jesus truly is God (John 1:1–3; Phil 2:6; Col 2:9; 1 Tim 3:16; Heb 1:3, among other scriptures). He is not merely a man, a good person, or a good teacher. Jesus is God, and so he is to be worshipped and obeyed as God. When Thomas touched his nail prints, he cried out, "My Lord and my God." Jesus Christ, our Lord, and our God.

Renounce and repent of lies concerning Jesus Christ:

___ I have often lived as if Jesus were not Lord of my life.

__ I have many areas that have not been submitted to the Lordship of Jesus Christ.

__ I believed that Jesus Christ was merely a good moral person and a good teacher.

__ I believed that Jesus Christ is fully human but not Divine.

__ I believed that Jesus Christ was *a* god, the first created, but not the one eternal God.

__ I believed that Jesus Christ was not eternally God but *became* God.

__ I believed that Jesus Christ is not one in being with the Father.

__ I believed that Jesus Christ did not literally and physically resurrect from the dead.

Now believe, receive, and confess these truths:

- Make a decision to agree with God's word that Jesus Christ is Lord, God, and the one mediator for salvation between God and humanity.

- Jesus Christ is fully God and fully human.

- Jesus Christ physically and literally resurrected from the dead.

- Jesus Christ died for the sins of the world.

- Jesus Christ is the one mediator sent by God for our salvation.

- Jesus Christ is Lord and God.

- Jesus Christ is my Lord and Savior.

- Yes, and Amen. I believe and receive these truths.

AFFIRMATION

Say aloud: The heart of humanity is deceitful and desperately wicked. Who can understand it? The good I want to do; I find that I do not do. The evil that I do not want to do, I find myself doing. There is a war inside of me between the good I want to do, and the sin that I do not want to do. Who can help me, but the Lord Almighty my Deliverer? I do not put my trust in my own understanding, my own goodness, or in my own ability, but I fully trust in the Lord who is my salvation and my strength. In Christ I find mercy for me and for others. I seek not to judge anyone but to offer them the same mercy that I seek from Christ my Savior.

MORNING REFLECTION

The M.E.E.T. Method—In the morning, purpose in your heart to:

M—Monitor your thoughts during the day and

E—Evaluate them. Do they align with God's word? Are they distortions of what is real?

E—Expel any thoughts that are contrary to the truth and replace them with the

T—Truth of God's word, created in the image of God.

EVENING REFLECTION—THE 7RS METHOD

1. Rest and Receive

Rest and receive God's truth. I entrust myself and others to God's grace and care.

- Receive the truth in your heart. We have all sinned and are in need of God's grace and mercy. Rest in this fact.

- Sit and relax in a quiet place. Calm and quiet your mind as you think on this truth.

- Breathe deeply through the nose and out the mouth repetitively, as you rest in what God has done for you. As thoughts of the day come into your mind let them go. Give each thought to God.

- Be mindful of God's goodness. Be mindful of the gift of this moment. Be mindful of the gift that you are.

- Imagine every care being taken into God's loving embrace. Let the cares, concerns, and details of the day unravel slowly, layer after layer. Give each thought to God. You are intentionally casting your cares on God. They belong to God and not to you.

- Give to Christ any thought that is contrary to the truth. Let him nail it to his cross.

- Pray that Jesus would come into your mind and shine the light on any area that he desires. Also ask Jesus to come and speak specifically to any situation that is on your mind.

- Listen to God speak through your conscience concerning your thought-life today. Do you need to repent, or offer thanksgiving or a praise? Do you need to resolve to do God's word?

- Write down what God is impressing upon you.

- Hear and receive the truth of God's voice as he speaks to your thought-life.

2. Repent

Turn away from the lies and turn toward the truth. Also repent of all acts that are contrary to the character of Christ.

- Identify any lies in your thought-life that would lead you away from God's mercy and grace or lies that tempt you to believe that you are better than others or others are better than you. Also identify lies that would say that your own goodness supplants the goodness of God.

- Uproot the lies by rejecting and casting them down.

- Renounce the lies by making a decision to renew your thoughts.

- Turn from believing the lies to believing the truth. Replace the lies with the truth.

3. Renew

Renew your mind with the truth. Plant the word of God in your heart and believe it personally for your life.

- Meditate on the Scriptures for this section.

- Read and declare those Scriptures several times.

- Agree with God's word by saying, "Yes" and "Amen" to what it affirms. "Yes, and Amen, we are all sinners in need of God's grace."

- Receive the truth. Own it. Personalize it and make it yours.

4. Recite

Confess and declare the word of God.

- Think God's thoughts. Say what God says in his word.
- Declare several times, "I have sinned and fallen short of God's glory and am in need of mercy and salvation. My neighbor has sinned and fallen short of God's glory and is in need of mercy and salvation."
- In the future, remember and confess boldly God's word.

5. Resolve

Resolve yourself to action. Be a doer of the word.

- Make a decision to put this truth into practice. Practice it daily in every area of your life. Make clear resolutions to manifest the truth in concrete actions that impact others and the world around you.

6. Repeat

Repeat the process.

- Repeat and strengthen your commitment to the previous five steps. Repetition and rehearsal strengthen the truth in you.

7. Reality

Repetition brings reality.

- After much repetition from thought → word → deed, the truth becomes experiential and a solid concrete reality in your life that will yield the fruit of wisdom and righteousness.

The Cross—It is finished.

Scripture:

- Isaiah 53:4–5 (NIV): "Surely, he took up our pain and bore our suffering, yet we considered him punished by God, stricken by him, and afflicted. But he was pierced for our transgressions, he was crushed for our iniquities; the punishment that brought us peace was on him, and by his wounds we are healed."

- Matthew 28:5–6 (NIV): "The angel said to the women, 'Do not be afraid, for I know that you are looking for Jesus, who was crucified. He is not here; he has risen, just as he said. Come and see the place where he lay.'"

- Mark 10:45 (NIV): "For even the Son of Man did not come to be served, but to serve, and to give his life as a ransom for many."

- Romans 3:25 (NIV): "Whom God hath set forth to be a propitiation through faith in his blood, to declare his righteousness for the remission of sins that are past, through the forbearance of God."

- Romans 4:25 (NIV): "He was delivered over to death for our sins and was raised to life for our justification."

- 1 Corinthians 1:17–18 (NIV): "For Christ did not send me to baptize, but to preach the gospel—not with wisdom and eloquence, lest the cross of Christ be emptied of its power. For the message of the cross is foolishness to those who are perishing, but to us who are being saved it is the power of God."

- Ephesians 1:7 (NIV): "In him we have redemption through his blood, the forgiveness of sins, in accordance with the riches of God's grace that he lavished on us."

REFLECTION

John Calvin:

> Our salvation may be thus divided between the death and the resurrection of Christ: by the former, sin was abolished, and death annihilated; by the latter, righteousness was restored and life revived, the power and efficacy of the former being still bestowed upon us by the means of the latter.[9]

Jesse Penn-Lewis, Welsh Revival leader and author:

> Calvary is the very pivotal point of the world's history. All prior things pointed forward to it; and all subsequent things point back to it.[10]

The single most important event in human history is the "Jesus Event," the cross. What we are calling the Jesus Event is the death, burial,

9. Calvin, *Institutes*, 2:447.
10. Penn-Lewis, *Cross of Calvary*, 5.

resurrection, and ascension of Jesus Christ, or what is often captured in the reference "the cross" in the fullest sense. In this one God-ordained event, God was reconciling the world to God's self by taking away the sin of the world that separates us from God. I am not contending here for any specific theory of original sin, transmission of sin, or atonement. It is sufficient to say that we have all sinned, sin separates us from a holy God, and because God loves us too much to allow the separation, God sent God's Son Jesus Christ to forgive our sins and to make us holy.

This event, which is the culmination of indeed the "greatest story ever told," is beyond total comprehension. The Creator becomes the creation. The eternal enters into time and dies at the hands of his creation. The depth of this mystery is only equaled and surpassed by the depth of God's love that is the reason for this mystery. All of time and human drama are strategically gathered into one place, on one stage at Calvary. In the Jesus Event, the incarnational drama reaches its climax. Tragedy crucifies the Son of God. Yet somehow the tragic does not triumph here, and death does not silence. The event turns as then does space and time upon the goodness of God, and no tragedy remains but is overcome. However, the turn is not immediate. No, there is a three day pause. Tension mounts, watching and waiting, until hope can no longer contain itself and erupts with realization. He is risen and we with him.

His breaking through the death barrier uniquely marks the event. A resuscitation does not quite accomplish the same goal. A dead body revived must once again eventually die. Christ's death and resurrection were an eruption of this age and the birth of the age to come, bringing the full embodiment of what is and is to come, a new heaven and a new earth. The Jesus Event is for all to experience freely. We participate in the Event by faith. When we trust in God's love in Christ, we are brought into Christ, and embraced in Christ. "If anyone is in Christ, the new creation has come." In Christ, we are a new creation.

NAMES OF GOD

Study and meditate on the names of God that relate to our teaching on the Cross. The names of God reveal God's nature and attributes. He *is* his name. And he extends the attribute represented by his name to us in covenant. For example, *Yahweh Shalom*, "the Lord God is peace." His name is peace. He is peace. And his peace he extends to us, so it becomes our peace.

Lamb of God—John 1:29, 36

Attribute: Sacrificial, Compassionate. The Lamb of God who takes away the sins of the world, have mercy on us. Although sacrificial imagery and language appear controversial to our modern sensibilities, the fact is that Scripture does contain many references to the sacrificial nature of the atonement. Love by nature is sacrificial, and Christ gave his life for our sins. Scripture does not endorse any one interpretation of the atonement but at times employs metaphors and images of sacrifice to communicate God's love and at times sacrifice as substitution. The Lamb, God's symbol of mercy, offers himself up for us to demonstrate God's love for us and takes sin and death upon himself and defeats it, freeing us from its power.

Advocate

Attribute: Advocate, Defender. At times we find ourselves helpless and defenseless. We seek advocacy. As sinners we stand guilty as charged and helpless to justify ourselves before God. However, Jesus forever lives to make intercession for us. God's will for humanity is accomplished through Christ on our behalf. The Holy Spirit extends Christ's intercessory work from the throne to our hearts. The Spirit ministers Christ to us. His comfort, counsel, advocacy, and empowerment are essential to edifying the body of Christ for every good work.

Deliverer

Attribute: Deliverer. Humanity is in bondage to sin. Jesus came to set us free. He who was without sin, took sin upon himself and destroyed it in the flesh upon the cross, so you and I can be free. So be free in Jesus. People are in bondage to themselves, to money, lust, power, etc. If we are in sin, then we are in bondage. Christ is greater than the devil and any bondage. He will lead us not into temptation but deliver us from evil.

Mediator

Attribute: Intercession, Deity & Humanity. Theology has always made classical distinctions between the Divine and humanity. God is eternal. We are temporal. God is infinite. We are finite. God is uncreated, and we are created. God is all-powerful, all-knowing, and all-present. We surely are not.

Many theologians have captured the radical "otherness" of God. God is so wholly other than God's creation. In many ways, the essence of God, who God is in God's self, is unknowable or apophatic. Yet, 1 John 5:20 states, "And we know that the Son of God has come, and he has given us understanding so that we can know the true God. And now we live in fellowship with the true God because we live in fellowship with his Son, Jesus Christ. He is the only true God, and he is eternal life." We can know the Son of God who gives us understanding of the Father, and we can have fellowship and eternal life with the Father. The only way this is possible is because the eternal became temporal, the infinite became finite, the uncreated became created, and God became human through the one mediator, Christ Jesus. Jesus Christ mediates God to humanity, and he mediates humanity to God.

Renounce and repent of lies concerning the Cross:

__ The cross did not cover all my sins.

__ The cross did not destroy the power of Satan.

__ I was not crucified on the cross with Christ.

__ The cross did not destroy sin, guilt, shame, death, and Satan.

__ The cross cannot deliver me.

__ Jesus Christ died, but it was not a sacrificial or atoning death.

__ Jesus Christ cannot take away my sin(s).

__ Jesus Christ really did not die. God would not let one of his prophets suffer defeat.

__ Jesus Christ did not resurrect from the dead.

__ Jesus Christ resurrected from the dead, but not literally. The resurrection was in the hopeful minds of the disciples.

__ The death and resurrection of Jesus Christ was not the means by which God chose to save the world.

__ Other

Now believe, receive, and confess these truths:

- Jesus Christ was crucified for our sins.

- Jesus Christ physically and literally resurrected from the dead.

- Jesus Christ died for the sins of the world.

- Jesus Christ is the one mediator sent by God for our salvation

- The Jesus Event was a real salvific event in history through which God reconciled the world unto God's self.

- Yes, and Amen. I believe and receive these truths.

AFFIRMATION

Say aloud: Christ came into the world to die for sinners, of whom I am chief. At the cross, Jesus took the sins of the world unto himself and destroyed the power of sin and the devil. When he was raised from the dead, he destroyed the power of death. Because I trust in Christ, sin and death have no power over me. Jesus has freed me from the law of sin and death. Jesus has invited all to the Jesus Event, where the old can become new again; where the blind will see; where the deaf will hear; where the sick will be healed; where the poor will be rich; where the weak will be strong; where the sinner will be saved; and where the dead will live. This is the Good News. Christ is calling for a new creation. His body, the church, proclaims this Good News to all.

MORNING REFLECTION

The M.E.E.T. Method—In the morning, purpose in your heart to:

M—Monitor your thoughts during the day and

E—Evaluate them. Do they align with God's word? Are they distortions of what is real?

E—Expel any thoughts that are contrary to the truth and replace them with the

T—Truth of God's word, created in the image of God.

EVENING REFLECTION—THE 7RS METHOD

1. Rest and Receive

Rest and receive God's truth. I entrust myself and others to God's grace and care.

- Receive the truth in your heart. We have all sinned and need God's grace and mercy. Rest in this fact.

- Sit and relax in a quiet place. Calm and quiet your mind as you think on this truth.

- Breathe deeply through the nose and out the mouth repetitively, as you rest in what God has done for you. As thoughts of the day come into your mind let them go. Give each thought to God.

- Be mindful of God's goodness. Be mindful of the gift of this moment. Be mindful of the gift that you are.

- Imagine every care being taken into God's loving embrace. Let the cares, concerns, and details of the day unravel slowly, layer after layer. Give each thought to God. You are intentionally casting your cares on God. They belong to God and not to you.

- Give to Christ any thought that is contrary to the truth. Let him nail it to his cross.

- Pray that Jesus would come into your mind and shine the light on any area that he desires. Also ask Jesus to come and speak specifically to any situation that is on your mind.

- Listen to God speak through your conscience concerning your thought-life today. Do you need to repent, or offer thanksgiving or a praise? Do you need to resolve to do God's word?

- Write down what God is impressing upon you.

- Hear and receive the truth of God's voice as he speaks to your thought-life.

2. Repent

Turn away from the lies and turn toward the truth. Also repent of all acts that are contrary to the character of Christ.

- Identify any lies in your thought-life that would lead you away from God's mercy and grace or lies that tempt you to believe that you are better than others or others are better than you. Also identify lies that would say that your own goodness supplants the goodness of God.

- Uproot the lies by rejecting and casting them down.

- Renounce the lies by making a decision to renew your thoughts.

- Turn from believing the lies to believing the truth. Replace the lies with the truth.

3. Renew

Renew your mind with the truth. Plant the word of God in your heart and believe it personally for your life.

- Meditate on the Scriptures for this section.

- Read and declare those Scriptures several times.

- Agree with God's word by saying, "Yes" and "Amen" to what it affirms. "Yes, and Amen, we are all sinners in need of God's grace."

- Receive the truth. Own it. Personalize it and make it yours.

4. Recite

Confess and declare the word of God.

- Think God's thoughts. Say what God says in his word.

- Declare several times, "I have sinned and fallen short of God's glory and am in need of mercy and salvation. My neighbor has sinned and fallen short of God's glory and is in need of mercy and salvation."

- In the future, remember and confess boldly God's word.

5. Resolve

Resolve yourself to action. Be a doer of the word.

- Make a decision to put this truth into practice. Practice it daily in every area of your life. Make clear resolutions to manifest the truth in concrete actions that impact others and the world around you.

6. Repeat

Repeat the process.

- Repeat and strengthen your commitment to the previous five steps. Repetition and rehearsal strengthen the truth in you.

7. Reality

Repetition brings reality.

- After much repetition from thought → word → deed, the truth becomes experiential and a solid concrete reality in your life that will yield the fruit of wisdom and righteousness.

Repentance

I turn from myself to God. I turn from my way to God's way. Scripture:

- 2 Corinthians 7:9–11 (NIV): "Yet now I am happy, not because you were made sorry, but because your sorrow led you to repentance. For you became sorrowful as God intended and so were not harmed in any way by us. Godly sorrow brings repentance that leads to salvation and leaves no regret, but worldly sorrow brings death. See what this godly sorrow has produced in you: what earnestness, what eagerness to clear yourselves, what indignation, what alarm, what longing, what concern, what readiness to see justice done. At every point you have proved yourselves to be innocent in this matter."

- Matthew 3:1–3 (NIV): "In those days John the Baptist came, preaching in the wilderness of Judea and saying, 'Repent, for the kingdom of heaven has come near.' This is he who was spoken of through the prophet Isaiah: 'A voice of one calling in the wilderness, Prepare the way for the Lord, make straight paths for him.'"

- Matthew 3:8–10 (NIV): "Produce fruit in keeping with repentance. And do not think you can say to yourselves, 'We have Abraham as our father.' I tell you that out of these stones God can raise up children for Abraham. The ax is already at the root of the trees, and every tree that does not produce good fruit will be cut down and thrown into the fire."

- Matthew 6:11–13 (NIV): "Give us today our daily bread. And forgive us our debts, as we also have forgiven our debtors. And lead us not into temptation, but deliver us from the evil one."

- John 16:8 (NLT): "And when [the Holy Spirit] comes, he will convict the world of its sin, and of God's righteousness, and of the coming judgment."

- Acts 20:21 (NIV): "I have declared to both Jews and Greeks that they must turn to God in repentance and have faith in our Lord Jesus."

- Read Psalm 51.

REFLECTION

St. Theophan the Recluse (1815–1894), Eastern Orthodox monk:

> What is repentance? It is a decisive change for the better, a breaking of the will, a turning from sin and a turning to God, or a kindling of the fire of zeal for exclusively God-pleasing things, with renunciation of the self and everything else. It is above all characterized by an extreme breaking of the will. Decisive and active resistance to sin comes only from hatred of it. Hatred of sin comes only from a sense of evil from it; the sense of evil from it is experienced in all its force in this painful break within repentance.[11]

Thomas Watson (1620–1686), prolific Puritan author:

> The two great graces essential to a saint in this life are faith and repentance. These are the two wings by which we fly to heaven. (pp.7)
>
> Repentance is a grace required by the Gospel. Some think it is legal, but the first sermon Christ preached, indeed, the first word of his sermon, was "Repent" (Matt 4.17).
>
> And his farewell that he left when he was going to ascend was that "repentance should be preached in his name" (Luke 24.47).
>
> The apostles did all beat upon this string: "They went out and preached that men should repent" (Mark 6.12)
>
> Repentance is a grace of God's Spirit whereby a sinner Is inwardly humbled and visibly reformed. For a further amplification, know that repentance is a spiritual medicine made up of six ingredients:
>
> 1. Sight of sin
>
> 2. Sorrow for sin
>
> 3. Confession of sin
>
> 4. Shame for sin
>
> 5. Hatred for sin
>
> 6. Turning from sin
>
> If anyone is left out it loses its virtue.[12]

Clement of Alexandria on repentance:

11. Theophan, *Path of Salvation*, 92.
12. Watson, *The Doctrine of Repentance*, 7–18.

There are two kinds of repentance. The more common is one of fear (of punishment) because of what has been done. The other kind, which is more special, is the shame that the spirit feels in itself, arising from the conscience. He that repents of what he did, no longer does or says the things he did . . . He, then, who has received forgiveness of sins should sin no more.[13]

Names of God

Study and meditate on the names of God that relate to our teaching on repentance. The names of God reveal God's nature and attributes. He is his name. And he extends the attribute represented by his name to us in covenant. For example, *Yahweh Shalom*, "the Lord God is peace." His name is peace. He is peace. And his peace he extends to us, so it becomes our peace.

El Roi, God who sees

Attribute: Omniscience. *El Roi* means the God or Mighty One who "sees." God sees everything everywhere. God sees us, and God knows our situation. We can be in a crowd and still feel alone. Though our lives are so busy, we often go unnoticed and untouched. However, God sees and knows our heart. God sees injustices and unrighteousness. Nothing escapes God's eye. He sees the past, the present, and the future. As we live, we live before God's presence. Nowhere can we go and not find God's presence or be seen by God, even in the midst of our sin. God is near and present to help when we call on the Lord who sees.

Just One

Attribute: justice and equity. Christ is called the Just One, perhaps because Christ will not only return to judge the living and the dead, but also because he who knew no sin became sin for us to make us just. He who is a justified and just judge is also the justifier of many. When we trust in Jesus, he makes us just before the Father who sends his Holy Spirit to dwell in us, enabling us to live justly and work justice in an upside-down world. We are called to be a manifestation of God's justice in all we do, especially toward those who have been victims of injustice. May we fight and pray for God's equity in an unequal world.

13. Bercot, *Dictionary of Early Christian Beliefs*, 556.

The Way

Attribute: Direction, Guide, Pathway. In an age of radical pluralism, it is easy to lose our way in the labyrinth of paths and ideas. Which way is right? Also, in a world of so many choices, how do I know which is the right one to choose? As with the truth, one can conceive of "ways" in the abstract—"this way or that way,"—but Jesus himself is the Way. He is the personal way. We are to come to Jesus, and he, the Way, will lead us in all the ways we need to go. Do we need guidance? Find Jesus and follow him. The Way will take us in the ways we need to go.

Renounce and repent of the following lies concerning repentance

__ My sin is not that bad compared to _.

__ It is okay to sin. We always sin in thought, word, and deed every day.

__ God does not really want me to repent every day for my sins.

__ God does not see what I do or hear what I think.

__ Everyone else is doing it.

__ Society thinks what I do is fine.

__ It is not hurting anyone.

__ I can never change.

__ Other _____

Now believe, receive, and confess these truths:

- The Spirit convicts us of our sins.

- We are commanded to turn from our sins and turn to God.

- Repentance involves seeing and feeling about sin as God does.

- God gives us the grace to repent.

- Repentance is an act as well as a lifestyle of turning from sin and turning to God.

- I repent of my sins _____ and turn fully to God and trust in his grace.

- Yes, and Amen. I believe and receive these truths.

AFFIRMATION

Say aloud: Lord, I come to you as a sinner. You know my heart, my thoughts, my words, and my deeds. They are laid bare before you. You even know the sins of which I am not aware. I cannot hide my sin from you. I cannot wash my own sins away. I cannot undo what has been done or erase the past. My sin and guilt are before me and before you. I know my sin is evil in your sight. Yet you desire to forgive and cleanse me. I desire to part with my sin and turn fully to your mercy and salvation. Lord I ask for forgiveness of my sins. Please take away my sin. I ask for a desire to hate sin and love your righteousness. Be Lord over every area of my life. I surrender to you and desire to serve you in all things.

I also ask that you grant repentance and forgiveness to _____. Grant _____ deliverance and freedom from every sin, sickness, affliction, and oppression. May you give ____ your grace and your Spirit to serve you in all things. Also grant grace for repentance to all nations, that your righteousness may be exalted, and the people be made right and free to live in your peace. In Christ's name—Amen.

The Collect for Purity—*Book of Common Prayer, 1979.*

> Almighty God, to you all hearts are open, all desires known, and from you no secrets are hid: Cleanse the thoughts of our hearts by the inspiration of your Holy Spirit, that we may perfectly love you, and worthily magnify your holy Name; through Christ our Lord. Amen.

MORNING REFLECTION

The M.E.E.T. Method—In the morning, purpose in your heart to:

M—Monitor your thoughts during the day and

E—Evaluate them. Do they align with God's word? Are they distortions of what is real?

E—Expel any thoughts that are contrary to the truth and replace them with the

T—Truth of God's word, created in the image of God.

EVENING REFLECTION—THE 7Rs METHOD

1. Rest and Receive

Rest and receive God's truth. I entrust myself and others to God's grace and care.

- Receive the truth in your heart. We have all sinned and need God's grace and mercy. Rest in this fact.

- Sit and relax in a quiet place. Calm and quiet your mind as you think on this truth.

- Breathe deeply through the nose and out the mouth repetitively, as you rest in what God has done for you. As thoughts of the day come into your mind let them go. Give each thought to God.

- Be mindful of God's goodness. Be mindful of the gift of this moment. Be mindful of the gift that you are.

- Imagine every care being taken into God's loving embrace. Let the cares, concerns, and details of the day unravel slowly, layer after layer. Give each thought to God. You are intentionally casting your cares on God. They belong to God and not to you.

- Give to Christ any thought that is contrary to the truth. Let him nail it to his cross.

- Pray that Jesus would come into your mind and shine the light on any area that he desires. Also ask Jesus to come and speak specifically to any situation that is on your mind.

- Listen to God speak through your conscience concerning your thought-life today. Do you need to repent, or offer thanksgiving or a praise? Do you need to resolve to do God's word?

- Write down what God is impressing upon you.

- Hear and receive the truth of God's voice as he speaks to your thought-life.

2. Repent

Turn away from the lies and turn toward the truth. Also repent of all acts that are contrary to the character of Christ.

- Identify any lies in your thought-life that would lead you away from God's mercy and grace or lies that tempt you to believe that you are better than others or others are better than you. Also identify lies that would say that your own goodness supplants the goodness of God.

- Uproot the lies by rejecting and casting them down.

- Renounce the lies by making a decision to renew your thoughts.

- Turn from believing the lies to believing the truth. Replace the lies with the truth.

3. Renew

Renew your mind with the truth. Plant the word of God in your heart and believe it personally for your life.

- Meditate on the Scriptures for this section.
- Read and declare those Scriptures several times.
- Agree with God's word by saying, "Yes" and "Amen" to what it affirms. "Yes, and Amen, we are all sinners in need of God's grace."
- Receive the truth. Own it. Personalize it and make it yours.

4. Recite

Confess and declare the word of God.

- Think God's thoughts. Say what God says in his word.
- Declare several times, "I have sinned and fallen short of God's glory and am in need of mercy and salvation. My neighbor has sinned and fallen short of God's glory and is in need of mercy and salvation."
- In the future, remember and confess boldly God's word.

5. Resolve

Resolve yourself to action. Be a doer of the word.

- Make a decision to put this truth into practice. Practice it daily in every area of your life. Make clear resolutions to manifest the truth in concrete actions that impact others and the world around you.

6. Repeat

Repeat the process.

- Repeat and strengthen your commitment to the previous five steps. Repetition and rehearsal strengthen the truth in you.

7. Reality

Repetition brings reality.

- After much repetition from thought → word → deed, the truth becomes experiential and a solid concrete reality in your life that will yield the fruit of wisdom and righteousness.

Deliverance and Forgiveness—Release to be Released

Throughout our lives, it goes without saying that we have been hurt by others, and we have hurt others. As it goes, hurt people, hurt people. Much of that hurt goes unforgiven. We hold each other in captivity. We need to release our debtors in order to be released by our creditors.

Jesus tells a parable of the "Unforgiving Servant" in Matthew 18:21–35 to illustrate the creditor-debtor relationship. One of the lessons learned in the parable is that unforgiveness empowers the devil to torment both the captive and the captor. Human conflict and pain are often the result of an unbroken chain of offenses resulting in unforgiveness that leads to revenge and further offence. Chain reactions and cycles of unforgiveness link much of our conflict and suffering, especially within families. Forgiveness is one of the greatest needs of humanity. Who can stand in the gap and break the cycles? Who can release us from the prison of our own unforgiveness?

We know the story in Matthew 18. The man who was forgiven his debt would not forgive his debtor. He is thrown in debtors' prison by his creditor until the debt is paid. The parable of Jesus teaches us that this debtor's prison, a cell of unforgiveness, is a place where people are tormented without escape until their creditor sets them free, or the debt is paid.

The parable is true to life. Many people are tormented because of unforgiveness. They hold each other in captivity and will not release them from their suffering. Counselors and pastors frequently encounter clients and parishioners who are tormented by their past and tormented by their current situations. They usually are on one side or the other of this creditor-debtor relationship. They have been hurt, wounded, and abused, or they have been the one who has inflicted hurt, wounds, and abuse. He/she is the one who needs to be released, or the one who needs to release. The sins we commit are against our neighbors, ourselves, and above all against God. We cannot take back the wrongs that we have done. No, we cannot undo what has been done. As it is often said, we cannot un-ring a bell.

If our sins merit an eternal debt, then we cannot pay them off. We deserve judgment and punishment because we are all lawbreakers of God's commandments, especially God's commandment of love. We have sinned against the one holy and eternal God. We have sinned against our neighbor who was made in the image of God. We all hurt and have been hurt. No one is innocent. There is no privileged class of people.

We are all infected by sin and infect each other. We cannot reverse the cycle. We cannot undo our broken relationship with God or our neighbors. Even looking past what we have done and to the future, we cannot fulfill God's righteous requirements to love God and our neighbor with a perfect love all the time. Still, we need to remember that there is no sin that we have committed that is outside the boundaries of God's grace and forgiveness. Our debt is great, but the riches of his grace are greater (Eph 2:7).

Despite our eternal debt, God is full of grace and mercy. His mercy triumphs over judgment. He gives mercy to souls but judgment to sin and Satan. God sent his only Son to die for us on the cross. Jesus died as a substitute for our cycle of torment, so that we may be forgiven. This is the Good News!

We can have our wrongs and our rights cancelled at Calvary. The right and the wrong, the offender and the offended, the prosecutor and the defendant, and the victor and the victim—for we are all of these—have died with Christ, so that the cycles may end. And we may begin a new life that exchanges cycles of torment for forgiveness.

We can be freed and set others free. Now that we are forgiven, the Lord calls us to do the same. We are called to forgive others (Eph 4:32; Col 3:13). As we have been released from our debts, so are we free to release others from their debts to us. As we have been liberated from debtor's prison, so should we release others who are in debt to us. We need to be intentional to release others whom we may have imprisoned in a cell of unforgiveness. Where there is no forgiveness, both parties finish in a prison of torment for an indefinite period until there is forgiveness.

Many mental illnesses, dysfunctional relationships, addictions, and cycles of sin are often rooted in and perpetuated by unforgiveness. I have seen countless people receive mental, emotional, and physical healing when they either decided to forgive or they received forgiveness. Release and be released. This divine exchange delivers us from debt and torment.

All deliverance begins with repentance and forgiveness. Jesus came to set the captives free. He plundered the prison cell of unforgiveness and liberated us from debt and torment. Freedom is a free gift for whoever wants it. But, if Jesus has set us free, then why do we hold each other in prison? Why do we hold debts over each other when Christ has wiped out our debts and our own credits?[14] Why do we hold on to past hurts and wrongs? Why must we continue to make people "pay" for their wrongs toward us? We need to be delivered from a spirit of vindication and vendetta.

Jesus is our Jubilee. He is our liberation. When we have been liberated by Christ, we are compelled by his Spirit to go and set the captives free, including our own captives, those whom we have imprisoned. Jailbreak! We are called to a ministry of forgiveness and reconciliation (2 Cor 5:18). We can choose to forgive and be forgiven. The forgiven forgive (Eph 4:32; Col 3:13). We are called to live a life of forgiveness.

Forgiveness is indeed lifelong and a lifestyle because we continue to hurt and be hurt. It is also a lifestyle because forgiveness can be a long-term process consisting of many tough decisions to forgive along the way—a seventy times seven practice (Matt 18:22). As Christ has sent us to heal the brokenhearted, he has sent us to forgive and be forgiven, for there is no more effective medicine or treatment for the soul than forgiveness, which is unconditional love in action.

Let us loose forgiveness wherever we go. Forgiveness is healing. As we stand beneath the cross and receive forgiveness, let us picture our creditors and debtors there also receiving forgiveness. It is much more difficult not to forgive when we sit together at the foot of the cross in need of the same mercy and grace. At the cross we hear Jesus say to us, "As I have forgiven you, so forgive others."

Take time in prayer to invite the Spirit to show you whom you need to forgive. Ask God for the grace and power to release your debtors. Release and be released. Let go of a spirit of unforgiveness that you may be delivered.

Wisdom on Praying against Addiction[15]

Many of the people who will come to your X-Team will be bound to some degree in addiction. We have become an addicted society.[16] It is imperative that deliverance ministers have a basic understanding of Addiction 101. I will try to keep this discussion simple, but the neuroscience of addiction is not simple. The basic dynamic that occurs with addiction of most types is

---

14. All our righteousness is filthy rags (Isa 64:6; Phil 3:8).

15. For a thorough treatment of the neuroscience of addiction, see Grisel, *Never Enough*.

16. Nikolovska, "44 Alarming Addiction Statistics," para. 1, 3.

that the neurocircuitry (brain wiring) that controls the mesolimbic system (reward and motivation) has been hacked and hijacked by addiction. The gratification system works normally with the executive function (in the frontal lobe of the brain) to regulate and prioritize self-sacrificial investments with long-term benefits over short-term immediate gratification.

Here is how the reward system is supposed to work. For example, when we go to college, we realize that we will be making many taxing sacrifices and burning the midnight oil to complete our studies. We realize that we cannot indulge in a lifestyle that will interfere with this deep commitment. We cannot afford the consequences of short-term gratification, binges and habits that will impede and interfere with our education and long-term goals. We sacrifice the immediate, short-lived, and negatively consequential gratification and benefits, and we make a long-term sacrifice to study hard in order to achieve long-term gratification, like graduation and a career. The reward system is regulated to prioritize long-term benefits over short-term gratification.

The executive function and other neurocircuits monitor and moderate the reward system, making sure proper priorities are considered and implemented. However, *genetic, epigenetic, environmental, behavioral,* and *stress conditions* can predispose someone to impulsive, risky behavior, which if unchecked can become abuse and then addiction. After abuse and addiction, the cycle continues into binge mode, negative withdrawal, and anticipation for the next high. Under addiction the brain changes, adapts (neuroadaptation), and learns to override its own system. The desire and drive for the reward or high increases (increased incentive salience), the rewards are not enough, and the executive function (their defense) is compromised. The person under addiction wants more, better, faster, and stronger rewards. Harder stuff is needed. The old stuff doesn't work anymore.

With addiction, this process of regulating gratification is compromised and dopamine levels are increased.[17] Addiction can increase the release of dopamine in the reward system (nucleus accumbens and dorsal striatum) in exorbitant amounts in a short period of time. The brain conditions itself (teaches itself) and remembers the stimulus-reward dynamic that attained the high (impacting memory in the hippocampus). And then a feedback loop is created to repeat the process, as you spiral down a vortex of devastation.

The "drug" whether it is substances, inappropriate internet content, sex, alcohol, etc. is never enough. One needs more and harder. Some studies

---

17. Dopamine is a neurotransmitter responsible for mood, feeling, and motivation impacting our reward and gratification system, among other functions. Some call dopamine the feel-good brain chemical.

indicate that dopamine does "not signal pleasure" but signals "the anticipation of pleasure."[18] It is the anticipating, savoring, and salivating that comes
before one eats a meal. Some get high off the pursuit more than the thing
itself.

Addiction wrongly teaches a person that they do not have to spend
years of sacrifice for a reward. Why work hard and long and wait for the
good feeling of a reward that comes with graduating college, waiting for
marriage, or saving and investing money? Why wait, when one can get the
same high and greater in a moment by pursuing one's addiction of choice.

Bypass sacrifice and suffering and get immediate gratification and
pleasure! But people don't read the small print that comes with addiction.
There is a price to pay. The small print states, "If you allow addiction to
hijack your system, then you will sell your soul and everything else for this
short-term destructive high."

The hijacking that occurs with addiction is like a virus entering your
computer. The virus will flood the system, take it over, corrupt it, and destroy it. Addiction is destructive to the spirit, mind, and body. With addiction, in the end, a person will sacrifice their soul and *everything* they love
for *one* thing that will destroy them. Recovery is giving up the *one* thing that
is destroying them to gain back *everything* that they love. Addiction cannot
heal the hurt that lies underneath. It only exacerbates it.

Consider the brain dynamics of addiction, as I shared above, when
you pray repentance, deliverance, and healing. Remember, there are *genetic,
epigenetic, environmental, behavioral,* and *overall stress components* at work,
leading up to the addiction. Under addiction, the main dynamics are the
hacking of the reward system followed by a feedback loop that perpetuates
the pursuit for a greater high Address these directly in prayer. Pray against
generational sin and curses. Pray for the compromised neural circuitry to
be restored and line up with God's created intentions. Pray for balance and
regulation in the reward system and dopamine levels. Pray for strength and
proper functioning of the executive functions. Pray for peace in the over-
reacting amygdala. You get the point. Pray with authority and informed
intercession.

Learn the Sciences

I encourage deliverance and healing ministers to take a beginner's course or
read some introductory material on the human anatomy and physiology, as

18. Grisel, *Never Enough*, 27.

well as neurology and neuroscience.[19] Having this basic information will give you wisdom and enable you to pray with more specificity and directness. When I was trained in healing ministry back in the 1980s at the Charles and Francis Healing School, medical doctors of every specialization were on staff to train practitioners and evaluate what was taught and practiced. They gave us guidance to understand how the body was intended to function. Their wisdom and instruction enabled us to pray more specifically and effectively.

The interdisciplinary approach was an early influence on my healing and deliverance ministry. I learned to co-work with the sciences. The sciences are not your enemy or an obstruction to healing and deliverance. An interdisciplinary methodology upped my game and my effectiveness because every intercessor knows if you want to be effective in your prayer life, pray more specifically. In your prayer and ministry learn to incorporate the sciences when you address addiction, mental health issues, healing, trauma, and other ailments.

Preparation Conclusion

In conclusion, let us review the task of the X-Team. Godly, mature leaders are selected, trained, and certified to minister deliverance:

- They have prayed and fasted in preparation over each area.
- They know how to use their spiritual weapons for warfare.
- They minister with humility and care.
- They know the four laws of deliverance.

Review of the Four Laws of Deliverance (Feel free to skip over, if you've got the Four Laws down.)

Deliverance is based on the finished work of the cross, true repentance, the liberation of the will, and executing the authority of Jesus Christ

Intercessors execute and enforce the finished work of Christ, as summed up in the name of Jesus, on behalf of the demonically bound person. Jesus destroyed the power and authority of Satan, sin, and death on the cross. Our enemies have been soundly defeated. We minister deliverance from a place of victory. The finished work of the cross is our basis for total defeat of the devil. We do not grope or strive to attain victory. The battle is already won. The war is over. We are merely enforcing the victory.

19. Amthor, *Neuroscience for Dummies.*

The X-Team operates in the authority of Christ and executes and enforces the finished work of the cross, where our Lord has already destroyed the works of the devil (1 John 3:8) and set the captives free. The cross provides the legal, finished, and objective grounds for the defeat of Satan. We merely apply what Christ has already accomplished. We bind the devil and take authority over him because we have been given the keys (authority) of the Kingdom (Matt 16:19; 18:18). And in Jesus' name we drive him out.

Those ministering enforce deliverance in the name of Jesus, the name that is given as power of attorney to believers to act on Christ's behalf in his power and authority. Intercessors co-work with the leading and power of the Spirit to break the powers of darkness that are controlling the bound person. The individual is then led to surrender to the delivering work of the cross. The saving and sanctifying work of God is embodied in the Son of Man and represented by the name of Jesus. The name of Jesus is the only name given to the world for salvation (Acts 4:12). All are summoned to bow at the name of Jesus (Phil 4:10). In Jesus' name, his disciples shall overthrow, trample underfoot, and cast out demons.

There is power in the name of Jesus. People chained are called to repent and renounce forever former practices and confess the Lordship of Christ. As in the ancient baptismal liturgy and covenant of the early church, believers are called to vocally renounce Satan, his power, and his works. Individuals are reminded that they willfully gave in to temptation and sin. Now, they need to recover their will by acknowledging that they freely chose to sin. They willfully surrendered to the power of the enemy. Now, they need to cooperate with God's grace, choose the truth and righteousness, and surrender to Christ. This act of turning is an essential part of repentance. People gain hope by recognizing as they once yielded their lives as instruments of sin, now they can yield their lives as instruments of righteousness Rom 6:12–19).

It is paramount that repentant people acknowledge their part in having surrendered to sin rather than blaming the devil. By the grace and power of God, they need to recapture their will. Recapturing the will begins by acknowledging that they willfully chose to rebel, but now by grace they can willfully choose to resist sin and Satan and obey God. Deliverance is carried out based on reversing The Law of the Will. This law determines and governs the nature and degree of bondage.

We remember that The Law of the Will is that, to the degree one submits one's will to sin and the demonic, to that degree they have authority over you. Conversely, to the degree one submits to the Lordship of Christ, to that degree Christ has authority over the person and manifests his authority.

Manifest authority. This is the Second Law of Deliverance. Jesus is Lord over all in our lives, or he is not Lord at all.

The degree of control in one's everyday life can in part be measured by the nature of the sinful practice or stronghold and the duration, frequency, and intensity of the practice. By way of illustration, we note the increased degree of influence in the life of the addict as a function of frequency, duration, and intensity of use of a particular substance. The law of habit strengthens the chains of addiction. Deliverance involves the liberating of the will and the reversal of authority.

In deliverance, God is transferring the control and authority over the will by sin and Satan to Christ and obedience. This process begins by God empowering individuals to recover their will in repentance, to own their compliance to sin, then to surrender that area to Christ. The intercessors begin to drive out the devil in the name of Jesus following repentance. People bound need to demonstrate a willingness to be set free, although it is God who supplies the grace and power for the heavy lifting of repentance and deliverance. Like a forklift. The lift does the heavy lifting, but the operator needs to be willing to turn the key and pull the levers. The grace of God does the heavy lifting. We just need to be willing and cooperate.

In the character, fruit, and Spirit of Christ, the intercessors are encouraged to minister deliverance with both humility and boldness. Special attention should be paid to the pastoral ministry and the pastoral moment (timing) of deliverance. The X-Team needs to be sensitive to all pastoral issues that arise specifically around protecting the integrity, dignity, confidentiality, and will of the person who will be receiving prayer.

Also, proper prayer preparation prior to deliverance sessions and intentional discipleship sessions following deliverance sessions are imperative to full restoration of those receiving deliverance. Practices of inner healing and belief and identity formation are essential *before and after* deliverance.[20] In fact, many demonic strongholds break easily following such careful and prayerful preparation. Remember, all the cracks in the soul where the devil can gain a foothold need to be sealed and the low areas built up with the Word, so that the house is repaired and can keep out sin and be filled with the Spirit, lest the devil return seven-fold (Luke 11:26).

---

20. See Bellini, *Truth Therapy* and other strategies of inner healing, belief and identity formation, and discipleship for pre- and post-deliverance. Repentance, forgiveness (giving and receiving), and accepting the truth concerning one's identity in Christ are indispensable practices for receiving deliverance.

Lesson 5

Deliverance Decorum

THIS CHAPTER MAY BE the most important one in the book. While many in deliverance ministry are concerned with casting the demon out, we also need to be concerned about treating the seeker with dignity, confidentiality, integrity, compassion, and care. This pastoral dimension of deliverance is often neglected. We must remember the Hippocratic oath and John Wesley's first rule for the early Methodists: "Do no harm." When trying to help, first, do not do any or further harm. *Helping begins with not hurting.*

I was once in a deliverance conference when a young man came to me crushed and in tears. He was devastated. I learned that he had several intellectual disabilities, and one of the workers had attempted to cast out the young man's learning disabilities as demons. He was told he had demons that made him "slow." I spent the rest of the afternoon caring for the young man and explaining to him that his disabilities were not demons. We all have different levels of ability and development. We are all limited to some degree as humans and are challenged to grow relative to our capacity. This person was hurting, and the person who attempted to help did further harm through their prayer.

DO NO HARM!

When a person needs help, they are already in distress. We need to be aware that, even with good intentions to help a person, we can inadvertently hurt them further. Our first priority should be to do no harm. We have all been challenged in the past to do no harm. Yes, we want the demon cast out, but not at the expense of the person's safety or dignity. Select caring and compassionate X-Team members, not weekend warriors or soldiers of misfortune.

It is the goodness of God that leads us to repentance. And it is the love and grace of God that delivers and saves us. Fragile! Handle with care!

I have witnessed deliverance ministries that were extremely physical, abrasive, rude, aggressive, and insensitive to seekers. We cannot imagine Christ acting in this manner. Of course, we want to be direct, bold, and authoritative with the devil, but not with people. Take the time to explain the process in detail. Share with the seeker that there may be times you are confrontational and stern with the devil, but this is not being directed at them. Carefully explain the process and get their permission for everything you do. Deliverance is uncomfortable enough. Go out of your way to show hospitality, gentleness, and understanding.

Think of how a nurse or a doctor informs you before, during, and after an exam or a procedure. They meticulously and caringly let you know what is going to happen, step-by-step, during the exam. They prepare you for what to expect. During the procedure, they ask questions. "How are you doing? Did you feel any pain?" Or they give further instructions. "I am going to ask you to relax, lift up your arms and cough," for example. After the exam is over, they may ask if you have any questions or whether you are experiencing any pain. We want to be thinking more like a nurse than a drill sergeant.

DELIVERANCE: A TIME TO WORSHIP CHRIST THE KING

The final item of decorum relates to the Lord and not to the seeker or deliverance team. A deliverance session is a time to glorify God and not Satan. We do not celebrate that we have authority over Satan. We celebrate that God has delivered and healed someone's soul (Luke 10:20). God gets all the glory. The deliverance session should begin and end by focusing on and exalting the King of Kings and the Lord of Lords. We put him first. Take time at the start and end of the session to worship and praise the one who was, is, and is to come.

The book of Revelation is about warfare and judgment, but it is also a book about worship. Chapter after chapter opens our eyes to the heavenly worship that occurs at the throne as the angels, elders, and saints behold the Holy One. Gazing at the exalted Christ inspires worship that releases power and authority in warfare. Warfare and worship are intertwined and interplay back and forth. Ultimately, worship even becomes a weapon of our warfare.

I often envision the warrior Jesus of Revelation chapters 1 and 19 when I worship and invoke Christ during a deliverance session. I invoke the warrior who rides on the white horse with a double-edged sword proceeding from his mouth to make war on the nations. He comes to judge and rule. He judges demons, the antichrist, the beast, the false prophet, and their followers, and rules over them with an iron rod. Christ, the Alpha and the Omega, the first and the last, the ruler of all, will come as a demon slayer (Rev 19:15). He will make war against his enemies. He will rule over and judge Satan and his hordes. He comes with all power and authority to set the captives free, demonstrating his Lordship. It is Jesus, the Lion of the Tribe of Judah, that we invoke to execute deliverance. He is a jailbreaking Jesus!

Deliverance is a time to enthrone Christ in our hearts as Lord. We submit and surrender everything to him. All of his enemies are his footstool. We recommit our lives to the absolute Lordship of Christ at this time. We give him glory and honor. The spotlight is now off the devil and on the Lord. I have often heard ministers and even seekers brag about their sessions and put more focus on the enemy and his works than God. A deliverance session is a session where we worship Christ the Victor!

THE EXTERMINATOR

Let me share an analogy that in part explains deliverance in terms of addressing the devil. We do not boast about having demons or about a deliverance session. Deliverance, in this sense, is like having cockroaches in one's apartment. No one advertises and brags about having roaches. You do not post it on Facebook and Twitter. "Hey, I got a mass quantity of huge roaches. They are so big that I am charging the neighborhood kids five dollars a ride."

Do not boast about having demons. If one has roaches in their apartment, they quietly call the exterminator and tell them to park ten houses down the block, so they are not near your abode, advertising your cockroach problem to the neighbors. You pray that the exterminator goes in and out as quickly as possible without being noticed by others. You are not proud that you have roaches.

The exterminator also informs you that the roaches (the demons) are only the symptom of a deeper problem. You must keep the place clean of anything that attracts them (sin). The exterminator may also instruct you to move out because you are in an apartment complex that is infested with roaches. In this case, the problem may be more with your neighbors (your circle of friends). The roaches originated from your neighbor's apartment and spilled over into your apartment.

You may need to change your circle of friends and influences (1 Peter 4:4). You may have to throw out some things, like infested pieces of furniture, and replace them with new furniture. You may have to throw out demonically attached objects, movies, images, games, files, books, paraphernalia, etc. (Acts 19:18–19). I have led witches (white and black), warlocks, and Satanists to the Lord who found total freedom when they burned the accessories and accoutrements of their former craft. Sweep the place clean and fill it with the Holy Spirit and the aroma of God's presence.

Meanwhile, the exterminator (the X-Team), I am sure, does not like roaches. The exterminator wakes up to roaches and has them on his mind day and night. Roaches are his life. "Roaches-Are-Us" is his tagline. I would venture to guess that he hates them so much that his own house is clean without any roaches. I would also venture to guess that when he gets home to his family and sits down for dinner, he is not talking about the rebellious roaches he chased around all day. He has better things to discuss. I am sure the fella working at Roto-Rooter would act the same. Keep the focus off the roaches and the waste in the toilet, and glorify Christ the dragon slayer!

FIFTY GUIDELINES FOR DELIVERANCE

Note: There is no strict formula or science to deliverance. Deliverance comes from the grace of God, revealed in the finished work of Jesus Christ on the cross, through the power of the Holy Spirit. Deliverance is Spirit-led and occurs through the faith of the believer, as he or she trusts in and implements the authority of the name of Jesus, given to them by Christ. Although there is no strict formula or magic phrase for deliverance, there are Biblical and Spirit-led wisdom and principles that can guide the process. Here are some guidelines and wisdom one can use for deliverance:

1. After answering TRUE on all 10 statements on the 10 Point Checklist, have the recipient fill out the release form. Remember not to administer deliverance if the person has not scored 10 on the Checklist. ___ Have them go over each area and repent individually for each sin. The person should take three to four weeks to do this while fasting. Also, both participant and team need to have fasted twenty-four hours prior to the session.

2. Assign the session to an available, well-trained, prepared, and certified deliverance team (of at least two people, preferably three or four, mixed sexes). ___

3. Recipient has filled out inventory, C1–13 assessment, and waiver forms. ____

4. Leadership has reviewed the results of the inventory and assessment with recipient. ____

5. Leadership has interviewed recipient about the problem, the inventory and assessment, the solution and deliverance procedures, and expectations. ____

6. It is good to have women take the lead with women and men with men. ____

7. Protect the dignity of the person above all. ____

8. Deliverance team with designated leader is prayed and fasted up. ____

9. Deliverance team has gone through a period of repentance, cleansing, and fasting over each area of sin identified by the C1–13. ____

10. Make sure deliverance team does not hinder the process in any way through improper dress, foul breath or odors, division, arguing, forcing of manifestations, or the like. Have breath mints and mouthwash in the deliverance room. ____

11. Set aside a special, private room for deliverance. ____

12. Have the following items available: Bibles, bottles of water, power or granola bars or healthy snack items, towels, tissues, a garbage can, praise and worship music, breath fresheners, and other useful items. ____

13. Saturate the room before, during, and after deliverance with prayer, praise, and worship. ____

14. Explain the process and ask permission at each juncture. ____

15. Set aside an initial time for worship and submission to God. ____

16. Plead the blood of Jesus over the room, the team, and the recipient. ____

17. Invite recipient to repent of all sins and renounce all practices from both the inventory and whatever comes to their mind. ____

18. Invite Jesus the Lion of the Tribe of Judah, the Dragon and Demon Slayer, into the room to release deliverance. ____

19. Ask for protection from warrior angels and release protection. ____

20. Bind all distractions and hindrances. ____

21. Bind and break powers over the area and the deliverance team. ____

22. Dismantle and deactivate all assignments and strategies of the enemy. ___

23. One person speaks at a time. Avoid confusion and distractions. ___

24. Expect the Spirit to reveal the gifts of the Spirit, especially discernment, healing, and words of knowledge and wisdom that will address names of spirits, types of afflictions, and strategies for victory (Ps 107:20). ___

25. Ask permission from the person to lay on hands or for anything attempted. Lay hands lightly. ___

26. When necessary, explain the process and its procedures to the seeker as you proceed. ___

27. Be pastoral even over being prophetic. ___

28. One should lay hands with permission, in only appropriate places, and on the same sex. ___

29. Do not allow demons to manifest or speak. They are liars. ___

30. Go through the 5 Step Deliverance Method in chapter 6. ___

31. Address each spirit from the inventory or otherwise specifically by name and command it to come out in the name of Jesus. ___

32. Break and renounce each of these spirits in Jesus' name. ___

33. Curse the demonic powers with the blood of Jesus. ___

34. Declare over the candidate repeatedly that Jesus is Lord; Insist that the demons acknowledge it as well. ___

35. Remind Satan that all authority has been given to you in Jesus' name to bind him and cast him out. He has been judged. ___

36. Throughout the session, as led by the Spirit, invite the candidate to repent of various sins and to renounce them, as well as to confess Jesus as Lord. ___

37. Only raise your voice if the Spirit leads, but it is not necessary for deliverance. ___

38. Be led. Allow for others to speak and take the lead for a time if the Spirit leads. But stay focused. Watch out for distractions from the enemy through the seeker or the team. ___

39. Do no harm! Be attentive to the person's dignity and honor. Do not hurt, harm, embarrass, or shame the person. ___

40. Do not get physical in a way that can harm, hurt, or violate the person. Be gentle but bold. ___

41. Heaviness can harbor and manifest in the chest area. Pray over that area. ___

42. Demons often nestle in the spirit that impacts the stomach area. Pray over that area. ___

43. Do not struggle, wrestle, or contest with demons unnecessarily or for prolonged periods. The person is either ready for deliverance, or they are not. The deliverance team knows their authority in Christ, or they do not. ___

44. Continue to praise and worship Jesus throughout the session. Actually, Christ is the main focus during the deliverance session and not Satan. ___

45. If the person is not willing to repent, renounce each spirit, or surrender to the point of breakthrough, do not force their will, but discontinue the session for a later date when the recipient is more open or ready. ___

46. Close all open doors and seal them with the blood of Jesus. __

47. If the person has repented and is set free, invite the person to accept Christ as their Lord and Savior (if they have not already) and pray for the person to receive the infilling of the Holy Spirit where a vacancy has been created by the deliverance. ___

48. Plead the blood for cleansing over all who have participated. ___

49. Pray protection against backlash over each person and all that pertains to the covenant in their lives. ___

50. Schedule a follow-up session before leaving and begin discipleship in *Truth Therapy* by Peter Bellini or a similar work. Other recommended reading: *Deliverance and Inner Healing*, John and Mark Sandford; *Christianity with Power*, Charles Kraft; *The Bondage Breaker, Victory over the Darkness, Who am I in Christ, Freedom From Addiction*, and other titles, Neil Anderson; *Deliverance from Evil Spirits*, Francis Mac-Nutt; *Biblical Guidebook to Deliverance*, Randy Clark; *How to Cast Out Demons*, Doris Wagner; *Demons: the Answer Book*, Lester Sumrall; *Deliverance and Spiritual Warfare Manual*, John Eckhardt; *Handbook for Spiritual Warfare*, Ed Murphy, among others. ___

THE TEN MOST FREQUENTLY ASKED QUESTIONS ABOUT DELIVERANCE:

#1 Can anyone cast out demons?

No. Unbelievers cannot. But a believer who knows their authority in Christ can. All believers have the authority to cast out demons and should receive training. Only local church trained, certified, and appointed people should engage in this very sensitive ministry. Deliverance is not the wild, wild west. We don't need self-appointed cowboys to shoot up Dodge. Proper training is essential. See chapter 4, "Qualifications for Deliverance."

#2 Can a Christian have a demon?

A Christian cannot be *possessed* by a demon. However, a Christian can be *influenced* by a demon, beginning with temptation leading to sin, leading to oppression and a stronghold or demonic attachment in an area of their life. An example of a believer needing deliverance was Peter when he told Christ he did not have to go to the cross. Jesus knew Satan was speaking through Peter (Matt16:23, Mark 8:33, Luke 4:8). The same disciple who said just prior, "You are the Christ, the Son of the living God" (Matt 16:16). Peter had a spirit of fear, and Satan spoke through him. He was not possessed, but the devil clearly had a degree of influence on him.

Judas was one of the twelve who preached Christ and worked miracles. Christ said to his disciples that their names were written in heaven, indicating that the disciples were believers. (Luke 10:20). Nonetheless, Satan entered into Judas and used him to betray Christ (Luke 22:3; John 13:2, 27). Randy Clark cites two other cases in which believers needed deliverance, the woman disabled for eighteen years (Luke 13:10–17) and the Syrophoenician woman's daughter (Mark 7:24–30).[1] It is noteworthy that many of the demons Christ cast out were in God's house (Mark 1:23, 39; Luke 4:33).

Also, there are some ministers who say you should not minister deliverance to an unbeliever, because if they are not converted, seven more demons will come back. This is true in a sense if the person does not repent and submit to Christ's lordship. But deliverance absolutely should be ministered to unbelievers upon their *repentance and submission* to Christ, as taught in this book, for both believer and unbeliever. Deliverance is evangelistic and part of conversion, like it was for the Gadarene man. Deliverance

---

1. Clark, *The Biblical Guidebook to Deliverance*, 53–55 and Arnold, *Three Crucial Questions about Spiritual Warfare*, 73–142.

is a sign and wonder that aids conversion and proclaims the gospel to others (see the Gadarene man, Matt 8, Mark 5, and Luke 8). We should not forbid it. It is an instrumental component of power evangelism.

#3 During deliverance, should we ask demons questions, like asking them their names?

This is a controversial subject. Some ministries do and some do not. I personally do not prefer to ask demons questions. They are all liars. They are worse than talking with some teenagers.[2] My experience has been that this is an effective distraction of the devil to lead people down a rabbit trail. Ministers can easily get off-track and lose the goal, which is liberation, not a conversation. Demons will make any excuse not to leave. They are like trying to put your six- and eight-year-old to bed at night. They run and hide. They make excuses. They want water, food, their favorite toy, this, or that. Anything but to go to bed. You cannot reason with them. You cannot reason with demons (Of course, that is the only similarity between them). There is only one biblical occurrence where Christ asked the demons their names (Legion) when ministering to the Gadarene man. In other instances, he told the demons to be silent (Mark 1:34; Luke 4:41). He also did not allow the demons to manifest uncontrollably or hurt a person.

One of our goals is to protect the seeker. They are not a subject for experimentation. Try not to permit demons to speak, manifest, or harm the person. Be bold and tell the evil spirit to be silent. Ministers ask demons questions because they are looking for clues and information that can help the deliverance process. The rationale is that if they know the name of the demon, then they have authority over it. This conclusion is erroneous. You already have authority over the demon in Jesus' name. Do not look to Satan for clues and information for deliverance. Rely on the Spirit and not demons.

If demons are willing to give you "insight," how much more is the Holy Spirit? The Holy Spirit will lead you. He will reveal the names of demons and other information if necessary. Also, you have the C1–13 that has already disclosed the type of demons that you will be facing.

I try not to get caught up in constructing a formal, sophisticated taxonomy or naming of demons when Scripture is not that clear or exhaustive on the matter.[3] Occasionally, Scripture will reference the name of a demon,

---

2. It is my humor again. Pray for me. I had teenagers years ago. I loved them then and now, and I love teens in general. Sometimes truth-telling seemed to be a challenge for them. We all have our hurdles to overcome.

3. I provide a general list of angels and demons from Scripture and Christian

but many ministers seem to go beyond Scripture. They have gone over the top with a name for every demon. Some get as creative as they would be if they were naming their own newborn son or daughter. "Honey, let's buy a demon name book and pick it out together." It may make people sound more "spiritual," but maybe bordering on the "spooky spiritual." We Spirit-filled types are often labeled as flaky, and some of that stereotype is warranted. I call it "spiritual granola" in charismatic churches: too many fruits, nuts, and flakes.

Let us not become superstitious, mythical, spiritualists, overdramatic, or extrabiblical. And we will become just that if we major in minors and get off-track. It is all about *Jesus Christ, repentance of sin,* and *forgiveness and salvation as revealed in Scripture by the Holy Spirit.*

We charismatics have often gone overboard on self-styled spiritual experiences that go beyond the simple boundaries that I expressed. Our Christian life looks more like a Marvel Universe movie than the scriptural life of Christ. Too many Dr. Stranges in the house. We do not have to be able to name a demon in order to cast it out. They respond fine to "devil," just like the person next to me turns toward me when I say, "Hey, you." I do not have to be specific. If the Spirit or Scripture gives a specific name to a demon, then so will I.

#4 Should we allow deliverance during worship services?

In order to protect the privacy and dignity of the seeker and the congregants, I would suggest not doing public deliverance sessions. Train your altar team to take the seeker to a special room designated for deliverance if demonic manifestation should emerge. Remember that demons can attack the innocent, like children, who cannot defend themselves. They should not be exposed to that environment.

#5 Can I address the devil directly or must I ask the Lord to do it on my behalf?

I think either way is scriptural. I use both approaches, depending on how I am led. We are given the authority to do both. Christ clearly commanded the disciples to cast out demons. So, the believer can directly address the devil to come out in the name of Jesus. The believer can also say to the devil,

---

tradition in Appendix A. However, it is not detailed and overly speculative. The list stays faithful to Scripture.

"The Lord rebuke you, Satan." Most often I address the devil directly with boldness and authority. Even then, let your words be scriptural, few, and authoritative (see Jesus in Matt 4). We are not there for a tea party. And we are not there in pride to mock the devil. Even Michael the Archangel did not do so (Jude 1:9). We cannot beat the devil by being like the devil. Be humble!

#6 What if the demon(s) does not come out?

There can be many reasons for resistance. It is not uncommon. A seeker's spiritual pipes are already clogged; that is why they came to you for spiritual Drano. Possibly, the seeker has not truly or thoroughly repented. Perhaps the deliverance team was not fully prepared and walking in manifest authority. During a session, there can be stuck points or blocks. Satan can create these as well as the seeker. The seeker can become fearful. Pray for peace. Seek to soothe their fear. Explain the process and what is occurring.

At times, the seeker may quit resisting the devil. This can happen because they are not aware that they are no longer resisting. Go back to coaching them to resist. Also, the seeker may stop resisting because he/she is tired. Deliverance is spiritually, physically, mentally, and emotionally grueling for all parties. Take a break for a couple minutes if necessary but stay on track. If the person has repented and is open, and the team is on-point, then the demon(s) should come out. Like a loose tooth, when it is ready, it will come out. When it is not ready, you can pull and pull, and it will not budge. When the apple is ripe, it falls. When the baby is ready, it can be delivered.

Coach and push through stuck points. Like in childbirth, make sure the seeker is breathing properly and sufficiently, in through the nose and out through the mouth, and, when it becomes difficult, short quick breaths. Watch at stuck points during the 5 Steps (chapter 6). Pay attention to when the block occurs during the 5 Steps. Pray for wisdom. Often you will be able to sense when and where the resistance is occurring. If the seeker or the team are exhausted, even after breaks, reschedule if necessary. If it is a chain of demons, they may not always come out in one session. You may need several sessions, depending on progress.

Beware of a *false or premature* deliverance. A false deliverance occurs when the manifestations have subsided, but the demon has hidden for cover deep within the flesh. The demon wants to go undetected, so that it can remain attached to the person. Therefore, it hides in silence undetected. The demon plays dead. The witness of the Spirit and discernment of spirits from a seasoned deliverance minister can easily pick this up. At this point, once one starts to pursue the demon aggressively, then it is forced to manifest. I always make one final aggressive pursuit before finishing a session to make sure the house is clean.

Another clever tactic is when the demon blows smoke to distract you and cause you to abort and prematurely end the session. Watch out for this trick. The devil uses it often. Once I was casting a demon out of a young woman. She was manifesting and writhing on the ground. Then she started to complain that I was hurting her, even though no one was touching her. She did not seem to be lying. She appeared to be in real agony. The evil spirit was actually causing the pain throughout her body to prevent further deliverance. It was hoping she would throw in the towel and quit the session. The devil was also tempting those present to feel sorry for her so we would quit. We took authority over the pain. I was not buying that cheap trick and pressed on until she was delivered. The young woman received Christ as her savior that night!

#7 How do I cast out demons?

There is no one exact formula. But we simply cast out demons with a command to leave the person in the name of Jesus. When the person is ready, we say, for example, "Spirit of fear, I command you to come out of Joe in Jesus' name." Just use the cross, faith, authority, and the name of Jesus. Continue reading for more details.

#8 How do I know if someone has a demon?

This type of knowledge with certainty can be tricky. Read chapter 4 and have the seeker take the C1–13. The X-Team and the seeker can know directly by the inner witness.[4] They will also know with the gift of discerning of spirits, and indirectly by demonic manifestations (presentations), sinful practices, seeker's testimony, and the C1–13.[5] Demonic manifestations may

---

4. The inner witness is when God's Spirit directly bears witness with our spirit about the truth (John 14–16, 15:26; Rom 8:14–16; Heb 10:15; 1 John 2:20, 27). The witness is immediate, direct, and self-evident. It is often a still, small knowing or voice that leads the believer into truth. It is our sixth sense, or spiritual sense by which we discern good and evil.

5. Discerning of spirits is a gift that allows one to detect and identify spirits (good and evil) through spiritual perception that can involve hearing, seeing, smell, or feeling. For me it works with the inner witness and allows me to pick up on demonic signals, identify the type of demon, track its movements, uncover demonic spirits when they hide in a person, and know when they have left a person.

My spiritual perception usually operates through spiritual sight and feeling. I see

include, but are not limited to: involuntary twitches or bodily movement not explained medically; eyes rolling back to the whites; cursing and blaspheming; rage and supernatural strength; scratching, cutting, or self-mutilation; speaking in a different voice; a foul scent; hissing; jerks, twitching, contortions, bloating, an abnormal swelling in a part of the body that when prayed for moves; bodily pain; slithering on the ground; yawning; repetitious licking of the lips or sticking out of the tongue; eyes change color or grow darker; growling; a sudden increase in strength that comes with rage; levitation; vomiting and others. The eyes are also a good indicator. Focus on them. Remember that these bodily activities can also be explained, at times, by other causes. Thus, we ask for medical evaluation prior.

Of course, these manifestations (presentations) are not all listed in the Bible and are debatable in themselves. The Bible does not give us much detail about these phenomena. That is why we make the connection with the demonic through sinful behavior that can be observed. I have witnessed these manifestations, and they were correlated with the demonic due to the behavior associated with the person. I also trusted the inner witness of the Spirit and the gift of discerning of spirits. Here, I rely on my years of deliverance ministry experience.

Our strategy is integrative and incorporate the biomedical and psychological models of explanation as well. We should verify that these manifestations, presentations, or symptoms cannot be explained otherwise by medical science. Refer to a medical professional when necessary. Even have one present if possible. After medical treatment, if the manifestations persist, then the seeker may need deliverance.

#9 What is the difference between oppression and possession and deliverance and exorcism?

See chapter 4 for details. Unbelievers can be oppressed or possessed. Believers cannot be possessed, only oppressed. Deliverance is for degrees of demonic influence like oppression. Exorcism is for possession when the seeker no longer has agency to act freely. The method to liberate one who is oppressed or possessed is the same.

---

and feel demonic presences. For me discerning of spirits, coupled with the inner witness, is like a cross between a demonic GPS tracking system, a demonoscopy, a DRI (Demonic Resonance Imaging), and a demon-seeking drone or missile. I am using figurative language, of course. This gift operates as the Spirit wills (1 Cor 12:10–11).

#10 How long or how many sessions does it take for a person to be liberated?

It depends on many variables. Has the seeker truly repented? Is the deliverance team truly on-point? How many demons are the team facing? What is the degree of demonization? Are the demons in chains and clusters? Deliverance can be immediate or progressive. Deliverance session(s) are finished when the person is free. We know one is free immediately by the inner witness of the Spirit through the team and the seeker. Those who have the gift of discerning of spirits can detect this immediately as well. We can also detect an immediate visible change in their countenance. Manifestations have ceased, and their countenance, *especially the eyes*, appear illuminated and lucid. The person will often weep and experience great joy. The evidence and signs are cumulative; freedom is not detected by merely one sign alone.

Wisdom. Do not rely on any one manifestation as a litmus test or indicator that one has been delivered. There is no single gauge that we turn to, but it is rather a cumulative witness of the Spirit, ceasing of manifestations over a period of time, a reversal in behavior, and the fruit of the Spirit. When I was a pastor, I had a congregant who always felt he had a demon. Even though I explained to him that the way of the cross was the normative way we are delivered from evil, he insisted on regular deliverance. He had learned this erroneous doctrine from his previous church.

He had another outlandish, quirky theory that he always knew when the demons left him because he would burp. No burp, no deliverance. That was his sign that he relied on absolutely. Nothing else. I should have given him Pepto-Bismol. For some it is vomiting, yawning, sighing, or crying. Eventually, I would not do sessions with him anymore. He ended up going weekly to another deliverance minister for his regular dose of Rolaids.

Be aware that the ceasing of a manifestation(s) in itself is not a clear sign of deliverance. A temporary ceasing of manifestations is an old trick of the devil.[6] Demons will retreat, go into hiding, and nestle deep in the

6. I was ministering deliverance to a non-denominational pastor who was bound in multiple areas of sexual addiction for quite some time. He was bound in one area since his teen years. The Spirit of God moved powerfully in our session and was breaking strongholds. The seeker had several strong manifestations, such as other voices, growling screaming, and hissing. At one point, we had a breakthrough, as spirits of perversion and confusion left, and the manifestations subsided. I regularly interviewed the seeker at various strategic points.

After this breakthrough, I asked how he was doing. I knew we had a major victory, but I also knew by the Spirit that we were not finished. He said he felt peace and knew he was fully delivered and smiled. I discerned that the remaining demon went underground and was hiding. He would not manifest and show his face, lest I realize that the

soul so they cannot be detected. They go under the radar. Their goal in hiding is to convince you that the seeker has been delivered so you will quit the session too early. Watch out for demonic camouflaging. Don't abort the mission. Another indirect long-term way to know the person has been delivered is that they no longer practice that specific sin anymore.

In terms of numbers of sessions, there is no hard rule. Many times I have led deliverances that occur instantly. On one occasion, a mother brought her teenage son to the altar following my preaching. It was a revival service. She said her son was a practicing warlock and had been oppressed by spirits for quite some time. He wanted to be free.

I did not intend to cast the demons out of him at that moment. I went to lay hands on him while listening and waiting for the direction of the Holy Spirit. As soon as I laid hands on him, he flew horizontally backwards in the air and landed about fifteen feet from where I first laid hands. The ushers and I went to the ground with him to pray and to check how he was doing. I was thinking, we may have to take him into a room for deliverance, but he was already delivered. Lucid, in his right mind, weeping with joy and confessing Christ. No prayer, no repentance, and no deliverance session.

At a later date, the church followed up to make sure his deliverance was genuine. I know I said not to hold deliverance sessions during worship service. Well, I did not intend to, and really, we did not hold a deliverance session. God did it all by himself!

On the other hand, I know of a man who received prayer for nearly thirty years to deal with an issue of rage that afflicted him. He was abused as a child by his mother. His mother's violent anger was transferred to him. Later, after he married, he would manifest rage spontaneously and uncontrollably at his wife for no apparent reason. Screaming and physical abuse accompanied each episode.

Things began to turn around when he received a candid dream that a violent spirit was attached to him like a flat disc against his back and would not let him go. He cried out in the dream for help but could not be loosed. He would try to escape but the spirit would stay attached. In the dream, the Lord showed him to seek deliverance, and that, in deliverance the evil spirit would be cut in pieces and easily removed by the hand of God.

---

work was not finished.

Well, praise God, we have the Holy Spirit who guides us in all truth. I told the pastor that we had had a big breakthrough and he felt peace, but we were not done yet. We still had to catch the biggest fish. He trusted me, and we went back to work. I commanded that devil to come out of hiding and show himself. It started to manifest, then I bound it, judged it, and cast it out. The pastor has been walking in freedom ever since. Glory to God!

After decades of oppression, he found freedom after I held only two short sessions with him. Praise God! Why then? Why only two sessions? I do not know. He indicated that for the first time, he truly owned his actions, and his repentance was sincere, which is quite possible. Ultimately, only God knows. The bottom line was he was delivered from a generational spirit of rage and murder, a Jezebel spirit, and a spirit of Leviathan.

In conclusion, as you minister deliverance, above all, do no harm! Handle with care! Think of PADS when it comes to deliverance wisdom. Padding is soft and protective. In sports, it can prevent injuries. PAD the deliverance session.

PADS:

P =Pastoral sensitivity
A= Authority in Jesus Christ
D= Discerning of spirits
S= Spirit-filled and led

Lesson 6

Operation Deliverance (5 Step Method)

[A]Deliverance Session
  5 Step Deliverance Method

1. Identify

2. Repent

3. Renounce

4. Expose and Bind

5. Judge and Evict

Deliverance should be done in private in a room set apart for such a ministry. The room should have comfortable chairs, even a couch. Have water and healthy snacks for post deliverance. Deliverance can be exhausting. There should be altar cloths and anointing oil available. Anoint the room and consecrate it for this special purpose. The oil is for the healing of deliverance. Anoint each member of the team and the seeker with oil before laying on hands. Some use crosses and Bibles in their session as symbols to mediate spiritual authority. Loose warring angels against the enemy and ministering angels to heal the seeker.

Turn on light worship music and begin to worship and invoke the Lord Jesus Christ.[1] Magnify the Lord. Put God in the center. This is about the Lord, not the devil. Let this be an act of worship. Praise him. Give thanksgiving. Confess the various names of God. Worship him. Then, pray a prayer of adoration, invocation (invite Christ the Deliverer), and cleansing

---

1. We recount how David's worship drove out the demons of rage and torment from Saul (1 Sam 16:14, 23; 18:10; Ps 18:1), and how the armies of God routed the enemy through the praise of Judah (2 Chr 13:14–15; 20:20–24). Worship is a weapon of war.

(for all). Pray a prayer against demonic backlash, covering each person, their families, possessions, and everything that pertains to the covenant with a hedge or firewall of protection and the blood of Jesus.

Make sure the person keeps their eyes open (as best as possible) throughout the session. The eyes are the windows of the soul (Matt 6:22). Regularly look into their eyes when you confront the devil. The eyes will often reflect the inner state of the person as they move from darkness to light.

THE 5 STEP METHOD[2]

1. Identify

Identify sins and demons from the C1–13 that need repentance and deliverance. Identifying is done by the team leader and the seeker. The team is also inviting the Holy Spirit to come and loose demonic strongholds and bring freedom. Throughout the session, the team needs to listen to the Holy Spirit who will manifest gifts, such as discerning of spirits, words of knowledge and wisdom, faith, and healing to lead the deliverance. He sends his Word to heal and deliver (Ps 107:20). *This process is to be spoken aloud.*

1. Identify demons that are influencing the person. Taken from their C1–13 assessment and the leading of the Spirit.

2. Identify degrees of demonization, C1–13.

3. Identify sins committed by the person that have opened a door. Legal access.

4. Identify sins committed against the person that have opened a door. Legal access.[3]

5. Make sure the seeker is aware of each sin and/or demon that will be addressed.

6. Have them open their hearts, yield, and focus on Jesus Christ as Lord.

---

2. In addition, feel free to pray ancient exorcism and deliverance prayers from St. Basil the Great and St. John Chrysostom, or another form prayers of deliverance. See Appendix C.

3. The deliverance team can pray repentance on behalf of the one who committed sins *against* the seeker. These sins specifically do not need repentance from the seeker but inner healing. Inner healing often loosens the demonic stronghold. Pray for Christ to transform the person's thoughts and self-talk regarding the event. Override the lies with the truth. If there have been sins committed against the person that subsequently led to the person committing willful sins, then one needs to repent of those sins.

7. Make sure this step is complete before moving on to the next step. Interview the seeker to be certain. [

2. Repent

Repentance is to be done by the seeker. The team is praying for the Spirit to convict. The team is also praying for an openness and willingness to repent on behalf of the seeker. They are also interceding for a release of the gift of repentance.

1. Confess aloud all the sins that have opened a door to the demonic, even generational sins.

2. Express aloud godly sorrow for each sin with the understanding that our sin deserves eternal punishment. Say what God's Word says about each sin. Use Scripture.

3. Express aloud a willingness to be set free from sin and demonic attachments.

4. Make a prayerful and intentional decision to cease from sinning, turn from them, and turn to God.

5. Submit aloud those areas to God, breaking all former legal access and authority of the devil. Humble and submit yourself to God.

6. Receive (and give) forgiveness and healing in those areas by faith. Release forgiveness to anyone who has wronged or hurt you. Receive forgiveness for the transgressions you have committed.

7. Following repentance, the X-Team will give the scriptural assurance that the seeker is forgiven.

8. Make sure this step is complete before moving on to the next step. Interview the seeker to be certain.

3. Renounce

Both the seeker and the team will renounce aloud each sin and demon one at a time.

1. Address and renounce every demonic tie, covenant, vow, curse, alliance, assignment practice, idol, false altar, ritual, and/or connection that has opened a legal door to these sins and strongholds. Use the C1–13 and the leading of the Spirit.

2. Renounce and break each one of these connections. Shut every legal door of access in the name of Jesus.

3. Apply the cross and plead the blood of Jesus over affected areas. Rom 8:3: sin is condemned and judged.

4. Claim your right in Christ that Satan has no more legal grounds or access in your life.

5. Repentance and renouncing break the legal ties with sin and Satan. With true repentance, there is legal ground to evict.

6. With true repentance (ceasing of sin) and renouncing complete, the person is ready for demons to be Exposed, Bound, Judged, and Evicted.

7. Make sure this step is complete before moving on to the next step. Interview the seeker to be certain.

4. Expose and Bind

Repentance has cancelled the legal ground of sin and demonic access. Renouncing each demon breaks the attachment. The will is no longer in cooperation with the demonic and is being recovered. It is time to expose, arrest, and bind the demon(s). The deliverance team and the seeker, as able, will go through these steps out loud.

1. Look into the eyes of the person (the windows of the soul) when you bind, judge, and cast out demons. Keep looking in the eyes throughout. At times you will be able to follow the demons through manifestations (presentations) in the body and eyes. They often begin in the stomach area and move up out of the mouth and/or eyes. They often exit through the mouth or eyes.

2. Call on Jesus the demon slayer to arise and slay the demonic with the sword (the Word) that proceeds from his mouth. It is a double-edged sword with truth as its point. One edge is mercy. The other edge is judgment. When the point of the sword of the Lord touches sin, it cuts between soul and spirit, giving mercy to the sinner and judgment to the devil.

3. Speak directly to the demon and cut off every demon, sin, and their work from the spirit of the person with the Sword of the Lord, the Word of God—Heb 4:12

4. Ask the Lord to put the Finger of God on every evil spirit in the person. Command every demonic spirit to come out from hiding, to come to the light, to be revealed, and to be exposed (manifest) in Jesus' name.

5. Demons may manifest or come out from hiding at this point. Control the manifestations. We want to know they are emerging, but with no harm to the person.

6. Take authority over these demons. As they emerge, arrest and bind them one at a time in the name of Jesus. Since repentance has occurred, the demons have no legal right. They are to be arrested and bound.

7. Bind the strong man, the ruling spirit, and every other exposed demon that is revealed in the name of Jesus. The ruling spirit is the controlling or root demon. Sometimes this demon is at the end of the chain.

8. Make sure this step is complete before moving on to the next step. Interview the seeker to be certain.

5. Judge and Evict

God gives judgment to sin and Satan but gives mercy to seekers. Mercy triumphs over judgment (James 2:13)! Since the demons have been exposed, arrested, and bound, it is time for judgment and eviction. The X-Team and the seeker, as able, will go through these steps audibly.

1. Declare, according to John 16:11, that the Prince of this World is judged and defeated by the Finger of God. Pronounce his judgment in Jesus' name. Sin has been judged on the cross (Rom 8:3), and Satan has been judged on the cross (John 12:31; 16:11, 19:30; Heb 2:14–15; 1 John 3:8)

2. Evict (cast out) every demon spirit by name, one by one in the name of Jesus. Break the chains. Break Satan's power. Drive out the enemy. Destroy his idols and tear down his altars.

3. Cast into outer darkness every demonic power and render them harmless and void never to return. Seal the soul with the blood of Jesus in every area.

4. Pray that every open door be shut and sealed with the blood of Jesus.

5. Command angels with flaming swords to guard every portal of the soul from any demons returning to the person (Gen 3:24).

6. Pray for an infilling of the Holy Spirit and inner healing in every affected area.

7. Pray and intercede until there is a witness of the Spirit in the team and the seeker that the work is finished. Examine the eyes for lucidity, an absence of oppression, and the presence of the Lord. The seeker will usually express liberation through tears and expressions of joy. Everyone in the room should experience the peace of God (peace acts as umpire and makes the call, Col 3:15) to indicate the demon(s) has been expelled, victory has come, and Christ rules in the seeker's heart.

8. Provide any comfort, care, hospitality, word, food, etc. needed.

9. Make sure this step is complete to finish the session. Interview the seeker to be certain.

IS THE DELIVERANCE SESSION FINISHED? 5 POINT CHECKLIST

1. All 5 Steps have been completed as stated above. ( )

2. Every member of the X-Team has an inner witness and/or a discerning of spirits that the work is finished and has peace. ( )

3. The seeker has an inner witness and/or a discerning of spirits that the work is finished and has peace. ( )

4. All demonic manifestations have ceased, and the person shows signs and testifies of salvation, love, peace, and/or joy. Their countenance has lifted. Eyes are lucid. ( )

5. The person is no longer walking in the sin(s) that opened the door to the demonic. The X-Team needs to hold them accountable over the *next month* to observe whether there is any fruit. Checking off the *first 4 points* will indicate that the deliverance session is *finished*. The *fifth point* determines that the deliverance is *complete*. If any of the first 4 points are not checked, then determine which of the 5 steps is incomplete and go back to that step. ( )

FOLLOW-UP

- I recommend pre-work preparation and post-work follow-up to accompany any deliverance session. See this book, *Unleashed! Truth*

Therapy by Peter Bellini, and similar works for direction. The newly
delivered soul needs their mind renewed, the cracks in the soul healed,
and their whole being filled with the Spirit. We do not want the demons to come back with seven more friends (Luke 11:26).

- This 5-Step process is based on the simple command from James 4:7–8
  to "submit to God and resist the devil and he will flee from you," and to
  draw near to God and repent.

- The key is the law of the will. To whatever degree one has submitted
  one's will to a power (Christ, a sin, an evil spirit), to that degree it
  has authority over them. The will needs to be recovered. As one has
  submitted one's will as an instrument of disobedience and sin, to that
  degree one needs to submit to Christ and righteousness.

- Follow-up with a counselor, pastor, or deliverance minister.

- Home cleansing—If needed, the deliverance team should go to the
  person's home for a cleansing. Take inventory of all demonic items.
  Make sure all demonic objects are permanently removed from the
  home. Play worship music in the house for at least twenty-four hours
  the day before the cleansing. Anoint the home, each room, door, doorway, bed, table, pets, etc. Also, anoint the outside of the house. Prayer-
  walk around the perimeter of the house. Use the 5 Step Method to
  identify sins and demons, repent of each sin, renounce each sin and
  demon, bind the demons, judge and evict them from the home and
  property into outer darkness.

Lesson 7

Post Deliverance (Post-Op): Renewing
of the Mind with Truth Therapy

INTRODUCTION

This chapter primarily provides a follow-up strategy for those who have gone through a deliverance session(s). It offers resources for renewing the mind. A deliverance minister can also read this chapter to learn how they can minister to someone who has gone through deliverance. This chapter provides specific devotional material for post-deliverance care and discipleship.

Post-delivery recovery is essential to deliverance and wholeness. I recommend that following deliverance a person follows up with several action items:

- Take an active part in one's own discipleship, accountability, and formation through a small group or one-on-one discipleship.

- Meet regularly with an accountability partner or sponsor.

- If needed, seek out a counselor or spiritual director to offer guidance and wisdom for your life.

- Find a mentor who is willing to spend time with you in intentional discipleship.

- Begin to delve into discipleship material that will keep you on the road to recovery.[1]

1. Hull, *The Complete Book of Discipleship*; Bellini, *Truth Therapy*; and Anderson, *Who I Am in Christ*.

- Participate in all the available means of grace, such as Bible study, prayer, worship services, Holy Communion, self-denial, fasting, giving, serving, and other forms that communicate the grace of God.

- Get immersed in a book that teaches you how to renew your mind, such as *Truth Therapy*.[2] Another shameless plug.

Renewing the mind with the truth is vital. Lies bind. Truth sets free. People who have been delivered need to *unlearn* the lies they have believed over a lifetime and begin to *learn* the truth. These practices are the fundamental goals of *Truth Therapy*. Identifying and expelling the enemy's lies and replacing them with the Word of God is no small undertaking. *Truth Therapy* is designed for those very tasks. It will provide tools to identify deceptive and destructive thinking, as well as offer resources to help you process and assimilate the truth in every area of your life. *Truth Therapy* works with basic Christian doctrine, the names of God, scriptural affirmations, and cognitive-behavioral theory to assist in *belief and identify formation*, which are vital to effective discipleship and healing the image of God within. It is time for a brand-new life! In this chapter, I have included some sections from *Truth Therapy* as a start.

AFFIRMATION OF FAITH

As a part of post-deliverance and recovery, it is important to affirm our faith in the Lord Jesus Christ of historic Christianity. Being rooted in historic Christianity helps to bring stability to our faith. The Nicene Creed is a universally recognized symbol of faith accepted by most Christian communities. The Creed has been generally accepted by the universal Christian church as the standard for orthodoxy. The creed was first hammered out at the First Council of Nicaea in 325 and amended at the First Council of Constantinople in 381. As the first step in post-deliverance recovery, let people affirm their faith by reciting the Nicene Creed and meditating on its words daily.

THE NICENE CREED

We believe in one God,
the Father, the Almighty,
maker of heaven and earth,

---

2. I also recommend Sandford and Sandford, *Deliverance and Healing*.

of all that is, seen and unseen.
We believe in one Lord, Jesus Christ,
the only Son of God,
eternally begotten of the Father,
God from God, Light from Light,
true God from true God,
begotten, not made,
of one Being with the Father;
through him all things were made.
For us and for our salvation
he came down from heaven,
was incarnate of the Holy Spirit and the Virgin Mary
and became truly human.
For our sake he was crucified under Pontius Pilate;
he suffered death and was buried.
On the third day he rose again
in accordance with the Scriptures;
he ascended into heaven
and is seated at the right hand of the Father.
He will come again in glory
to judge the living and the dead,
and his kingdom will have no end.
We believe in the Holy Spirit, the Lord, the giver of life,
who proceeds from the Father (and the Son),
who with the Father and the Son
is worshiped and glorified
who has spoken through the prophets.
We believe in one holy catholic and apostolic church.
We acknowledge one baptism
for the forgiveness of sins.
We look for the resurrection of the dead,
and the life of the world to come. Amen.

SEVEN TRUTH THERAPY PRINCIPLES

Lies Bind

The enemy's power is singular and simple, *deception*. The power of the lie is deception. All the devil's strategies are based on lies. He is the *father* of all lies (John 8:44). The nature of a lie is not reality but illusion. Satan is the master at creating illusions. He accomplishes this feat through witchcraft. The Devil is the first sorcerer, creating deception (spells) with his words, a form of witchcraft and sorcery.[3] When he deceives, he casts spells and incantations that alter one's perception of reality. His spells hypnotize, blind, deafen, paralyze, trap, and cage people into submission (Isa 42:22).

Scripture warns that Satan is extremely cunning and crafty (Gen 3:1; 2 Cor 11:3) and even uses the scriptures (Matt 4:6), false signs and wonders (Mark 13:22; 2 Thess 2:9), and a disguise of light (2 Cor 11:3) to blind people's minds. He traps, binds, and destroys his victims with sophisticated, well-crafted, tailormade lies specifically and personally designed to bait you. Take away deception and you have defanged the serpent. Victory comes when we recognize deception, reject it, and replace it with the truth. Truth is the antidote to the serpent's venom.

The first step in identifying lies is to monitor our thinking. Sinful thinking, wrong thinking, or distorted thinking can trap us in a world of deception and destruction. Two practices are key to uncovering lies. First, Satan often camouflages his voice as our own self-talk. Many times, it is the devil speaking to our minds, but we think it is our own voice. Recognize and be aware of the enemy's voice and our ongoing inner monologue or self-talk, especially as it reveals itself in automatic thoughts and deception. Beware of ANTS—automatic negative thoughts. Stamp out your ANTS!

Automatic thoughts are those quick, reactive, and under-the-radar thoughts that determine our emotional life. We become aware of our self-talk by noting that we do indeed have self-talk, and that our self-talk or thought-life can be identified and critiqued. Second, through critical reflection, we can learn to identify deceptive and destructive thought patterns, known as cognitive distortion or stinking thinking. The challenge is to uproot stinking thinking and replace it with truth-based thinking. Truth-based thinking is biblical thinking.

---

3. Revelation 18 depicts the fall of Babylon, the Great Whore. Revelation 18:2 (NIV) claims that Babylon "has become a dwelling for demons and a haunt for every impure spirit." Demons inhabited and used Babylon to seduce the world with its riches, luxury, and harlotry. Verse 23 states that this demon-infested city was inundated with witchcraft. We should not be surprised that demons practice witchcraft through human vessels. Witchcraft originated in the heart of the devil. Demons are sorcerers: "By your magic spells all the nations were led astray." The NKJV translates "magic spells" as "sorceries." It reads, "for by your sorcery all the nations were deceived." Deception and witchcraft are related. They both create a false reality with words. And they both intend to trick or bewitch the hearer into believe the lie or false reality. Deception or witchcraft is Satan's only power. Witchcraft is crushed by the truth and humility.

Truth Sets Free

Thinking that is truth-based (biblical, rational, realistic, and hope-filled) can liberate us from evil, sin, worry, fear, depression, anxiety, and other damaging conditions and practices. We repent of deception-based thinking and turn toward truth-based thinking. It is a choice! I have counseled so many people who used to be trapped and imprisoned in their own minds. Their thought-life was negative, fearful, hopeless, and despairing. They claimed that they were helpless to change what seemed to be an insurmountable barrage of ANTS. At first, they were unaware that they were allowing this onslaught. But when I taught them to listen below the surface of their conscious awareness to their inner monologue, they realized the source of their trouble. They were able to track the source. Their negative, anxious feelings were flowing from their distorted self-talk. Our inner monologue often goes under the radar; we do not recognize it. But if one monitors closely their thoughts and feelings, they can detect and track it quietly working. They learned to detect, intercept, and correct their stream of consciousness-like self-talk.

I would teach them how to test or critique their inner monologue and not accept it as gospel. Test your thoughts (2 Cor 13:5; 1 John 4:1). Ask if the thought lines up with Scripture. Ask if the thought is based on evidence that is sufficient, conclusive, realistic, objective, and true, or is it based on fear, irrationality, or stinking thinking? Ask if the thought is based on hope or hopelessness? If the thought is not biblical, evidenced based, and hopeful, then cast it out. Change the channel of your mind to a different station. Adjust your thinking. Replace the stinking thinking with the truth. What does God's Word say about that matter or issue? If you do not like what you are watching on the screen of your mind, then change the channel. Your will is the remote. Take back the remote and change the channel. And replace sinful thinking with righteous thinking. Switch the channel!

Freedom begins by identifying the lies that have chained and imprisoned us. The standard of God's Word enables us to discern our thoughts and evaluate them for their truth-value (Heb 4:12). The truth sets us free from the stronghold and bondage of deception. The truth sets us free, while the lies of the enemy bring us into bondage. Your ears are not Satan's garbage cans.

The truth liberates. Jesus said that "the truth will set us free." If that is true, then so is the opposite. Lies will bring us into bondage. Lies bind, but truth liberates. The Word of God is truth (John 17:17). It is a sharp double-edged sword able to penetrate flesh and soul and separate them from spirit. The Sword of the Lord separates what is of God from what is of the flesh. The truth has the power to free our minds from the binding lies of the devil.

The truth can penetrate the areas where lies have been forged and have chained a person to destructive thought patterns. The Word discerns and reveals our thoughts and our intentions, whether they come from the flesh or the Spirit. The truth of God's word can unshackle a person by exposing the lie through the truth's inherent light. The brightness of the light of truth exposes the darkness of the lie. It reveals the lie for what it is. Remember, the power and strength of a lie is its power to deceive.

I counseled a person for years who was crippled by lies and fear. Any pain imagined or real they concluded it was cancer or some other disease they discovered on the Internet. In their mind, every person they encountered hated them and did not accept them. Any perceived setback, they concluded, was the end of their life. Any information that came into their mind, they distorted it and framed it in a negative light. They would only believe and retain negative interpretations, thoughts, and images. They lived in crippling dread, terrified to attempt anything. Years of *Truth Therapy* helped set them free, but it was not easy. They created a vicious cycle of believing lies and fear that was difficult to break.

What makes a lie binding? First, the lie has the power to deceive. It is a grandiose, unrealistic, seductive, inflated, illusory promise. It is attractive. It allures one into accepting that the mirage is real. Second, a lie is bound to our hearts when we receive and believe that it *is* true. We give deception power when we believe it. Otherwise, it has no power. Stop giving power to the enemy! The law of sin, misery and death is no longer your life sentence!

Surrender to the power of the truth. The power of the truth is its ability to penetrate and shine light. It goes to the root of the lie and exposes it for what it is. When the truth exposes darkness and the destructiveness of the lie, then deception's power is deactivated and dismantled. When the person rejects the lie and believes the truth, then the alliance and the tie with the stronghold and the lie are broken and the person is free. The truth creates and shapes a new God-given reality, a Christ-like reality, and a Kingdom reality in the heart of the believer. Righteousness, peace, and joy begin to reign in the heart. You are a new creation in Christ!

We Cannot Control Others, Our Circumstances, or the World around Us

Many of us are controlled by the desire to control. *Controlled by control.* I, too, am a recovering control addict. Control gives us the illusion of absolute security. Of course, only trust in God can bring us true security. It is difficult to unlearn the unrealistic notion that we can control anything in an ultimate sense. We cannot control the stock market. We cannot control our teenagers. We cannot control our tongues. We cannot control the economy. We cannot control our spouse. The list goes on.

When we acknowledge regularly that we cannot control anything outside of ourselves., then we can begin to be liberated from this powerful deception. Letting go is a lesson that seems simple at first glance but is a lifelong challenge. Not only can we not control our circumstances, but also often we cannot even control ourselves. Try to stop "petting" your cell phone for at least an hour. Don't even look at social media. Good luck! Our weakness humbles us to not only recognize our frailty but also to surrender and trust in the Lord with all our heart; don't trust in our own limited, sinful, and irrational understanding—Proverbs 3:4–6.

We Can Control our Thought-Life

Although we *cannot* control the world around us, we *can* control ourselves, at least in a limited way. Of course, we cannot control involuntary processes within our bodies, like our heartbeat. We also cannot control our expiration date and a host of other variables. But in a limited sense we can control our decisions and our thought-life. "Yes" or "No" are under our purview. Our control is limited to what thoughts we let in, and what thoughts we reject. God has given us the grace and freedom to choose to reject lies, sin, and distorted thinking and to accept the truth.

Our limited control comes in the form of freedom to choose the content of our thought-life. Liberation and transformation begin when we recognize that we *do* have the ability to choose life or death, truths or lies (Deut 30:19). We are not helpless and hopeless. Recovering our responsibility to choose and not to be passive about our thought-life can be revolutionary. Freedom begins to be experienced when we begin to identify our power to choose, a recovering of the will.

We are Transformed by Renewing our Minds with the Word of God

There is an instrumental connection between our thinking and our being. Our inner conversation greatly determines who we are and who we will become. Our being is transformed by renewing our mind. Change begins with the thoughts and meditations of our hearts (Rom 12:1–2). If we think fearful thoughts, then we will become fearful. If we choose to think selfishly, then we will become prideful and selfish. There is a vital connection between our thinking and our feelings, will, and actions. When we meditate and act on the truth, then we will experience the blessings of God's promises.

Today, our society is in a truth crisis. We do not know where to turn for the facts. Truth is a rare commodity. Although truth comes in many forms (all truths are God's truths), truth that brings salvation comes from Scripture, God's Word. We trust the truth found in God's Word. God's Word has power to reset and revolutionize our lives. God sanctifies us with the truth, and God's Word is truth (John 17:17). The Word cleanses us and separates us from evil and deception and purifies our heart, so that we can see God and experience God's holiness. It is the pure in heart who see God (Matt 5:8). Sanctification clarifies spiritual vision and spiritual hearing. It gets rid of the carnal static that prevents us from discerning and hearing God's voice. God's word is also a lamp unto our feet and a light unto our path. Scripture has many metaphors for the Word. It likens it to food, both milk and meat, to nourish and strengthen our spirits. Put some muscle on your inner man/woman. Live off every Word that continually proceeds from God's mouth.

Grace and Truth: God's Balance

Two correctives are needed when applying God's word. First, God's Word is not magical. We do not put the Bible under our pillow and sleep on the Bible in order to receive wisdom or healing. We do not believe that, because we quote the Bible, we are reciting some magical recipe or incantation of success. Scripture invites us to have faith in God. We hear the word of God and believe God. And we believe what he has promised. We mix our faith with God's Word and believe in the God of the Word (Heb 4:2). We trust what God is saying to us with all our heart. Then we act on what God is telling us. The answer from God's Word comes from a personal God and not some force or law in the universe. Nor is faith some sort of self-hypnosis by which we convince ourselves through endless positive confession. Faith trusts God and not our own confession.

Through the Word and the Spirit, we have a personal relationship with God, a covenantal relationship. God keeps his end of the covenant. God is faithful to his Word. Our part is to believe and obey. Without faith we cannot please God (Heb 11:6). The Word works for those who work with the Word. When we hear God's Word, we mix our faith with the Word and receive God's promise. It is true that God responds out of God's own nature and faithfulness, and often answers prayer and moves in our lives without any faith, which is a gift itself. However, God chooses to work with us and is pleased when we respond with trust.

Second, throughout history, religious groups have used the truth to divide, to hurt, to abuse, to control, to sin, and even to make war. The truth can be dangerous because it is powerful. Just like nuclear power is dangerous and can be used constructively or destructively, so is truth, and therefore both are to be handled with care. The Word is to be shared and received in meekness. The temptation can be toward legalism or Bible-beating. Scripture reveals grace and truth inseparably. John 1:14–18 states that Moses came with the law, but Jesus came as God's revelation of grace and truth to us. Moses came with truth. Jesus came with grace and truth. He did not come merely with law like Moses. He did not come with a salvation that is based on performance or good works. Instead, he brought grace. He brought a gift, salvation. Remember, our works, don't work!

We do not have to work toward attaining this gift. A relationship with God is a free invitation, unlike most relationships. We do not work toward salvation, but we begin with it by grace. It is not a reward or a goal of our striving and working. It is a gift given to us as a base, a starting point, a basis for life. From this place of security in God's grace, we grow in our identity in Christ. We grow in strength and in the knowledge of God. Our identity in Christ affects our relationships with others. We do not grope for approval, acceptance, or affirmation based on our performance toward others or God. We start with God's approval, acceptance, and affirmation.

Jesus came into the world with grace and truth. Grace means he gives us the gift of salvation and life. He does not hold the carrot of performance in front of us, and then drives us like a taskmaster to get it. And then makes us feel overburdened with guilt when we do not attain it. Acceptance, approval, and affirmation become our starting point and not our finish line. Jesus also gives us truth not just an easy "greasy gravy grace" that allows for any belief or behavior. Christ reveals to us truth that transforms us into his image of righteousness and true holiness. We learn that he has made each of us a new creation in Christ. He has taken our sin away from us and has given us a new nature, which is just like his. He takes away our sin, so that we will not return to it. He loves us right where we are at but loves us too much that to leave us there.

He then gives us the power to overcome ourselves, sin, and life's challenges (1 John 5:4) Through the Holy Spirit we learn to live a new life empowered by his grace. As disciples, (disciple = disciplined learners and followers of Jesus Christ) we learn a disciplined life that exercises our faith, our hearts, and our spirits by obeying God's word. We learn to overcome daily by walking in the Spirit and obeying God's will.

Grace and truth function as the Carpenter's building square to build a balanced foundation for our Christian life. *Grace without truth is license to do whatever we want. Truth without grace can lead to legalism and rules and regulations that enslave.* Grace and truth are the balance that keep us from the extremes of legalism and license. With grace and truth, God gives us the content of our faith and the direction for our lives. And he supplies us with the power to accomplish both. Grace gives us divine ability to obey the truth that God requires of us. We need the balance of grace and truth in our reading of Scripture, in our walk with God, in our ministry, on our jobs, in our parenting and relationships, in our discernment and in our decision-making. Grace and truth measure proper balance for all aspects of our faith and practice.

Self-Denial: Say "No" to your Will and "Yes" to God's Will

Self-denial is simply to say "no" to our will when it is contrary to God's will, and to say "yes" to God's will (Luke 22:42). In order to hear and receive the truth it is necessary to put God first. We need to be willing to hear and obey God over our own will and the will of others. Following Christ is predicated on an open and willing heart. We need to be willing to say "no" to self and "yes" to God. Luke 9:23 is the crux of the Gospel and is essential to becoming a disciple of Christ. Jesus said, "*If any want to become my followers, let them deny themselves and take up their cross daily and follow me.*" When our will is contrary to God's will, we simply need to say "no" to ourselves and "yes" to God, not my will but your will be done. At times, this is quite easy, but other times it can be quite difficult, as it was for Jesus in the Garden of Gethsemane.

Self-denial is virtually unheard of today, whether one is inside or outside of the church. No one likes to deny self. We like to feed self. We are more accustomed to hearing messages that encourage us to indulge and do what feels good or do what we want to do. Our culture promotes permission. We have no boundaries or checks. Our flesh is permitted to do whatever it feels. Today, our culture allows us to do things that we would have never done twenty or thirty years ago. Everything goes. Nothing is forbidden, except to say that something is forbidden. The moral slope has sure been slippery.

A spirit of lawlessness has been released in our society that despises law, order, authority figures, moral absolutes, the Word of God, the exclusivity of Christ, the witness of the church, life itself, and fear of God. But it unquestioningly welcomes any lie, opinion, confusion, perversion, and absurdity as the truth. There is a truth crisis that is not only in the church on theological matters about God but also in the hard and soft sciences, in the medical field, in our academic institutions, in the education system, in the political system, and in our governmental institutions. We do not know who to trust anymore for the facts. These institutions seem to no longer prioritize truth or virtue as they once did. They will distort the facts or even lie to reinforce their ideological narratives.

Institutions, like the sciences, journalism, or the medical field, that normally have been trusted and once relied on the truth for their day-to-day operations will now deny, cancel, suppress, twist, or change the truth if it does not fit the prevailing, political, ideological narrative in the culture. They create the reality that they want to hear and believe. The truth is not Play-Doh or a Rorschach test. Truth is non-negotiable! We are not free to twist it into any configuration. Nor are we permitted to interpret it anyway that we feel. Sounds familiar, like someone else we know who twists the truth and invents lies.

We should be open to testing every message that we hear. Test the spirits and the voices that we hear to see if they line up with God's truth (1 John 4:1). In a world of information overdose, not every voice we hear is right. The volume, repetition, dispersion, and consensus of the voices do not make them true either. Fact-check the fact- checkers who fact-check the fact-checkers. Not everything we hear is true, good, right, or healthy. We surely are in a truth crisis. So, vet sources. Use logic. Gather evidence by which you can draw reasonable conclusions.

Test the spirits and say "no" to anything that is contrary to the Word of God or even contrary to our wellbeing. Self-denial is one of the most difficult disciplines to master. It takes serious dedication and intentionality along with all the grace and strength that the Spirit can provide to equip us to be consistent and thorough in denying self and surrendering to God. However, if we do not deny self, it is impossible to allow Christ to be Lord and to follow him.

Keep in mind, self-control is a fruit of the Spirit. As we go through this book, it is important to yield to the Spirit of Truth, total consecration. As you begin to process the truth, you will often experience the conviction of God's Word. Conviction is that act of the Spirit that gently but convincingly touches those areas of sin or pain to remove or heal, so the Lord can change us. God's conviction requires our cooperation. We need to work with God's Word, so God's Word can work in us. Submit to the Spirit's nudging and prompting toward the truth. Repent of the things that the Spirit shows you. The word "repentance" in Scripture is *metanoia*, which means a change of mind or attitude. Repent means "change your mind" and "turn around."

"Change your attitude," and thus change the direction of your life concerning that area or issue.

Think what God's Word tells you to think about that issue, and then act on it. It is important to weed out the garden of our hearts and uproot the lies that grow in the soil of our minds before we plant the fresh seed of God's Word (Mark 4). We need to have the hardened soil of our minds and hearts broken up by the plow of the Spirit's conviction before we can plant the truth concerning our identity in Christ (Jer 4:3; Hos 10:12). We will begin to grow in the image of Christ when the truth is planted and watered regularly by the Spirit, and we exercise the spiritual disciplines.

John Calvin wrote on self-denial:

> We are not our own; therefore, neither is our own reason or will to rule our acts and counsels. We are not our own; therefore, let us not make it our end to seek what may be agreeable to our carnal nature. We are not our own; therefore, as far as possible, let us forget ourselves and the things that are ours. On the other hand, we are God's; let us, therefore live, and die to him (Rom xiv.8). We are God's; therefore, let his wisdom and will preside over all our actions . . . For as the surest source of destruction to men is to obey themselves, so that the only haven of safety is to have no other will, no other wisdom, than to follow the Lord wherever he leads. Let this, then, be the first step, to abandon ourselves, and devote the whole energy of our minds to the service of God.[4]

John Wesley preached on self-denial:

> The "denying" ourselves and the "taking up of our cross," in the full extent of the expression, is not a thing of small concern. It is not expedient only, as are some of the of the circumstantials of religion; but it is absolutely, indispensably necessary, either to our becoming or continuing his disciples. It is absolutely necessary, in the very nature of the thing, to our "coming after him" and "following him," insomuch that as far as we do not practise it, we are not his disciples. If we do not continually "deny ourselves," we do not learn of him but of other masters. If we do not "take up our cross daily," we do not "come after him," but after the world, or the prince of the world, or our own "fleshly mind." If we are not walking in the way of the cross, we are not

---

4. Calvin, *Institutes of Christian Religion.*

following him; we are not treading in his steps, but going back from, or at least wide of, him.[5]

WARRIORS NOT WORRIERS!

Let us continue to apply *Truth Therapy*. Philippians 4:4–9 exemplifies what *Truth Therapy* is all about; replacing anxious thoughts with prayer and peace.

> Rejoice in the Lord always; again, I will say Rejoice. Let your reasonableness be known to everyone. The Lord is at hand; Do not be anxious about anything, but in everything by prayer and supplication with thanksgiving let your requests be made known unto God. And the peace of God, which surpasses all understanding, will guard your hearts and your minds in Christ Jesus. Finally, brothers and sisters, whatever is true, whatever is honorable, whatever is just, whatever is pure, whatever is lovely, whatever is commendable, if there is any excellence, if there is anything worthy of praise, think about these things. What you have learned and received and heard and seen in me—practice these things, and the peace of God will be with you. (ESV)

What can we learn about renewing our minds from this passage in Philippians? Let us break down each verse and reflect.

4:4

Have an attitude of joy of the time, not sometimes or when things are going well, but all the time. How is that possible? The verse says to rejoice in the Lord *always*, even in circumstances that are not always joyful. God is always the same yesterday, today, and forever. Joy is not based on your feelings. It is not circumstantial. Joy comes from the Lord! The joy of the Lord is a well that never runs dry. We need to think on the Lord and the promises, and we will continually have joy, not our joy but the joy of the Lord, as our gift.

Also, we are called to verbalize our joy by "rejoicing." The verse commands us to rejoice. Give thanksgiving, praise, and testimony for all God has done, is doing and will do. Have an "attitude of gratitude" and exercise "thanks-living," a lifestyle of thanksgiving. Sometimes we try to rejoice, but life can get us down, so Paul repeats the command: "Again I say rejoice." We

---

5. Collins and Vickers, *Sermons of John Wesley*.

need to be reminded and to remind ourselves, again and again. Even David had to encourage himself in the Lord when no one else would encourage him (Ps 43:5). Encourage yourself!

4:5

Let us paraphrase verse 5. "Jesus is returning soon, and eternity is forever; so be reasonable, moderate, and considerate in the way you live. Weigh out all things temporal in the light of eternity." Not only is Jesus returning, but also, through the Holy Spirit, his presence is already here with us. We should always live in the presence of the Spirit and walk in the Spirit's fruit. Treat others with mercy, gentleness, and respect. The ESV translates the word "reasonableness," but the original language conveys mercy, gentleness, and respect toward others. Taking our minds off ourselves and being mindful of others is a good way to stop worrying and being anxious.

4:6

We are called not to be anxious or worry about anything, not today or tomorrow, not for food or clothes, not for money or jobs or houses, not for this or for that, etc. Fill in the blank. God simply commands us not to worry or be anxious. Anxiety and worry are sins. They are sins because they are transgressions of God's will for us. God wants us to have peace and joy. Our Heavenly Father wants us to trust that all things are taken care of today and tomorrow (Matt 6). While we wait on God's will and God's promises, the Spirit brings us peace and joy to keep us and guard us against anxiety, worry, fear, and other temptations.

God also knows that fearful and anxious thoughts are toxic. They can raise our blood pressure and cholesterol level. Anxiety and fear are bad for the heart. They weaken our immune system. They also cause us to be reactive and impulsive and to make poor choices in life. A mind on anxiety does not operate properly. We make foolish decisions under the influence and impulse of anxiety and worry. Anxiety can even stifle our memory. Stressed out people become forgetful people. God tries to protect us from the contagion of anxiety. The Lord directs us not to worry but redirects us to pray. Do not be worriers. Be warriors, prayer warriors.

We waste a ton of energy on worrying. We think worrying can change things. Often when we give things up to God, we become faint hearted, lose trust, and take those things back. We feel God cannot take care of the situation as well as we can. We believe if we can just worry about that problem a little longer, then things will change, and the solutions will come. If that is the case, we should create special worry-closets and worry-rooms in our homes and churches, so that we can intercede by worrying. We would not need prayer closets or prayer rooms. We will not admit it, but we often believe in worry as a form of intercession. Our self-talk in essence is saying as much when we worry.

No! God calls us to be *warriors* and not *worriers*. It is time to overcome by taking all that worry-energy, anxiety-energy, and fear-energy and converting it all into prayer energy. Prayer takes our weights and problems and makes them God's weights and problems, and for God, that is no problem. When we put our weights in God's hands, we can trust that God will take care of them and work all things out according to the Lord's perfect wisdom and plan (Rom 8:28). Since God has resolved our problems, we no longer need to worry or have anxiety (1 Peter 5:7). We can be rid of stinking thinking and convert all that wasted time and energy into prayer energy. Imagine praying and believing as much as we fear and worry.

Fervent, effective prayer is often challenging because our mind roams, and our flesh never sleeps. Here is some incentive to pray. Try considering prayer as an exchange. We are exchanging our anxiety for God's promises. We are giving God all our worries, fears, anxieties, and problems, and God is giving us his promises. Promises for problems—not a bad deal. Through prayer not only do we give God our problems, and God gives us his promises, but we also experience an effective means of processing our thought-life. Of course, prayer is primarily communicating with God, but secondarily it provides a means for reflection and self-awareness.

From a human standpoint, prayer helps to alleviate worries and stress because it allows us an opportunity to examine our hearts and identify and name our problems. Sometimes we can be weighed down in our spirits and not know why. When we identify the problem, put a label on it, and communicate it, the problem becomes manageable and loses its omnipotence. When issues stay hidden and buried, they remain unidentified, and we feel anxious without knowing why. And the problem remains unresolved.

When we pray from our hearts, we are bringing the hidden things to light, giving them a name, and communicating them. In this way we are better able to manage our thought-life and destress our lives. Even though prayer is directed toward God, it can indirectly act as a type of talk therapy that helps us process our issues and straighten out our stinking thinking. People pay up to three hundred dollars an hour for the same process with a therapist.

Finally, we are encouraged to couple our prayer with thanksgiving. Thanksgiving is an attitude and a lifestyle, thanks-living. Thanksgiving is saying to God, "As I pray, I am believing that you have already answered my prayers according to your word, and so I am thanking you now in advance because your promise is true, and by faith it is already accomplished." Not only is the Lord pleased with such an attitude of faith and thanksgiving, but thanksgiving also ministers truth therapy in our hearts. Thanksgiving refuses to foster a hard heart, a negative attitude, or a mindset of entitlement, but it substitutes stinking thinking with hopeful, grateful praise.

4:7

Prayer is communication, an exchange. We exchange thoughts and words with the Divine. We also give God our problems, and God our Savior gives us his promises. Specifically, God gives us peace, *shalom*. Our God is the God of peace. Jesus is the Prince of Peace, the Prince who embodies peace rules by peace. His peace makes war on anxiety, delivering us from unease and providing rest. Where Jesus rules there is peace. Evil and sin are defeated, and God rules over our mind. When God gives us peace, he gives us his own peace, not the false peace of the world (John 14:27). The world's peace is often false: a temporal peace, a circumstantial peace, and at best a ceasefire. Only God can give us true peace. God's very nature is peace, and we can experience this type of Divine peace.

Shalom, or God's peace (Judg 6:24), is not only a cessation of evil, but it also signifies right relationships, fulfillment of purpose, and perfect order. With God's peace, the cosmos and everything in it is in right relationship with God and with itself. The cosmos is fulfilling its purpose and operating in God's perfect intended order. God promises us this kind of peace. Yet, the context of peace in this passage in Philippians is saying even more. The peace of God will guard and protect us against anxiety and worry.

Peace protects. The word translated "guard," *phrourein*, is actually a military term that is used to describe a Roman garrison that is assigned to protect a village or stronghold from attack. God's peace acts as a garrison of well-trained soldiers that are assigned to protect our hearts and minds against fear, worry, and anxiety. When we pray through our problems, God sends a garrison of peace to hedge our hearts and minds against the onslaught of the enemy of our soul. Since God is the Lord of Hosts, his garrison is probably a garrison of angels that surround and protect our minds. That is Good News. The Lord of Hosts wants to protect our thoughts and emotions from anxiety if we would submit our hearts to him in prayer.

4:8

In this verse, Paul instructs the believers to cease from being anxious and to redirect their energy to prayer. God's peace will protect them from further anxiety. In 4:8, Paul moves the Philippian church on to the next step. He wants to redirect their thinking. Now that they are no longer worrying but praying, the Philippians need to establish a healthy spiritual thought-life. St. Paul offers 8 virtues as a prescription for a healthy spiritual thought-life.

The Apostle Paul's final instruction is to think on the virtues that come from God. Paul wants us to fill our minds with good things, things that are virtuous and advance God's glory in our lives. How often we allow nonsense, fear, worry, or vanity to rent space in our mind. Each thought is a seed that will reproduce after its own kind. Each thought is a seed that we plant in our minds, and the fruit will be harvested in our lives.

Philippians 4:8 says to think about truth, honor, justice/righteousness, beauty, excellence, purity, and praise. Think on the things that will produce such virtues. Thus, we can think of these virtues as seeds for our thought-life: truth, honor, righteousness, purity, beauty, excellence, goodness, and praise. These virtues are enough to occupy our minds throughout the day with the right thoughts. The eight Philippian virtues:

1. Truth

2. Honor

3. Righteousness

4. Purity

5. Beauty

6. Excellence

7. Goodness

8. Praise

A virtuous thought-life will produce Kingdom fruit. When the weeds of worry, anxiety, fear, and depression are uprooted from the garden of our hearts, then we can begin to plant real fruit that will nourish our lives and the lives of those around us. We are commanded to "Think on these things," to "Fix our thoughts on these things." The Greek word means "to calculate, take into account, consider, and reckon," and also can be extended to "ruminating" or "letting one's mind dwell on" these things. Such thinking involves careful and intentional reflection, meditation, and evaluation of the things that can produce these godly virtues.

4:9

Of course, all the virtues point to God and are exemplified in Christ. These virtues reflect God's nature. However, the virtues also point to our thought-life and our actions. We are called to embody these virtues not just think on them. It is not enough that Christ is holy. We are called to *be* holy. It is not enough that we think holy thoughts, but our actions need to be holy. Virtues begin with thoughts, develop into actions, and culminate in habits or regular practices. Our faith should work—no unemployed faith.

Our thoughts and intents need to be completed in godly actions that reflect the love of Christ. Paul stressed that the Philippians needed to embody continuity between what they had heard and what they had seen; what they had been taught and what they practice. These have to be aligned, and they should be practiced with regularity regardless of circumstance. The verb in this verse indicates repetition and practice. One of the most difficult virtues to master, and one of the most valued, is consistency. It is interesting how this passage on virtuous thinking is seated within a larger context of discipleship. Paul was discipling the Philippian believers and was exhorting them to practice in thought and deed what he had modeled before them. *Truth Therapy* needs to be a spiritual discipline practiced within the context of discipleship and modeled before those we teach.

DISCERNMENT AND TESTING THE SPIRITS

Discernment is vital to a renewed mind. We need to be able to discern which thoughts to keep and which thoughts to expel from our mind. We must build upon the Rock. The thoughts we keep are building blocks that reconstruct a wall or bulwark around our temple (the heart). Like the wall around Jerusalem, this spiritual wall prevents invaders from reentering into the holy place of our soul. It keeps out sin and the devil. We begin with discerning which stones to keep and which stones to discard.

Let us move to our foundational text found in 2 Timothy 1:7—"For God has not given us a spirit of fear, but of power, and of love, and of a sound mind (self-discipline)."

An essential practice for renewing the mind and living the overcoming life is hearing God's voice. Throughout Scripture, "hearing" is a central practice for faith and obedience (Deut 6:4; Rom 10:17). We are called to hear and obey God's word (*shema*). Faith comes by hearing God's word. God's sheep are led by hearing God's voice (John 10). Hearing is the Christian's primary mode of spiritual perception. We are called to hear the voice of the Spirit for guidance, as God leads us by the still waters and the still small voice of the Spirit, the Spirit of Truth (Ps 23). The Holy Spirit, who is truth, will lead us and guide us into all truth (John 16:13). For as many as are led by the Spirit of God, they are the daughters and sons of God (Rom 8:14–16).

As believers hear the voice of God, they are filled with life and renewed. We do not live by consuming mere physical bread but by consuming every word that proceeds from God's mouth to our ears (Matt 4:4). Hearing brings the word and the illumination of God's word to our minds and activates our faith. The seed of faith is in the word of God (Luke 8:11). It is planted in our hearts by hearing. When the word is planted in a heart that has been weeded of sin, anxiety, and worldly care, it then produces much fruit.

What we hear will produce fruit. If we hear God's word it will produce revelation, faith, the gifts and fruit of the Spirit, and the works of God. If we hear lies, those words will produce fear, anxiety, depression, worry, anger, and other works of the flesh. We need to make sure that we hear the truth but resist lies by guarding our heart and mind.

It is not easy to stay fixed on the truth. The problem is that 8–10-inch space between our ears. It all comes down to the battle of the mind. The problem is the old mind. We need to lose our mind (yes) and gain the mind of Christ. Have you lost your mind yet? We put on the helmet of salvation and guard our minds against the fiery darts of the evil one (Eph 6:16–17). If we are unguarded those thought-darts stick in our mind and set our whole head on fire with unbelief, fear, and doubt. Some are running around with heads like the devil's pin cushion. Put on that helmet!

Set up a watch and monitor thoughts (Prov 4:20–24; 1 Pet 1:13; 5:8). Scripture admonishes us to cast down every thought that exalts itself against God and bring them into captivity to obey Christ (2 Cor 10:4–5). Capture those thoughts speedily before they take over the mind. Capturing the mind is crucial for Satan to establish control. If he gets the mind, then he gets the person. If the Spirit controls the mind, then God has the whole person. Take *every* thought captive, not just some. It only takes one thought to slip through your guard and knock you out. Take no thoughts from the flesh or the enemy. Build an appetite for the Word of God and meditate on it day and night (Ps 119). Train and program your mind for righteousness (1 Tim 4:8).

Another vital practice for renewing the mind is discernment. We are commanded to test the spirits, test the voices that we hear, and test our thought-life (1 John 4:1). Are they of God, self, the world, or the devil? 2 Timothy 1:7 offers us some guidance for the discernment process. God does not give us a spirit of fear. First, Scripture concludes that *fear is a spirit*. It is not merely an irrational thought, though in part it is an irrational thought. Fear, at least unhealthy fear, is a spirit. Fear of God is a healthy fear, along with other healthy fears and legitimate concerns that cause us to prepare and be vigilant. Fear of God leads us to him. Demonic fear drives us away from him. Unhealthy fear is a spiritual force. It comes from the spirit world and is used as a spiritual weapon by the enemy to destroy us.

Fear is quite destructive once we let it into our minds. It comes in like a powerful flood and washes away everything in its path like a hurricane (Isa 59:19). When terror comes into our minds, we know it is not of God. God does not give us a spirit of fear, a cancer of the soul that eats away at our faith. When we sense the first intimation of fear, we should drive it out immediately. Drive it out with all that we have in the name of Jesus. God did not give it to us. Reject it. No matter how right or true it seems, and it often does. Satan is no fool. His temptations are not obvious. He comes as an angel of light, and his lies masquerade as truth. We are aware of the wiles of the devil. Do not be duped by the wily devil (or the wily coyote).

Most things we fear are irrational and never come to pass. Fear is False Evidence Appearing Real! The old anecdote goes something like this: *Fear knocks at the door. Faith answers. There is no one there!* Demonic fear is based on deception. Deception is the only language the devil speaks. Do not be deceived by fear. If it produces fear, then it is of the devil, period!

Jesus taught us how to test the spirits. We can know a tree by the fruit it produces (Matt 7:20; 12:33). We can discern the spirits and our thoughts by the fruit they produce. If they produce fear, then they are not of God. God does not lead us by unhealthy fear that brings anxiety, depression, worry, condemnation, and terror (Rom 8:1). No, God leads by the still waters (Ps 23:2). God leads by his peace (Isa 26:3). Colossians 3:15 encourage us; *Let the peace of Christ rule in our hearts.* The word "rule" means to be an arbiter in the public games, or an umpire. God's peace acts as umpire in our hearts to make the call whether the voice is of God or not. We know that a voice or a thought is of God because we know the fruit of the Spirit, the fruit that the Spirit produces in our hearts. Thoughts that produce love, joy, peace, patience, gentleness, goodness, faithfulness, meekness, and self-control are of God.

God gives us his fruit. By the fruit we can discern the voice of God. God does not give us a spirit of fear, but instead he gives us a spirit of power, a spirit of love, and a spirit of self-control or a sound mind. God gives us his ability, his dynamic power (*dunamis).* He empowers us with the Holy Spirit to preach and teach the word, to move in the gifts of the Spirit, to walk in holiness, to work miracles, and to raise the dead. He gives us his *own* power.

He also gives us his unconditional love to share with all people, even our enemies. God enables us to love the unlovable. It is a gift. Further, we can recognize God's voice in our minds by the fruit of love. He leads us by and into love. Finally, God gives us a sound mind or self-control. The Greek word is *sophronismos* or *sophroneo* (sof-ro-nay-o). *Sophroneo* means to have a healthy mind of self-control. It means to be in one's right mind, to be sober minded, to exercise self-control and self-discipline, to think sensibly, to be temperate, to come to one's senses, to be able to reason and think properly and accurately, to think straight, to curb one's passions, to have intellectual soundness, to use good sense, to be reasonable, to have a measured and ordered way of life, to have understanding of practical matters, to use good judgment, to have a moderate estimate of one's self, and to be moderate in behavior. What a gift!

God gives us the "mind of Christ" as a gift (1 Cor 2:16). You have already been given this wonderful gift that money cannot buy. God gives us a healthy productive mind that can think God's thoughts and carry them out. We are enabled to discern the spirits and our thoughts through a sound mind of *sophroneo*. If our thought-life is producing perfect peace, then it is of God, because God has given us a sound mind that produces self-control. It is God's will that our minds are sound, healthy, and full of the truth. It is God's gift to us that we have such a mind. We receive a sound mind by faith. Throughout our study let us be reminded that a sound mind is both God's gift and goal for us. Receive it.

YOU ARE A NEW CREATION IN CHRIST

Essential to renewing the mind is to know "who you are in Christ," and "what you can do through Christ." The fact is that you *are* a new creation in Christ. And you can do all things through Christ. We will process those two truths through the *Truth Therapy* method. Scripture:

- 2 Corinthians 5:17 (NKJV): "Therefore, if anyone is in Christ, he is a new creation; old things have passed away; behold, all things have become new."

- Ephesians 4:22–24 (NLT): "Throw off your old evil nature and your former way of life, which is rotten through and through, full of lust and deception. Instead, there must be a spiritual renewal of your thoughts and attitudes. You must display a new nature because you are a new person, created in God's likeness— righteous, holy, and true."

- Romans 6:6 (NKJV): "Knowing this, that our old man was crucified with Him, that the body of sin might be done away with, that we should no longer be slaves of sin."

- Romans 8:5–6 (NIV): "Those who live according to the sinful nature have their minds set on what that nature desires; but those who live in accordance with the Spirit have their minds set on what the Spirit desires. The mind of sinful man is death, but the mind controlled by the Spirit is life and peace."

Reflection

John Wesley (1703–1791), Founder of Methodism:

> It is the change wrought in the whole soul by the almighty Spirit of God when it is "created anew in Christ Jesus," when it is "renewed after image of God," "in righteousness and true holiness," when the love of the world is changed into the love of God, pride into humility, passion into meekness; hatred, envy, malice, into a sincere, tender, disinterested love for all mankind. In a word, it is that change whereby the "earthly, sensual, devilish" mind is turned into "the mind which was in Christ." This is the nature of the new birth. "So is everyone that is born of the Spirit."[6]

Jessie Penn-Lewis (1861–1927), Welsh Revival Leader:

> The Cross of Christ is the sinner's cross. And why? Because the whole Adam life of nature is absolutely fallen. It cannot be improved. It is fallen and poisoned by the serpent in root and branch. The whole scheme of redemption lies in the fact that God must begin again, so to speak, and make a new creation. Through the Cross He plans to bring to an end the old Adam life of the fallen race and build again a new creation in the midst of its ruin.[7]

Our baptismal covenant with Christ points to our identification and union with Christ in his death, burial, and resurrection. Romans 6:1–7 speaks to this spiritual reality of how we receive salvation and become a new creation in Christ. By now you should know the principles of Romans 6 like you know your shoe size. As we stated the Romans 6 reality above, when Jesus died, we died. When Jesus was buried, we were buried. When Jesus resurrected, we resurrected as new creations in Christ. Jesus not only took our sins on the cross, but he also took the sinner and our old life and crucified it and gave us new life.

---

6. Outler, *Works of John Wesley*, 2:194.

7. Penn-Lewis, *Centrality of the Cross*, 5.

Jesus did not come to improve our sinful nature or make us better. He is not giving us a makeover. He came to put to death sin and the old life on his cross and to resurrect a new beginning in us. Everyone who repents and believes in Christ becomes a newly created being that is restored in the image of God, and that image is Jesus Christ. Your past life of sin ended on the cross. God forgives you of all your sins and remembers them no more (Ps 103:12).

As a new creation, you have a new life, a new heart, a new mind, a new future, new spiritual eyes and ears, a new family (the Church), new power, and new authority. Believers start with the reality of the new creation. It is the point where we begin. It is our position and our inherited status in Christ. We do not try to attain God's approval, affirmation, and acceptance by our good works. These blessings are not our goals to attain by our performance on the moral treadmill. As a new creation in Christ, we begin with God's approval, affirmation, and acceptance as a gift and a starting point not an unattainable goal. We do not work toward becoming a new creation, but we begin with the new creation on the inside of us. God gives it to us as a gift, and then we can grow more and more in this new life. We work from it and not to it.

Becoming a new creation in Christ is just the beginning. The new creation begins as a seed. It is not complete yet. The seed needs to grow. The new creation is a potential that is actualized as we walk out who we are in Christ by faith. In Christ, we have inherited all things that pertain to life and godliness. The blessings of the covenant and all the promises of God are ours (2 Cor 1:20). Jesus has purchased our forgiveness, salvation, deliverance, sanctification, healing, authority, and victory, but this inheritance and new life is just beginning We stand in a position of favor and grace (Rom 5:2). However, the seed of new creation needs to be watered and fed with the Word by faith, so that we can grow.

We grow by walking in faith and obedience to God. We acknowledge that we are dead to sin, and daily we choose to yield to God and not to sin. We decide to put off the old creation when we are tempted to go backwards and to put on the new creation, daily (Eph 4:22–24). Even though God has deposited this awesome potential within us, we must choose to resist temptation and the old ways and to "put on," or intentionally receive, this new life. In every situation we have a choice to follow the flesh or the Spirit (Gal 5:16–18). We *choose* to be spiritually minded and to be controlled by the Spirit and to be under the influence of the Spirit (Rom 8:5–6). It is our choice to allow ourselves to be instruments of righteousness for the advancement of the Kingdom in every sphere of influence that we are placed.

Knowing who we are in Christ is paramount to forming our new identity. How is our identity formed? Usually family, peers, education, community, or church help us to form our identity for better or worse. It is God's will that God forms our identity in Christ. He wants us to know who we are *in Christ*. We exist and are identified only as we are related to him. Without Jesus, we can do nothing (John 15:5). When we abide in the True Vine, we participate in covenant blessings. We share in all that God has, and we can do all things in Christ. When we know who we are in Christ, then we can know what we can do in Christ. All these blessings come because we are a new creation in Christ.

Struggle emerges when we allow other voices or influences to define our self-concept instead of the Word. There are so many influences that contribute to shaping who we are, but not all those influences are godly, healthy, or truthful. It takes keen discernment to sift through all the voices and determine which ones are truth-based. Influences that tend to bind and condemn us to our past failures, disappointments or traumas are not to be embraced. Also, influences that tend to shape us in an image that is anything less than Christ-like are not to be embraced. When we begin to learn who we are, then we begin to discern and resist what we are not. We learn to resist sin and the devil. Jesus has put to death our old life and has resurrected a new one in us. We are brand new creations in Christ, and nothing less will satisfy.

Names of God

The names of God reveal God's nature and attributes. He is his name. And he extends the attribute represented by his name to us in covenant. For example, *Yahweh Shalom*, "the Lord God is peace." His name is peace. He is peace. And his peace he extends to us, so it becomes our peace.

Image of God—2 Cor 4:4

Attribute: Humanity & Divinity. When we see the Son, then we have seen the Father, for he is the very image of God. Jesus is the icon of the Father, and when we gaze upon Christ in faith, then we are transformed from glory to glory in his image. The image of God is a mirror into which we gaze and contemplate, and the reflection of Christ shapes our very image, so that when we so ourselves and even others, we see Christ.

Author and Finisher of our faith—Heb 12:2

Source and Goal: See #8. The title "Author and Finisher" attributes our beginning and end to Christ. Jesus Christ is the source, sustenance, and goal of our faith. Nothing else will suffice but to put Jesus first. We put our trust fully in the Son of God. As we trust, it is important to realize that faith is not our work or merit but is found in our relationship with the source of our faith, Jesus Christ. Christ is the author or originator of our faith. When we read God's word and open our hearts to the Holy Spirit, we find that God releases faith in our hearts to believe God. Faith is a product of our intimate relationship with Jesus Christ. God inspires faith in our hearts, and God also brings our faith to completion. The good work that God has begun will be made complete. God has no unfinished jobs or projects. God is faithful to complete what God has started. The Lord births our faith and completes our faith.

Alpha and Omega—Rev 1:8; 22:13

The Word is the beginning and end of all things, the original creation and the new creation. The Word also became human for us and is our beginning and end. Our faith and life begin and end with Jesus Christ our Lord. Jesus is the first and last Word for all things in this life and in the life to come. Let Jesus become the Alpha and Omega, the beginning and end, of our faith. He is making a new creation and will complete his work in us. Since we are new creations in Christ, our life begins and ends in Jesus. He is the beginning and end of everything in our lives. He also initiates and completes all of God's work in us.

Repentance of Stinking Thinking

Identify Your Stinking Thinking

___ Prejudice and hatred

___ Unrealistic expectations

___ Predicting the future

___ Disqualification

___ Doublemindedness

___ Defeated

__ Unforgiveness

__ Unbelief

__ Competition

__ Plain lies and errors

__ Judging

__ Guilt and shame

__ Self-condemnation

__ I struggle to see myself as a new creation because of my past.

__ My past has really defined me.

__ I do not feel like a new creation.

__ I see myself as less than other or not as good.

__ I feel like I have to perform to feel good about myself or as good as others.

__ I feel like I have to work to get others to accept and approve of me.

__ I did not know that I was a new creation in Christ.

__ Other _____

Change Stinking Thinking

- How has stinking thinking impeded your walk as a new creation in Christ?
- Renounce the stinking thinking that has been identified.
- Make a decision to agree with God's word that you are a new creation.

Faith Formation, Truth-Based Thinking:

Identify the Truth:

- I am a new creation in Christ.
- My old life is gone, and a new life has begun.

Believe and Receive the Truth:

- Yes, and Amen. I believe and receive this truth.
- My self-concept is defined by my identity in Christ and not by others or my circumstances.

Affirmation

Say aloud: I died to sin with Christ on the cross. I am dead with Christ. I am buried with Christ. I am resurrected with Christ. I am a new creation in Christ. My past sins have been forgiven. God has given me a fresh new start. I have been recreated in the image of Christ in righteousness and holiness. I have a new heart and a new mind and a new destiny in God's Kingdom. I am accepted, affirmed, and approved by God through Christ. I am not trying to attain these things by my works. God gives them to me as a gift. I will realize all God has for me by walking in faith and not by sight. I am led by his Spirit, and I obey his word. In God's eyes, I am complete and am seated in heavenly places with Christ, and all my enemies are under Christ's feet. God will lead me into my destiny in Christ by walking out this new creation. I also pray for the new creation in others and in every facet of life in the world.

Morning Reflection

The M.E.E.T. Method—In the morning, purpose in your heart to:

M—Monitor your thoughts during the day and

E—Evaluate them. Do they align with God's word? Are they distortions of what is real?

E—Expel any thoughts that are contrary to the truth and replace them with the

T—Truth of God's word, created in the image of God.

Evening Reflection—The 7Rs Method

1. Rest and Receive

Rest and receive God's truth. I entrust myself and others to God's grace and care.

- Receive the truth in your heart. We have all sinned and need God's grace and mercy. Rest in this fact.

- Sit and relax in a quiet place. Calm and quiet your mind as you think on this truth.

- Breathe deeply through the nose and out the mouth repetitively, as you rest in what God has done for you. As thoughts of the day come into your mind let them go. Give each thought to God.

- Be mindful of God's goodness. Be mindful of the gift of this moment. Be mindful of the gift that you are.

- Imagine every care being taken into God's loving embrace. Let the cares, concerns, and details of the day unravel slowly, layer after layer. Give each thought to God. You are intentionally casting your cares on God. They belong to God and not to you.

- Give to Christ any thought that is contrary to the truth. Let him nail it to his cross.

- Pray that Jesus would come into your mind and shine the light on any area that he desires. Also ask Jesus to come and speak specifically to any situation that is on your mind.

- Listen to God speak through your conscience concerning your thought-life today. Do you need to repent, or offer thanksgiving or a praise? Do you need to resolve to do God's word?

- Write down what God is impressing upon you.

- Hear and receive the truth of God's voice as he speaks to your thought-life.

2. Repent

Turn away from the lies and turn toward the truth. Also repent of all acts that are contrary to the character of Christ.

- Identify any lies in your thought-life that would lead you away from God's mercy and grace or lies that tempt you to believe that you are better than others or others are better than you. Also identify lies that would say that your own goodness supplants the goodness of God.

- Uproot the lies by rejecting and casting them down.

- Renounce the lies by making a decision to renew your thoughts.

- Turn from believing the lies to believing the truth. Replace the lies with the truth.

3. Renew

Renew your mind with the truth. Plant the word of God in your heart and believe it personally for your life.

- Meditate on the Scriptures for this section.

- Read and declare those Scriptures several times.

- Agree with God's word by saying, "Yes" and "Amen" to what it affirms. "Yes, and Amen, we are all sinners in need of God's grace."

- Receive the truth. Own it. Personalize it and make it yours.

4. Recite

Confess and declare the word of God.

- Think God's thoughts. Say what God says in his word.

- Declare several times, "I have sinned and fallen short of God's glory and am in need of mercy and salvation. My neighbor has sinned and fallen short of God's glory and is in need of mercy and salvation."

- In the future, remember and confess boldly God's word.

5. Resolve

Resolve yourself to action. Be a doer of the word.

- Make a decision to put this truth into practice. Practice it daily in every area of your life. Make clear resolutions to manifest the truth in concrete actions that impact others and the world around you.

6. Repeat

Repeat the process.

- Repeat and strengthen your commitment to the previous five steps. Repetition and rehearsal strengthen the truth in you.

7. Reality

Repetition brings reality.

- After much repetition from thought → word → deed, the truth becomes experiential and a solid concrete reality in your life that will yield the fruit of wisdom and righteousness.

The Christian Life—You Can Do All Things Through Christ.

We know who we *are* in Christ. Our being comes before our doing. Now, let us look at what we can *do* through Christ. Scripture:

- Philippians 4:13 (NKJV): "I can do all things through Christ who strengthens me."
- Ephesians 6:10 (NIV): "Finally, be strong in the Lord and in his mighty power."
- Joshua 1:9 (NLT): "I command you- 'Be strong and courageous! Do not be afraid or discouraged. For the LORD your God is with you wherever you go.'"
- Isaiah 40:31 (NLT): "But those who wait on the LORD will find new strength. They will fly high on wings like eagles. They will run and not grow weary. They will walk and not faint."

Reflection

Charles Wesley (1707–1788) Methodist poet and hymn writer:

> Strong, I am, for he is strong;
> Just in righteousness divine:
> He is my triumphal song;
> All he has, and is, is mine;
> Mine,- and yours, whoe'er believe;
> On his name whoe'er shall call,
> Freely shall his grace receive;
> He is full of grace for all.[8]

Smith Wigglesworth (1859–1947), Pentecostal Apostle:

---

8. Wesley, *Collection of Hymns*, 193.

There is power to overcome everything in the world through the name of Jesus.[9]

In my recreational time, I powerlift and box. I even teach a class in boxing in my old age. A while back when I had already turned 50, I bench pressed 405 lbs., which was a major achievement for me at half a century. Yet even though God has gifted me with strength, I daily realize how weak I am. Over the years, I have found that I cannot bench press my past, my present or my future. These weights are much too heavy for me or any other lifter. At the writing of this book, the current raw bench press record is just 782 lbs., and the equipped record is at 1,120 lbs. Even these record holders cannot lift their own life's weight. Life is too heavy to lift. We are weighed down by stress, worry, anxiety, financial pressures, medical issues, among others. I do not know how people make it without Jesus. The good news is that we are not required to bench press our past, present or our future. We are not called to live our life without Jesus. He presses our weight for us (Ps 55:22).

When we give our lives to Christ, then our lives are not our own. We have been bought with a price (1 Cor 6:20; 7:23). We belong to him. Paul said, "It is no longer I that live, but Christ that lives in me." Our life is in Christ alone. We rely on him for everything. We do not lean unto our own understanding or strength, but we participate and trust in Christ's understanding and strength. In fact, when we are weak in our own ability, then we are strong in Christ, because his grace is sufficient for us (2 Cor 12). God is our strength, and whatever is impossible for us is possible for God. All things are possible for God who is Almighty.

So, whatever we need to do, we can rely on God's grace and strength to accomplish it—whether it is praying, working, parenting, studying, serving, suffering, leading, or obeying. We are drawing from Christ's strength. We are commanded to be strong by depending on God's strength which is infinite. God is eternal. He never grows tired or weak. He never runs out of love or power (Isa 40:27–31). There is nothing that God cannot do. Do all you can, and God will do what you can't. What I cannot do, he can. The weak become strong (2 Cor 12:9)! Depend on Christ for the big and small in your life and believe Christ to do a new and great work in the world around you.

Names of God

The names of God reveal God's nature and attributes. He is his name. And he extends the attribute represented by his name to us in covenant. For

9. Wigglesworth, *Ever Increasing Faith*, 15.

example, *Yahweh Shalom,* "the Lord God is peace." His name is peace. He is peace. And his peace he extends to us, so it becomes our peace.

The Lord my Strength

Adonai Uzzi. God's name here means strength. His names reveal his attributes and character, and through his covenant we are allowed to participate in these benefits. His strength becomes our strength. We are strong because God is strong. Even when we are weak, we are strong, because we do not rely on our own strength but on his infinite power and might that never weaken.

King of Kings—1 Tim 6:15

Jesus is the King of Kings. This name reveals his supreme royalty and his ultimate power and authority over all things. There is nothing that can defeat Jesus Christ. He has defeated sin, death, and the devil. The weapon formed against us can't prosper. Jesus also has the final say over the destiny of the world order and its kingdoms. The nations shall become the kingdoms of our God. As King of Kings, he rules over all. As disciples, we are members of his Kingdom and partake of its blessings.

DELIVERER—ROM 11:26

Attribute: Deliverer. Humanity is in bondage to sin. Jesus came to set us free. He who was without sin, took sin upon himself and destroyed it in the flesh upon the cross, so you and I can be free. So be free in Jesus. People are in bondage to themselves, to money, lust, power, etc. If we are in sin, then we are in bondage. Christ is greater than the devil and any bondage. He will lead us not into temptation but deliver us from evil. God is able.

Repentance of Stinking Thinking

1. Identify Stinking Thinking

___ Doublemindedness

___ Defeated attitude

___ Unbelief

__ Self-disqualifying

__ Lack of confidence

__ Self- condemnation

__ Fearful

__ Worried

__ Anxious

__ How will I be able to do ____?

__ I cannot make it.

__ I am not smart enough

__ I am not good enough

__ God will not help me with ___.

__ This is impossible.

__ There is no way that ___ will happen.

__ I cannot do it.

__ Other _____

2. Change Stinking Thinking:

- How has stinking thinking prevented you from doing what God has called you and empowered you to do?

- Renounce the stinking thinking that has been identified.

- Make a decision to agree with God's word about God's ability through you.

Faith Formation, Truth-Based Thinking:

Identify the Truth:

- I cannot live the Christian life on my own.

- I cannot live the Christian life in my own ability.

- God will provide me with the strength and ability to accomplish whatever the Lord has for me to do.

Believe and Receive the Truth

- Yes, and Amen. I believe and receive these truths.
- I am weak, but the Lord is strong.
- I can do all things through Christ who strengthens me.

Affirmation

Say aloud: The Lord is my strength. There is nothing God cannot do. Even when I am weak, I am strong. For the Lord does not grow weary. God will give me the power to do all that God has called me to do. I have strength to pray, strength to witness, strength to work, strength to overcome adversity, strength to love, strength to forgive, strength to serve, and strength to worship God. I am courageous and will not fear anything because my God is with me wherever I go. I will not worry, be anxious or doubtful, because God is working all things for good on my behalf. My life is in the Lord's hands. Even the nations are in God's hands. Lord advance your Kingdom reign in the earth and over the nations. Bring righteousness and justice. Let your Kingdom come.

Morning Reflection

The M.E.E.T. Method—In the morning, purpose in your heart to:

M—Monitor your thoughts during the day and

E—Evaluate them. Do they align with God's word? Are they distortions of what is real?

E—Expel any thoughts that are contrary to the truth and replace them with the

T—Truth of God's word, created in the image of God.

Evening Reflection—The 7Rs Method

1. Rest and Receive

Rest and receive God's truth. I entrust myself and others to God's grace and care.

- Receive the truth in your heart. We have all sinned and need God's grace and mercy. Rest in this fact.

- Sit and relax in a quiet place. Calm and quiet your mind as you think on this truth.

- Breathe deeply through the nose and out the mouth repetitively, as you rest in what God has done for you. As thoughts of the day come into your mind let them go. Give each thought to God.

- Be mindful of God's goodness. Be mindful of the gift of this moment. Be mindful of the gift that you are.

- Imagine every care being taken into God's loving embrace. Let the cares, concerns, and details of the day unravel slowly, layer after layer. Give each thought to God. You are intentionally casting your cares on God. They belong to God and not to you.

- Give to Christ any thought that is contrary to the truth. Let him nail it to his cross.

- Pray that Jesus would come into your mind and shine the light on any area that he desires. Also ask Jesus to come and speak specifically to any situation that is on your mind.

- Listen to God speak through your conscience concerning your thought-life today. Do you need to repent, or offer thanksgiving or a praise? Do you need to resolve to do God's word?

- Write down what God is impressing upon you.

- Hear and receive the truth of God's voice as he speaks to your thought-life.

2. Repent

Turn away from the lies and turn toward the truth. Also repent of all acts that are contrary to the character of Christ.

- Identify any lies in your thought-life that would lead you away from God's mercy and grace or lies that tempt you to believe that you are better than others or others are better than you. Also identify lies that would say that your own goodness supplants the goodness of God.

- Uproot the lies by rejecting and casting them down.

- Renounce the lies by making a decision to renew your thoughts.

- Turn from believing the lies to believing the truth. Replace the lies with the truth.

3. Renew

Renew your mind with the truth. Plant the word of God in your heart and believe it personally for your life.

3. Meditate on the Scriptures for this section.

4. Read and declare those Scriptures several times.

5. Agree with God's word by saying, "Yes" and "Amen" to what it affirms. "Yes, and Amen, we are all sinners in need of God's grace."

6. Receive the truth. Own it. Personalize it and make it yours.

4. Recite

Confess and declare the word of God.

- Think God's thoughts. Say what God says in his word.

- Declare several times, "I have sinned and fallen short of God's glory and am in need of mercy and salvation. My neighbor has sinned and fallen short of God's glory and is in need of mercy and salvation."

- In the future, remember and confess boldly God's word.

5. Resolve

Resolve yourself to action. Be a doer of the word.

- Make a decision to put this truth into practice. Practice it daily in every area of your life. Make clear resolutions to manifest the truth in concrete actions that impact others and the world around you.

6. Repeat

Repeat the process.

- Repeat and strengthen your commitment to the previous five steps. Repetition and rehearsal strengthen the truth in you.

7. Reality

Repetition brings reality.

- After much repetition from thought → word → deed, the truth becomes experiential and a solid concrete reality in your life that will yield the fruit of wisdom and righteousness.

CONFESSING OUR FAITH: FIFTY AFFIRMATIONS

The early church invested much of its time in the instruction of catechumens or young believers in training. A spiritual parent or mentor devoted up to three years of their lives facilitating the spiritual formation of the catechumen before baptism. The didactic, or teaching, approach of the catechumenate was holistic and involved a variety of pedagogies or teaching methods and strategies. The main instructional methods of *Truth Therapy* are belief formation through learning doctrine and affirmation of the faith. The book draws from various Christian doctrines and the scriptural names of God to create a context for spiritual formation, specifically belief formation. Belief formation is the transforming of our belief system and worldview from a secular one to a Christian one. We move from false beliefs about God, the world, the future, ethics and moral, the self, and others to Christian beliefs about these subjects. Further, belief formation relates to how our orthodox Christian beliefs then shape the development of the Christian life. The premise is that truth-based belief formation contributes to Christlikeness, effective discipleship, a healthy emotional life, quality decision-making, and productive and even virtuous living.

One cognitive strategy that is beneficial in constructing a sound thought-life is the use of affirmations or affirmations of faith. These statements are related to our faith in God. Affirmations of faith accomplish what one would suspect. They build our faith up. Affirmations are also self-directed statements intended to shape our minds or cognitive worlds. "Self-talk," specifically affirmations or self-directed statements are extremely influential in determining our self-concepts and how we see and feel about God, ourselves, others, and the world, as well our decisions and responses to the world we perceive. We remember that self-talk is the ongoing conversation in the recedes of our mind that we have with ourselves. We usually engage in a self-conversation about God, ourselves, others, and the world. It shapes and directs who we are and how we perceive God, others, and the world around us. In this section, we are taking a proactive role in shaping what we believe and don't believe.

Since self-talk is such a powerful and influential phenomenon, it is vital that we monitor our self-talk and take a proactive and intentional role in shaping and reshaping it. A great deal of our self-concept has already been constructed through the influence of family, community, peers, school, and others. Therefore, it is not always easy to be restructured and live as a new creation in Christ. We have much unlearning to do. Unlearning begins with the way we think, and the way we think is evident to us empirically through our self-talk. We can examine our own thought-life and unlearn sinful thinking. However, deeply entrenched scripts of self-talk are challenging to unlearn. We can begin now by self-monitoring for scripts of wrong or stinking thinking as well as sinful thinking. We can follow through by changing those stinking thinking patterns into hope-filled patterns by confessing and rehearsing various affirmations of our faith. In this section we will confess our position in Christ as a new creation.

One way to be intentional and proactive in scripting our self-talk is to make regular confessions, affirmations and declarations based on who we are in Christ; tell ourselves what God's word says about us. Affirm what God affirms. The Psalmist David regularly found that he had to encourage himself in the Lord. He also would often ask his soul, "Why are you so discouraged and downcast?" He had to talk to himself under the leading of the Spirit (Ps 42:5,11; 43:5; 88:14). In this next section we will be intentionally aligning our self-talk with God-talk. We are going to say what God is saying.

Affirmations and self-statements are some of the building blocks that God uses to construct our faith, our self-concept, and ultimately the framework for how we view and interpret life (worldview). From a Christian perspective, affirmations can assist in building our self-concept in Christ, which is actually our identity in Christ. From a strong identity in Christ, we begin to see others and the world through the lens of Christ, and finally we can walk in the life of Christ. Two essential affirmations in the Christian life are *knowing who we are in Christ, and what we can do through Christ.* Both affirmations stem from a greater reality, the new creation. We reviewed those two affirmations above through *Truth Therapy.*

In this section, we will be declaring and rehearsing various affirmations that are consequential to our new life in Christ. Read through the affirmation several times out loud. Let some readings be done more slowly than others. The purpose at this point is to integrate these truths into our faith-system. The word of God is not a magical spell or mantra that if we just speak the bare words something happens. The truth of God's word needs to be believed upon and trusted with one's whole heart.

We are challenged to keep the truth in our heart throughout the day. Let it influence our attitude and our actions. We are encouraged to make these declarations in both first person singular ("I" statements) and first-person plural ("We" statements). Too often in our Western Christianity we have privatized and subjectivized Christianity to its detriment. Christianity is a social practice that points our faith to act in love toward others.

We remember that affirmations build our faith. They assist in constructing belief and meaning by personally confirming the truths in Scripture. When we construct and verbalize right thinking (affirmations), we are building healthy frameworks for interpreting God, self, and the world around us. Our faith is built on hearing the truth (Rom 10:17). Faith comes by hearing the word, so we must both read the Word and read it aloud. When we read it aloud, our reading must be transformed into confessing and finally to doing. Reading is to recite objectively what is printed before us, but to confess is to add faith, conviction, and our personal testimony to the word. The word becomes our own. It is a part of us, living epistles.

From the dawn of the early church, it has been the church's DNA to confess her faith. When we testify or give testimony to the word by confessing it as our own several things occur. Our testimony is a liturgical act of worship and praise as we declare the goodness and greatness of our God. Our testimony is also an evangelistic proclamation to the church and the world that our God is good, and our God is great. Finally, our testimony functions as a witness, to God, the world, and ourselves of the gift of God's salvation that has been bestowed upon us. Finally, personally, the witness functions epistemically giving knowledge, meaning and assurance to reinforce our faith.

God's word is grafted in our hearts as we begin to trust who God is, and that God has the power to perform what God has promised. Our trust grows in confidence to the point that we act on God's word. Like the good farmer in the parable of the sower in Mark 4, we are called to hear the word, receive or accept the word, and then act on it and produce or be fruitful. Let us be hearers and doers of the word as the Apostle James exhorts (James 1:22).

Say aloud these fifty affirmations:

1. God is Father, Son, and Holy Spirit.

2. God created all things.

3. Jesus Christ is Lord and God.

4. I believe in the Holy Spirit, the Lord, the Giver of Life.

5. Christ died for the sins of the world.

6. It is finished.

7. Christ has risen from the dead.

8. Christ has ascended and will come again.

9. The church is the body of Christ.

10. We are the body of Christ.

11. I am fearfully and wonderfully made.

12. I am forgiven.

13. I am righteous in his sight.

14. I am saved.

15. I am delivered.

16. I am free.

17. I am healed.

18. I am a son/daughter of God.

19. I have been redeemed.

20. I have victory over sin and Satan.

21. I am justified.

22. I have been born again.

23. I am sanctified.

24. I have the witness of the Spirit.

25. I am called by God.

26. Jesus is my Lord.

27. I submit my whole life to him.

28. I am filled with the Spirit.

29. I am led by the Spirit,

30. I can hear God's voice.

31. I can love God and my neighbor.

32. I can love my family with the love of Christ.

33. I can love my enemies with the love of Christ.

34. I can obey God in all things.

35. I am covered and protected by the blood.

36. I am a servant of God.

37. I will decrease so he can increase in me.

38. My mind is renewed with the Word of God.

39. I am a new creation in Christ.

40. I can do all things through Christ who strengthens me.

41. I am an overcomer and more than a conqueror.

42. Nothing shall separate me from the love of God in Christ.

43. I am crucified with Christ.

44. I die daily.

45. I will deny myself and take up my cross.

46. I can pray without ceasing.

47. Through the Spirit, I can cast out demons, heal the sick, and work miracles.

48. I have been given the fruit of the Spirit.

49. All of God's promises are yes and amen.

50. Christ is my sufficiency in all things. [

Deliverance, affirmation of our faith, and renewing the mind are often followed by inner healing.

HEALING THE IMAGE OF GOD WITHIN

Inner healing begins with healing the image of God within. Genesis 1:26–27 pronounces that we are created in the image of God. We reflect the nature of God and are God-compatible. *We were built by God for God.* The image of God means that we were made to communicate and fellowship with God. We were specifically built for these tasks. The hand of God imprinted his own image on us so we can relate to him. Tragically, the image has been damaged by the fall in Adam. But God is restoring his image in us. The hand of God is reshaping, reforming, and healing the soul (mind, will and emotions) The Spirit of God, the finger of God, is crafting a new creation on the inside of us. The divine artist is making a *poiema* (Eph 2:10, handiwork), a work of art of your life (a masterpiece, poetry, symphony, great novel, from the Greek word "to create"). *Poiema* is the Greek word that means "to create" or "to craft." It is where we get our word "poem." You are fearfully and wonderfully made, divine poetry in motion. A work of art. A song. A poem. An epic. A symphony. A masterpiece. And above all, you are meant to be the embodied image of God. He made you to look like him. Do you? That is his intent.

God's goal for us is to restore us to the original image that he intended (Eph 4:22–24; Col 3:10), a new creation made in righteousness and holiness. Righteousness and holiness mean to be like Christ who is righteous and holy. The indwelling Holy Spirit is crafting our soul to look like Christ and to manifest his holy character. We call this sanctification. The Holy Spirit is the Spirit of sanctification (2 Thess 2:13; 1 Pet 1:2). He cleanses us and sets us apart. "Holy" is the Holy Spirit's first name. It is what he does. He makes us holy. The Holy Spirit gives us God's own holiness as a gift by faith. He baptizes us with fire! It is a refiner's fire that burns up everything that does not look like Jesus (Mal 3:1–3; Matt 3:11; Rev 3:18). The church and the world today need a baptism of fire to consume all our carnality and sin (Matt 3:11, Acts 15:9–10; 1 Thess 5:23–24; Heb 12:29).[10] Holiness is the missing ingredient in the church today!

As we surrender to the Spirit, he cleanses and removes our sin and fills us with the divine nature, the fruit of the Spirit. He gives perfect love (1 John 2:5; 4:12,17–18). The work of sanctification accelerates once one has been through deliverance. The impediments of sin and Satan are removed so the believer can grow freely in the image and likeness of God. The exact image and likeness of God is Christ (Heb 1:3). He is the goal, Christlikeness. God wants to imprint his divine nature on our soul and restore the image of God within. That image is Christ.

Today, *image is everything*. It does not matter who or what you really *are* but what you *appear* to be or what you *claim* to be. Descartes' idiom, "I think; therefore, I am," can be revised to, "I self-identify; therefore, I am." Many are attempting to craft and project an image of something that they are not. They are projecting not their *true* self but their *constructed* self. And they are trying with all their strength to hold that image together, but it runs like water through their fingers. Why are we spending so much energy constructing images? We grovel for *likes* and *followers*. The reason is that for most of us, the image of God within has been shattered and fragmented.

---

10. For a good exposition of entire sanctification or the baptism of the Holy Spirit and Fire, see any of the following holiness works: Wesley, *A Plain Account of Christian Perfection*; Hegre, *The Cross and Sanctification*; Keen, *Pentecostal Papers*; Knapp, *Lightning Bolts from Pentecostal Skies*; Carradine, *The Sanctified Life*; Steele, *Love Enthroned*; Wood, *Perfect Love*; Brengle, *Helps to Holiness*; Chadwick, *The Way to Pentecost*; Ruth, *Entire Sanctification*; Roberts, *Holiness Teachings*; and Palmer, *Way of Holiness*, among others.

And we observe life, ourselves, others, and God through this shattered lens. We do not know how the pieces fit back together, and we cannot put them back together even if we knew how to do it.

The image of God can be wounded, broken, disfigured, shattered, crushed, and tainted by sin. Sins committed and sins committed against us disfigure the image within. It can be wounded by the impact of a destructive environment like our family of origin. Dysfunctional families that abuse wound the soul. Mental, emotional, verbal, physical, sexual etc., all of it is physical abuse (neurological) at some level is toxic to the image of God within.

Pieces of our soul are scattered on the timeline of our lives broken off from a part of us that died along the way. *Truth Therapy* teaches us that we *cannot* change our past. But we can change *how we think* about our past. Experts in trauma contend that our thoughts and response to the trauma are what shape trauma more than the traumatic event itself. Often after trauma the devil tells us that we are unlovable, worthless, and we deserved the abuse. Traumatic self-talk increases the trauma of the event. But God has created the human psyche with such resilience and has built neurogenesis (the birth and growth of new brain cells and new neural circuits) and neuroplasticity (the ability of the brain to continually reform, reshape, and rewire itself) into the brain so that we can recover and survive traumatic events. And more so, he has given us his supernatural Holy Spirit to heal and restore us to the image of God in Christ.

He is healing the image of God within. He is mending our inner brokenness that we thought could never be healed. The Lord Jesus can speak his truth into our souls and override the destructive self-talk. He sends a healing word down the hallway of our soul's memories (Ps 107:20). Such a word from the mouth of Christ can heal past trauma and change how we think about our past. I have seen this occur time and again in my life and in the lives of others. Christ will speak truth directly to the lies one believed about their trauma and/or sin. The Lord takes them back to that place in their mind where they were lying dead on the road and are now dragging a dead body around. He goes to that wounded place to heal and resurrect what was once just a shell of life. People can retrieve their selves and walk in wholeness. Image healing. When he speaks his truth into that event, it rewires and renews their mind about the event. They see the event from God's redemptive perspective. God's Word overrides their own self-talk about the traumatic event. New neural pathways of life are created.

They can experience deliverance and healing and move on. God wants to renew our mind to reflect the mind of Christ. He heals the image of God within to look like Jesus. This process is central to post-op deliverance. This healing, restoration, and renewal is an ongoing work of the Word and the Spirt. As we yield to the work of the Spirit, he will rebuild the walls around our soul that guard our mind, will, and emotions one brick at a time.

We live in a hundred-year-old Tudor. My wife picked it out. Beautiful house. One day when I was on the porch, the Lord spoke to me and pointed out the brickwork on the arch that upholds our porch. It was beginning to give, and some mortar joints were eroding. At first, I ignored it. I did not want to deal with it. But the Lord warned me not to ignore what was happening, that it would be costly and hazardous if I did. Okay, Lord I will attend to it. At that time, I had yet to have any brickwork repaired on my house. For most of my decades of ministry, we lived in church parsonages. It was not my concern. We only owned two houses. The first house had vinyl siding. So, I had yet to deal with brickwork and the cost.

I examined the brick arch, and said to myself, it does not look that bad. I saw a few bricks that were failing and a few spots where the mortar joint was eroding. Shouldn't cost too much, five hundred to a thousand dollars. Ha! Not exactly. I wanted a cosmetic repair. I just wanted the image to look good, do the job, and move on. Looking at the big picture, I was unaware what was really going on at the foundation of that arch. Professionals who can see what I cannot see showed me why the bricks were giving way at the top. The foundation of the arch was damaged and shifting, causing the whole arch to pull to one side, causing the top to give. I only saw the top giving a bit, the cosmetics, the image. I just wanted to repair the image and get away cheap, no cost. God warned me for a reason. Getting away cheap would be a job half done and done poorly. The arch needed more than an image makeover, and so do we!

There was no way to repair the existing arch. The entire arch had to come down and be rebuilt from the ground up. God said to me, "Does this sound familiar? By the way I called this to your attention because it is prophetic. This is not just about the bricks." I replied, "Okay, God. I get it." And so much for five hundred to a thousand dollars. How about $13,600. It is going to cost. We may want cosmetic image makeovers that have no cost. But God will not let us get away cheap and remain broken. He will do the job right. He will destroy the old and build the new, starting with the foundation. You have to go to the roots. And it will cost you . . . everything. I am a professor, and I earn a professor's salary. Thirteen thousand dollars to be paid in one amount after the one-week job was finished was more than this meager earning professor wanted to fork out. But it had to be done. I received three other estimates, same story. So, we did it. I was blessed, though. The owner of the construction company was in recovery (AA). I shared Christ with him. He was very receptive. He even gave me a discount on the brickwork. Thank you, Lord!

The Holy Spirit reconstructs the image of God in us, building on the foundation of Jesus Christ. The Spirit wants to build your house (soul) on the Rock, a firm foundation. The workers mixed their mortar mix with sand, cement, and water to the right ratio. Then they begin to lay the brick and rebuild the arch. The Spirit builds the house and co-works with us as we mix our faith with the Word and put the Word into action one brick at a time (1 Pet 2:5). Kingdom building is with the Word of God, Jesus Christ as the chief cornerstone (Eph 2:20). Like Peter, we get a revelation of who Christ is (Matt 16:16). He is the Son of the living God. That revelation becomes the foundation upon which Christ builds our lives and the church. Revelation becomes the revolution and the rock upon which he builds (Matt 7) our soul and his Kingdom. The Holy Spirit builds on the foundation of revelation (of Christ). Revelation provides the specific blueprint that the Spirit follows to craft you in the image of Christ. Deliverance means new hope and a chance to start over again, a chance to take back your life. As we begin to pray and delve into scripture to seek God, the Spirit will reveal Christ's image within us and sanctify us. He will reveal our call, gifts, assignments, and ministries and how to carry them out. This ongoing work is all a part of post-deliverance and renewing our mind. I encourage the reader to continue faithfully along this path by the grace of the Father, Son, and Holy Spirit.[11]

---

11. Bellini, *Truth Therapy.*

THE X QUIZ

Take the X Quiz to see if you qualify as an X-minister (deliverance minister). You need 70 percent or higher. Take it the first time without the book. Grade the quiz. If you do not pass, then take it a second time without looking at the answers.

1. What is the difference between possession and oppression (degrees of influence?)? (2 pts.)

2. Can a Christian be possessed? Why or why not? (2pts.)

3. Can a Christian be oppressed? Why or why not? (2 pts.)

4. What are the 4 variables that determine degrees of demonization? (4 pts.)

5. What are the Four laws of deliverance? (4 pts.)

6. What are the 5 steps in deliverance? (5 pts.)

7. What is our basis or grounds for an effective deliverance ministry? (1 pt.)

8. What is the normative or standard way to be delivered from evil? (1 pt.)

9. Casting out demons should be our first resort when we see that someone seems to be oppressed by a demon. ( ) True or ( ) False? (1 pt.)

10. We need deliverance ministers who are more like a demolition crew than a team of nurses. ( ) True or ( ) False? (1 pt.)

11. Mental disorders and demons are not synonymous. They are not the same thing. ( ) True or False ( )? (1 pt.)

12. In the C1–13 assessment instrument, what is a Bondage Quotient? (1pt.)

13. Name at least 4 weapons we can use for warfare. (4 pts.)

14. What breaks the legal bond of sin subjectively in a person's life? (1 pt.)

15. What are 3 important necessary practices for preparing for deliverance? (3 pts.)

16. What is the Hippocratic Oath or Wesley's first rule for Methodists, and our first rule when we seek to help someone? (1 pt.)

17. What is one of the most important practices needed following deliverance or post-deliverance? (1 pt.)

18. Name 3 ways one can know that a seeker has been delivered from a demon. (3 pts.)

19. Should we interview demons and ask them their names and their assignments? (1 pt.)

20. Name 3 professionals that we can refer a seeker to for help. (3 pts.)

21. Name 4 characteristics of a qualified deliverance minister (4 pts.)

22. A person can be demonized by committing certain sins just one time. ( ) True or ( ) False? (1pt.)

23. All demons should be cast out in only one session. ( ) True or ( ) False

24. It is not possible for a problem, such as addiction, to have both a spiritual and a scientific cause ( ) True or ( ) False? (1 pt.)

25. Ultimately, in a deliverance session, who is the one casting out the demon? (1 pt.)

ANSWERS

Grade your quiz. There are a total of 50 points.

1. Possession is total demonic control. Unbelievers only can be possessed. Degrees of influence is partial demonic control. Both unbelievers and believers can be influence.

2. No. They have the Holy Spirit.

3. Yes. They can be influenced in an area.

4. Generational, Duration, Frequency, and Intensity

5. The Cross, the Will, True Repentance, and Authority

6. Identify, Repent, Renounce, Expose & Bind, Judge & Evict

7. The Cross

8. The way of the cross, sanctification, or resisting the devil. Any one of these

9. True

10. False

11. True

12. The value or terms that determines how bound one is. Determined by generational, duration, frequency, and intensity. Anyone of these is correct.

13. Word of God, blood of Jesus, worship, the armor of God, humility, fasting, the name of Jesus, prayer.

14. Repentance

15. Repentance, prayer, fasting, forgiving.

16. Do no harm.

17. Renewing the mind or Truth Therapy

18. Inner witness of the Spirit (peace), discerning of spirits, manifestations cease, stops sinning, fruit of the Spirit.

19. No

20. Medical doctor, therapist, social worker, pastor, spiritual director, psychiatrist, psychologist, recovery group.

21. Saved, filled with the Spirit, faithful, humble, teachable, fruit of the Spirit, wisdom etc.

22. True

23. False

24. False

25. God, the Father, Jesus Christ, or the Holy Spirit are correct.

GRADING

47/50 = 95%
45/50 = 90% > Excellent
42/50 = 85%
40/50 = 80% > Good
37/50 = 75%
35/50 = 70% > Passing. Congrats X-Ministers!
34 and below = Failing (retake it)

Excursus

Church and Community Deliverance

There are times that deliverance does not involve an individual but occurs on a broader scale. New levels, new devils! What does one do with evil in a church or community that is not localized at merely a personal level? It would take an entire book to engage the subject of church and communitywide deliverance and transformation. And many good books have been written on the subject.[1] However, I thought I would share a few anecdotes that illustrate that the *same principles* that apply on a personal level can apply on a social level, whether in a church or in a community. In this case, we move from individual will or agency to collective will or agency.

Begin with the C1–13 instrument. One can employ this tool for spiritual mapping. The C1–13 process is a type of spiritual mapping at an individual level. It works on a larger social scale as well. One can similarly evaluate or spiritually map a church, a block, a community, a city, a state, or a nation as you would an individual. Spiritual mapping is a term intercessors use for getting a profile or lay of the land of the area that is being targeted for intercession and warfare. Spiritual mapping usually involves getting a historical, socio-cultural, psychological, and demographic profile of a designated institution, area, or region that you are targeting. Such a profile is a combination of both supernatural spiritual insights, including prophetic words over the area, as well as hard historical and socio-cultural data on that area. This profile is an "intelligence report," providing vital information that will shape our prayer and warfare strategy and tactics.

Further, the intercessory team should regularly go onsite to the targeted location for prayer and discernment. The onsite prayer and observation

---

1. For example: Otis, *Informed Intercession*; Wagner, *Breaking Strongholds in Your City*; Silvoso, *Prayer Evangelism*; and Dawson, *Taking Our Cities for* God, among others.

(reconnaissance) will yield more data and discernment to be added to the intelligence report. With data in hand, one analyzes information from a targeted area to identify key leaders, groups, events, practices, and symbols related to sinful and/or demonic activity and to blessing and godly influence. The targeted areas we pray for usually have had a history of blessing and cursing. We are trying to map those activities historically. Under the guidance of the Holy Spirit, God will lead the intercessory team to target various key demonic strongholds that have caused a spike in the crime rate or that have impeded revival and citywide transformation. These focal points become the target for intercession and warfare.

As in personal deliverance, larger scale deliverance has similar preparation with long term prayer and fasting often onsite, targeting one or several strongholds. The Four Laws of Deliverance still apply: the cross, the will, repentance, and authority. The major difference is that the law of the will and the law of repentance apply at a larger scale. We are not dealing with an individual's will repenting, but that of a church or a community. Frequently, the intercessory team in a local church or a citywide intercessory team and association of pastors will pray repentance on behalf of the entire church or community (Dan 9 and Ezra 9).[2] This type of repentance is what I call an identificatory intercessory repentance. One identifies with the sins of a group and prays as if they are their own. Thus, a group is praying repentance on behalf of a larger group as well as for their own repentance.

The team is "standing in the gap," standing in between where people are in their current state and where God desires them to be. We partner and participate with Christ and the Spirit in their priestly and intercessory role for the salvation of the church and community and the breakthrough of the Kingdom of God.

We know that sin is already paid for at the cross but needs to be received through repentance and faith. Identificatory intercessory repentance seeks repentance on behalf of the church or community. The intercessory team then uses their authority to pray against strongholds "on the ground" and prays for angelic hosts to do battle "in the air." When I was ministering at the Ohio State University, God gave me Mark 11 as a strategy for large scale deliverance. If you read Mark chapter 11 carefully, you will find that the context is about Christ the King, God's judgment, the power of prayer, mountain-moving faith, and divine authority.

Let me provide a quick overview of the narratives in Mark chapter 11 as background for the prayer strategy that God revealed to me. The peculiar

2. For accounts of regional transformation across the world, see the documentaries *Transformations 1* and *Transformations 2* by the Sentinel Group with George Otis Jr. See also Otis, *Informed Intercession*.

story of the cursing of the fig tree is our focus. Mark 11:1–11 captures the triumphal entry of Christ the Messiah and King into Jerusalem, as palm branches are laid on the ground before him in this royal ceremony. He will gradually make his way to the temple. In verses 12–14, along the way he passes by a fig tree. Christ is hungry and looks for fruit on the tree even though it is out of season. He curses the tree because it is unproductive. In verses 15–19, he enters the outer court of the temple, reserved for prayer and the Gentiles (Court of the Gentiles). He finds it littered with the bargaining, bartering, and thievery of the moneychangers. His heart burning with righteous indignation, Christ whips the moneychangers and turns over their tables (also John's version 2:13–17). He indicts the religious leaders for turning the house of prayer for all nations into a den of thieves.

In verses 20–25, Jesus and the disciples pass by the same fig tree. They notice that the tree was dried up and withered to the roots. Peter remembered that Jesus had cursed it. Christ then uses the occasion to teach about prayer and faith. If we have faith, we can speak to mountains to be removed and cast into the sea. The chapter concludes with verses 27–33 with the religious leaders questioning Jesus' authority to minister. Jesus answers a question with a question, and in the end will not reveal his source of authority because they were seeking to trap and indict him.

Let us return to the cursing of the fig tree, which is our focus for this lesson. As we know historically, the fig tree is symbolic of Israel. The Son of God came to the world looking for faith. He came to the fig tree, Israel, to find fruit (fitting for repentance). He did not find it. The people of Israel did not repent. They should have been looking for the Son of Man even when least expecting him. Jesus judged the tree and Israel for not being ready for his coming. The Messiah and King came into Israel, and the people shouted, "Blessed is he who comes in the name of the Lord." They gave him a King's welcome with their lips but denied him with their actions, later crying in Mark 15:13–14, "Crucify him. Crucify him!" Israel refused their Messiah. Judgment was pronounced over the temple and the people, as Jesus mourned outside of Jerusalem (Matt 23:37). As the fig tree dried up and produced no more fruit, so the temple would be destroyed and Rome besieged Jerusalem in 70 A.D. Jesus was inspecting for fruit and did not find any. Even today, he examines the church and other institutions for fruit.

God expects everything to bear fruit for his glory and for the common, public good. People, institutions, churches, organizations, even nations will be judged by God based on their fruit bearing. He judges our fruit (Matt 7:20; 12:33; John 15). He will judge and uproot a fruitless institution and replace it with one that bears fruit. The Lord first offers people mercy to repent. He longs to deliver and judge the works of darkness in the church and in community institutions. We are called to pray for institutions and communities so that the Kingdom will invade every sphere of society and bear fruit; for God shines his sunlight on both the evil and good, and he sends rain on the just and the unjust alike (Matt 5:45). God is so good that he blesses, in some sense, everyone, regardless of their faith. However, if the people consistently do not repent, God may remove his favor. In this case the fig tree can symbolize a nation, a church, a city, a community, an institution, or an establishment.

Currently, I believe our nation and many of its institutions are in this predicament. Throughout our nation's history, we have been blessed with the favor of the Lord. But in recent decades, we have staunchly resisted the Lord, his righteousness, and our nation's inheritance. There is no fear of the Lord! As a result, we have been sent a strong delusion and have believed the lie because we have forsaken the truth and delighted in lawlessness (2 Thess 2:11–12). Repentance, deliverance, and healing are needed more than ever.

This book is being written in the heart of the COVID 19 pandemic. We are divided politically, racially, and spiritually as a nation. We are experiencing unprecedented disease, civil unrest, violence, and hopelessness. God is trying to get our attention by allowing these calamities. He is quarantining us for a season of repentance so that we may experience deliverance and healing. The world, the nation, its communities and institutions, and the church need the fervent prayer of the righteous.[3] We pray that God would have mercy on the people but uproot systemic evil and demonic strongholds. Everything in heaven and earth is being shaken. Only what is grounded in the unshakeable Kingdom will not be uprooted (Heb 12:25–29).

In some cases, when there is no repentance or fruit for a period of time, God judges the tree. It is at this point where his judgment goes to the root, even uprooting the institution itself. When God uproots evil (curses the fig tree), he is doing a new thing, tearing down establishments that do not bear fruit. He will start new ones. He will even allow churches to dry up and build new ones. It is part of his prophetic mission to judge, uproot, tear down, and build again (Jer 1:10). We implemented this strategy and witnessed its fruit at the Ohio State University (see preface) and the Dixie Strip (see chapter 3) and other places. We discerned God was ready to do a new thing.

---

3. Not the political or religious self-righteous.

GOD CLEANS UP A COMMUNITY
LITTERED WITH CRIME

At a church where I pastored (in Columbus), the surrounding community was inundated with crime, violence, drug and sex trafficking, and even murder. Much of it was coming from illegal immigrant gang activity among the youth in the neighborhood. In fact, one of the street gang's hangouts was down the street from the church. Routine trafficking occurred out of this house. I would regularly find drug needles on the sidewalk in front of the church. Scantily clad women were often picked up on the corner in front of one of their main houses and in front of the church. One time, I witnessed a man and a woman on top of a car in front of the church at 11 a.m. in broad daylight doing something that should only be done in privacy by a married couple. We heard gunshots fired day and night. I had to teach my wife how to army crawl below the windows when we would hear gunfire. Several people were murdered in the neighborhood from rival gangs. I am trying to give you a real, graphic, but cleaned-up version of where we ministered.

My family lived in the parsonage on one side of the church. And on the other side of the parsonage was a two-story double. On one half of the double, there was a woman who was prostituting and selling drugs out of her house at all hours of the day and night. I saw boys as young as eight years old patronize that house. On the other half of the double, a young man and two young ladies were running an afterhours strip club out of their living room. The women were regular workers at a strip club, but in their off hours, they stripped out of their house. The young man put a three-fourths inch piece of plywood over their pool table, and the women went at it. How do I know? Their concerned neighbor on the other side could see through their windows, which were uncovered. The other side of the double facing our house had twenty-four-hour traffic going in and out, and their windows were also uncovered. They did not keep it a secret. There is much more that I can share, but space is limited, and I am trying to give the reader a true but sanitized version.

Everything came to a climactic conclusion when our church's intercessory team began to apply the lessons of this book, specifically the cursing of the fig tree and spiritual mapping. We discerned that God was ready to do a new thing. After around five years of powerful intercession, the Lord shut the gang houses down. The authorities arrested many of the street-gang members. Soon after, the hangout was razed to the ground. It withered to the roots. The other houses were vacated. In the same time period, the woman next door to our parsonage was arrested on prostitution and drug charges. And on the other side, the young man and two women of the makeshift strip club moved out and left the neighborhood.

With the main suppliers of drugs to the community gone, new establishments moved in to better service the community. And the old holiness church where I pastored, which was dying and down to thirty members when I arrived, experienced revival and grew to over 250. We experienced two years of spontaneous revival at the same time and of the same nature as the famous revivals at the Toronto Airport, Smithton, Missouri, and Brownsville in Florida. People were saved, sanctified, filled with the Holy Spirit, delivered, healed, and were recipients of angelic visitations, gold-fillings, spiritual drunkenness, holy laughter, and other miracles. The church would reach out and lead many to the Lord from that and start new outreach ministries to help restore the community.

THE CASE OF THE WOULD-BE SCHOOL SHOOTING.

Following the mass shooting of 2019 in Dayton, Ohio, I held a prayer meeting at our Seminary, followed by a prayer walk at the sight of the shooting in the Oregon District.[4] God told me to call the meetings "A Prayer Shield Over Dayton." Our goal was to pray repentance and healing over the community and the land and for protection against future violence. At the conclusion of our prayer walk through the Oregon District, the Holy Spirit spoke a clear word of wisdom to my heart. It was Sunday, September 15, at around 9:15 p.m. He informed me that at that moment a person was planning a school shooting, and he was calling us to pray and intervene to thwart the effort. The Lord also revealed that the person had secured a semi-automatic rifle in preparation for the mass shooting. I quickly informed the intercessory team what the Lord had shared.

This prayer group was mostly made up of teens and young adults with a few older adults. The group was inexperienced in the gifts of the Spirit, spiritual warfare, and intercession. Originally, I made a general call for the prayer walk, but only a little over a dozen responded. I led the small group in prayer for God's intervention. I loosed angels to intercept and apprehend the would-be shooter and the firearm. I took authority over the devil and

---

4. On August 4, 2019, nine people were killed and seventeen others were injured at the hands of extreme left-wing gunman, 24-year-old Connor Betts in the Oregon District of Dayton, Ohio. The gunman was fatally shot by Dayton Police, who responded in remarkable time (32 seconds from the first shot). (See "Dayton, Ohio, Mass Shooting.") This was also the year of the El Paso, Texas, mass shooting in which twenty-three people were killed and twenty-three injured. In 2019, there were more mass shootings (417) than days of the year (365). (See Silverstein, "More Mass Shootings.")

over this horrific scheme. I prayed that the enemy's plans would be dismantled, and that God would send the right people to uncover this devious plot. The group agreed. After praying through, I told the group to watch the news in the following days for answered prayer.

Sure enough, the next day the news revealed that an eighteen-year-old woman had secured an AK-47 and was planning to shoot up the local high school of four hundred students. She claimed she had been bullied when she attended the school. Authorities were informed, and the woman was arrested.[5] I posted the news article along with information about our prayer walk on Facebook, giving God glory. One of my spiritual sons saw my post and got in touch with me. He shared some startling information.

I hadn't realized it, but his daughter attended that high school. He pastored the local Methodist church there in that small town. The youth group was led to pray for the school a week earlier. Also, a mutual friend of ours has a daughter who worked with the eighteen-year-old woman. The woman was flashing a picture of the gun on her cell phone to her coworkers. Our friend's daughter slipped away and informed the police. The event happened at around the *same time* that we were interceding! Praise God! God was looking for an attentive ear in that crucial moment to heed his warning and pray for help. God intervened and saved many lives.

What if we were more attentive to crises such as this in our intercession? When events like a school shooting occur, people ask, "Where is God?" I question, "Where is the church?" If we would tune in to hear God with such specificity and accuracy, perhaps we would be able to prevent a host of tragedies from occurring. If we stopped playing church and exercising the gifts of the Holy Spirit solely on each other every Sunday morning and took the power of God into the marketplace, we would see some larger scale supernatural transformation. However, the church is frequently too inwardly absorbed. I liken some in the body of Christ to bodybuilders when it comes to the gifts of the Spirit. It can be mostly for show.

I lift weights. I am a recreational powerlifter. I never wanted to body build because it was not for me. Forgive me, bodybuilders, it is just my opinion. In my estimation, one works hard but does nothing productive with all that muscle. For what are we training? Posing and looking at ourselves in the mirror? Flexing and showing off to friends who are likewise trying to outflex us? And finally, one competes in a show on stage before judges in a Speedo (the number one reason that I don't like bodybuilding). One poses on a stage against other posers to see who looks the best. I may be wrong. It may be for some, but not for me. Train for something greater than yourself.

---

5. Fieldstadt, "Oklahoma Teen Accused," para. 1–3.

Do something with those muscles. In the church, we flex and show off our gifts to each other and pose every Sunday. "Look at my word of knowledge." "Well, I see your word of knowledge and raise you a word of wisdom." As you read, picture me doing a bodybuilding pose with each reference to a gift of the Spirit. "Look at my prophecy!" "No, look at *my* prophecy!" "But I got a tongues and interpretation." Everyone flows with deadly accuracy and power when they use the gifts on other saints on Sunday morning. That is great! But if you have that kind of firepower, why don't you take it outside the four walls to the streets and fight some crime with it. Stop posing and flexing at each other and do something with those big guns. Empty some hospitals. Shut down abortion clinics. Prophesy hope to the suicidal. Stop hurricanes. Transform streets with those gifts! Let's really flex the muscles of the body of Christ and show the world Jesus.

SMOKE ON THE WATER AT 3:15 A.M.

Taking the gifts outside the four walls of church reminds me of another astounding occurrence of God being God. I was a young Christian. It was 3 a.m. I was fast asleep. The Spirit woke me up. I asked God why. He said, "Remember when you prayed that you want to be obedient to my voice at all times and even in the small things?" I responded that I remembered. He said, "Well, this is one of those times." He told me to get up. I asked, "Why?" He said, "You are on a need-to-know basis, and right now, you do not need to know." He reminded me again of my prayer. "Okay, God, I am getting up."

God said, "Get your keys. You are going for a ride." "Okay God." "Oh, and get your guitar." "Okay God." I was still questioning God in my heart, but, nonetheless, going along for the ride. He instructed me to drive downtown. So, I did. He said go to the park by the river and the bridge. So, I did. He said get out of your car and sit at that stone table on the far end. So, I did. He further instructed me to sit down and begin to play. I asked, "God what am I supposed to play out of the clear blue sky? And it's 3:15 in the morning. I am half dead." I was not a professional or accomplished musician. I just did it for a hobby. So, am I supposed to just play *Smoke on the Water* at 3:15 a.m.? God said play. So, I did.

With the strumming of the first chord, the Spirit erupted powerfully over me, like a tsunami. And I felt the Lord taking over. I began to sing spontaneously a song that the Spirit was giving me. I prophetically sang of a man who had everything but lost it all. Alcohol took over his life. In the end he lost his wife, kids, job, his money, and friends, and he was about to take his own life. I sang the blues about a man's tragic life from beginning to end.

It was a heavy, sad number that the Lord gave me. As I finished the song, I felt a presence behind me, as if someone were there. I turned around and beheld an older man in his sixties next to me, weeping profusely.

I greeted him and asked who he was. Through the tears, he cried out that he came down to the park and then heard me singing from a distance. So, he approached me and listened. He wept, "You don't know me, but you sang my whole life in that song." He cried, "You sang my life. That was me. I had everything, and I lost it. My wife, my family, my job, everything. I came here last night to jump off that bridge over there and end it all. I heard a voice say to me to wait. Wait twenty-four hours. Wait! I did not want to wait, but I did. Twenty-four hours is up, and I came here to finish the job. My time is up, and I came to jump off that bridge. That's when I heard you playing." At that point, I shared Christ with him. He was so open, and the power of God was overwhelming. I cast out the spirit of suicide and addiction and led him to the Lord. His conversion was overpowering. We were both drenched in tears. God's love is unfathomable! What a glorious victory for Christ. God is looking for open and obedient people. It could be a matter of life and death!

GOD TEARS DOWN AND BUILDS ANEW

My last anecdote is about a church that my friend pastored on the East coast. This church is an example of when God moves according to Jeremiah 1:10, "See, today I appoint you over nations and kingdoms to uproot and tear down, to destroy and overthrow, to build and to plant." The church was an elderly, traditional congregation and was running between thirty and fifty on a Sunday. It used to have over five hundred in attendance on Sunday in its heyday in the 1950s and 60s. My friend, Robert, was sent there to revive and grow the church. He soon learned that some older, dying, traditional Protestant churches say they want to change and grow, but what they really want is the *end result* of change without having to go through the *pain* of change. When they say that they want to grow, they really mean that they want the pastor to bring people into the church who are exactly like them, people over sixty who like pipe organ music and do church as if it were 1955. It's not going to happen.

Although the pastor was faithful and led by the Spirit, he did everything wrong in the eyes of the people. He would not wear a clergy robe when preaching. He would not preach from the high church pulpit. He preached from the Bible. He did not preach itching ear sermons. He was led by the Spirit and proclaimed the truth. They opposed him from day one.

Before Pastor Robert arrived there, I received a frightening vision in prayer. I saw a mammoth, archaic church building implode, like when a building is dynamited and demolished. I knew by the Spirit that this was the church that Robert would pastor. The entire structure caved in and collapsed. Out of the dust and smoke, I saw an image of a woman's face emerge. Following her image, the word "adultery" formed out of the smoke. The Lord revealed to me that woman was the choir director. Following the word "adultery," I saw the faces of many men emerge who the Lord revealed were leaders in the church and involved in this affair. The Lord then proclaimed that the church would close in a year due to unrepented sin. God was judging the church. He spoke to the fig tree.

I shared the revelation with Pastor Robert. He began to preach repentance. He kept a closer eye on the choir director. She was one of the few people in the building throughout the week. It was a dying church with little activity. Before they hired an outreach minister, the building was usually empty all week, except on Sundays. After the outreach minister started doing mission, more adults and children frequented the building. The choir director, Susan, was not accustomed to this new schedule and would forget that she and her man friends were not alone in the building. It was not long before the outreach minister accidentally caught her twice in compromising situations with church leaders in one of the many rooms that occupied the labyrinthine building.

The pastor began to document the incidents. Meanwhile, it became more contentious on Sundays, as the leaders regularly confronted the pastor about his sermons being too harsh. "He needed to preach on love more," was their complaint. One Sunday Pastor Robert preached on love from 1 Corinthians 13. Even then they were not happy. My wife and I were visiting the church that Sunday. In fact, one of the leaders got up in the middle of the sermon and began to shout and scold the pastor, pointing his finger and ranting and raving against the pastor's "version of love" that he was preaching. The ranting man went on and on. It seemed like he would never finish. We were all embarrassed. My wife whispered in my ear, "I pray that the ceiling falls in." I replied, "I am praying that it doesn't." I felt led to stand up and confront the man and defend the pastor. I did so. He finally sat down, but I felt a spirit of judgment in the house. I prayed mercy for this misguided man.

When the service ended, the pastor came down the middle aisle and waited in the back of the church for the people to pass by, so he could shake their hands as was the Sunday custom. I know this sounds hard to believe. It was hard for me to believe. When it was time for the disgruntled man to shake Pastor Robert's hand, in the spirit, I saw a presence appear behind the man. By the witness of the Spirit, I interpreted this presence as an angel. This angelic presence touched the back of the disgruntled man's shoulder, and, at that instant, his pants fell to his ankles in front of the whole church. He was quite overweight and had a difficult time pulling his pants back up. They fell to his ankles two more times. Obviously, he was red with embarrassment. And I did all I could to avoid bursting into laughter.

The rest of story was not so amusing. After the pastor confronted local and district church leadership about the documented incidents with the choir director, things began to spiral. The choir director left her husband and ran off with another man, who was a leader in the church. They both still attended the church and maintained their leadership positions. Instead of losing their positions, they corralled the rest of the leadership at the local and district level and had a kangaroo court church trial to remove the pastor. They were successful. How they managed to accomplish this was clear to Pastor Robert. He discovered that Susan had been with other leaders in the church. It was a secret they needed to keep. There are many more details that could be told, but due to space and dignity, I will leave it here.

The church ended up closing. The tree dried up down to the roots. It *closed a year to the date* that God gave me the vision, as The Lord said it would. There was a small independent Pentecostal congregation that needed a building. They had been meeting in other church buildings for some time. They were a small, faithful, Spirit-filled church that had a vision for the community. They ended up buying that building for less than half price. Unrepented immorality by church leadership was met with God closing one church and opening a door for another church to flourish. All that time, Robert and I prayed for repentance and revival. The leadership was not willing to repent. On the other hand, revival would hit that small Pentecostal church. Meanwhile, Pastor Robert moved to another church. He went on being faithful, leading other receptive churches into renewal. One church died, and another was resurrected.

Appendix A

The X-Manual Summary

The Four Laws of Deliverance

Law #1—The Law of the Cross

Law #2—The Law of the Will

Law #3—The Law of True Repentance

Law #4—The Law of Authority

7 Qualities of an X-Minister

1. Humility

2. Teachability–Apprenticeship of Sons and Daughters

3. Caring and Compassionate

4. Does no Harm

5. Maturity

6. Filled with the Fruit of the Spirit

7. Gifted and Called by the Spirit to Deliverance

Preparation for Deliverance

1. Praying and Fasting

2. Scripture Study

3. Repentance

4. Forgiveness

5. Take the C_{1-13}

Degrees of Demonization: 4 Variable Bondage Quotient (BQ)

1. Generational

2. Frequency

3. Intensity

4. Duration

5 Step Method of Deliverance

1. Identify (Sins and Demons)

2. Repent

3. Renounce

4. Expose and Bind

5. Judge and Evict

Follow-Up

1. Renewing the Mind with the Word of God

2. Truth Therapy Principles

3. Affirmations of Faith

4. Discernment and Testing the Spirits

5. Healing the Image of God Within

Appendix B

Angelology and Demonology: A Hierarchy

There are vast and varied lists of angelic and demonic hierarchies that stem from Christian and Judaic traditions and their multiple sources. There is no "authorized" list. Some of the lists are in part derived from Scripture, while others are from various traditions. The most influential Angelologies in the Christian tradition have come from Pseudo-Dionysius the Areopagite from his *On the Celestial Hierarchy* (fourth or fifth century AD) and Thomas Aquinas' *Summa Theologica* (1265 and 1274). Taken from Aquinas, the hierarchy below is divided into three spheres with there being three orders or choirs in each sphere, a total of nine orders. This hierarchy is not strictly derived from Scripture, coming more from tradition, and is speculative.

In terms of demons and their hierarchy, they are fallen angels, and so they once stood in the heavenly ranks. Even as fallen beings they have power, though limited and fallen. Their power no longer serves its original purpose, but it is self-serving to deceive, kill, steal, and destroy. Demons, as fallen angels, are still organized and well-structured in their attempt to thwart the purposes of God, to tempt and destroy humanity, and to bring chaos to the invisible and visible created order.

Some would hold that the hierarchy of demons still resembles the order of angels prior to falling, except it is a separate governmental hierarchy of darkness rather than light. Demons, though fallen angels, are still angels in essence. Demons, as created beings, remain in the same genus or created order as angels, though fallen. Angels and fallen angels are pure spirit, rational beings, incorporeal (not physical bodies), with volition (or will, though the probation period of choosing to follow God is finished). Throughout the Christian tradition there have been attempts to classify demons, by connecting a demon with a particular sin, such as Satan-Pride, Mammon-Greed,

Leviathan- Envy, Beelzebub-Gluttony, Jezebel- Witchcraft or Lust, Python-Lying, and so forth.

Some scriptural references for angels and demons are Genesis 3:24; Exodus 25:17–22; 1 Kings 6:23–28; 2 Chronicles 3:7–14; Psalm 91:11; 103:20; Daniel 9:21; 10:12–14, 12:1; 28;14–16; Zechariah 5:9; Matthew 12:24–27; 18:10; 22:24–33, Acts 8:26; 12:15; 1 Corinthians 4:9; Galatians 3:26–28, Ephesians 1:21–23; 6:10–17; Colossians 1:6; 2:18; Hebrews 1:14, 13:2; Jude 1:6,9; Revelation 2–3; 5:11; 12; 9:10.

First Sphere: These angels worship and serve God face-to-face in the throne room. Their presence and service are in the third Heaven to God directly. Fallen angels also occupied this sphere prior to their rebellion.

- Seraphim: "burning ones." They have six wings and human hands. They are caretakers of the throne. (Isa 6:1–3; Ezek 28).

- Cherubim: They have four faces: man, ox, lion, and eagle (Ezek 1:5–11; Rev 4:8). They guard the Tree of Life (Gen 3:24), the ark of the covenant, and God's throne. Satan is a fallen cherubim according to Thomas Aquinas. So is Beelzebub (Matt 12:24–27).

- Thrones or Elders: They have four wings and four faces. See Ezek 1:13–19 and Col 1:16. They send God's judgments out (throughout the book of Revelation), even his law (Acts 7:53; Gal 3:19). Also, their demonic counterparts are spiritual wickedness in the heavenly realms (Eph 6:12).

Second Sphere: These angels are in high places over creation. They are guiding and ruling spirits. They govern creation. Fallen angels also occupied this sphere prior to their rebellion.

- Dominions or Lordships: They are over domains of angels, governing them (Eph 1:21; Col 1:16). Their evil counterparts are demonic rulers of the darkness of this world (Eph 6:12).

- Virtues: They are over the elements, over motion, and assist with miracles (Eph 1:21). Belial is a fallen one (2 Cor 6:15).

- Powers or Authorities: They rule over evil powers (Eph 3:10). Their fallen counterparts are identified as demonic powers or authorities (Eph 6:12), such as the prince of the power of the air (Eph 2:2).

Third Sphere: These angels are protectors, guides, helpers, and messengers on earth to human beings. Fallen angels also occupied this sphere prior to their rebellion.

- Principalities or Rulers: They govern, protect and guide nations, groups of people, institutions, and the church (Eph 1:21, 3:10). One example of their demonic counterparts is the Prince of Persia, a ruling demonic principality (Dan 10:20). Demonic principalities (Eph 6:12).

- Archangels, "chief angels": Michael (Jude, 6, 9, and Rev 12) and Gabriel (Dan 8:16–18; 9:21; Luke 1:19, 26, 28) are the only angels mentioned in Scripture. Also see 1 Thess 4:16. Uriel is mentioned in the apocryphal 2 Ezra, and Raphael is mentioned in the Book of Tobit.

- Angels (including guardian angels Matthew 18:10): They are messengers, which is what the word "angel" means. Angels are beings and ministers of light, flames of fire (Heb 1:7, 14). They are involved in our daily affairs and minister salvation. (They minister God's Word, anointing, healing, and comfort.) Angels are tightly organized in God's Kingdom government. They have orders, hierarchies, stations, assignments, wisdom, information, and power to carry out the Father's executive orders in the name of the Son and through the ministry of the Holy Spirit. They operate at various levels from personal, familial, to cities and states, regions, nations, and at a global level.

Fallen angels attempt to counter the elect angels. They also are involved in our daily affairs tempting us to sin. Demons are well-organized into a government of darkness with hierarchies and networks from the ground to the air (Eph 2:2) that work to bring chaos and destruction. Though fallen, they have intelligence concerning our past and present, our personal affairs, and the affairs of cities, states, and nations, and the systems, institutions, and dynamics at every level from personal to national to global (Dan 10:12–20). However, they are no match for the elect angels (1 Tim 5:21), let alone God. They are one-third less than the elect angels in number and do not have the power of God backing them. Satan is a defeated foe, working on borrowed time, until the end when his sentence will be given and served in the lake of fire.

Appendix C

Eastern Orthodox Exorcism Prayers[1]

ST. BASIL AND ST. JOHN CHRYSOSTOM

First Prayer of Exorcism and Healing
St. Basil the Great—(330 -379AD)

Let us pray to the Lord.
Lord, have mercy.

O God of gods and Lord of lords, Creator of the fiery spirits and Artificer of the invisible powers, of all things heavenly and earthly: Thou Whom no man has seen — nor is able to see; Thou Whom all creation fears and before Whom it trembles; Thou Who didst cast into the darkness of the abyss of Tartars the angels who did fall away with him who once was commander of the angelic host, who disobeyed Thee and haughtily refused to serve Thee, do Thou expel by the terror of Thy name the evil one and his legions loose upon the earth, Lucifer and those with him who fell from above. Set him to flight and command him and his demons to depart completely. Let no harm come to them who are sealed in Thy image and let those who are sealed receive dominion, "to tread on serpents and scorpions and all the power of the enemy." For Thee do we hymn and magnify and with every breath do we glorify Thy all-holy name of the Father and of the Son and of the Holy Spirit now and ever and unto ages of ages. Amen.

---

1. *Exorcism: Orthodox and Roman Rituals*, 44–51, with permission.

Second Prayer of Exorcism- St Basil the Great

Let us pray to the Lord.
Lord, have mercy.

I expel you, primal source of blasphemy, prince of the rebel host, originator of evil. I expel you, Lucifer, who was cast from the brilliance on high into the darkness of the abyss on account of your arrogance: I expel you and all the fallen hosts which followed your will: I expel you, spirit of uncleanness, who revolted against Adonai, Elohim, the omnipotent God of Sabaoth and the army of His angels. Be gone and depart from the servant/handmaid of God _____.

I expel you in the name of Him Who created all things by His Word, His Only-Begotten Son, our Lord Jesus Christ, Who was ineffably and dispassionately born before all the ages; by Whom was formed all things visible and invisible, Who made man after His Image: Who guarded him by the angels, Who trained him in the Law, Who drowned sin in the flood of waters from above and Who shut up the abysses under the heaven, Who demolished the impious race of giants, Who shook down the tower of Babel, Who reduced Sodom and Gomorrah to ashes by sulfur and fire, a fact to which the unceasing vapors testify; and Who by the staff of Moses separated the waters of the Red Sea, opening a waterless path for the people while the tyrannical Pharaoh and his God-fighting army were drowned forever in its waves for his wicked persecution of them; and Who in these last days was inexplicably incarnate of a pure Virgin who preserved the seal of her chastity intact; and Who was pleased to purge our ancient defilement in the baptismal cleansing.

I expel you, Satan, by virtue of Christ's baptism in the Jordan, which for us is a type of our inheritance of incorruption through grace and sanctified waters: the same One Who astounded the angels and all the heavenly powers when they beheld God incarnate in the flesh and also revealed at the Jordan His beginningless Father and the Holy Spirit with Whom He shares the unity of the Trinity.

I expel you, evil one, in the name of Him Who rebuked the winds and stilled the turbulent sea; Who banished the legion of demons and opened the eyes of him who was born blind from his mother's womb; and Who from clay fashioned sight for him, whereby He re-enacted the ancient re-fashioning of our face; Who restored the speech of the speechless, purged the stigma of leprosy, raised the dead from the grave and Who Himself despoiled Hades by His death and Resurrection thereby rendering mankind impervious to death.

I expel you, in the name of Almighty God Who filled men with the inbreathing of a divinely inspired voice and Who wrought together with the Apostles the piety, which has filled the universe. Fear and flee, run, leave, unclean and accursed spirit, deceitful and unseemly creature of the infernal depths, visible through deceit, hidden by pretense.

Depart wherever you may appear, Beelzebub, vanish as smoke and heat, bestial and serpentine thing, whether disguised as male or female, whether beast or crawling thing or flying, whether garrulous, mute or speechless, whether bringing fear of being trampled, or rending apart, conniving, whether oppressing him/her in sleep, by some display of weakness, by distracting laughter, or taking pleasure in false tears whether by lechery or stench of carnal lust, pleasure, addiction to drugs, divination or astrology, whether dwelling in a house, whether possessed by audacity, or contentiousness or instability, whether striking him with lunacy, or returning to him after the passage of time, whether you be of the morning, noonday, midnight or night, indefinite time or daybreak, whether spontaneously or sent to someone or coming upon him/her unawares, whether from the sea, a river, from beneath the earth, from a well, a ravine, a hollow, a lake, a thicket of reeds, from matter, land, refuse, whether from a grove, a tree, a thicket, from a fowl, or thunder, whether from the precincts of a bath, a pool of water or from a pagan sepulcher or from any place where you may lurk; whether by knowledge or ignorance or any place not mentioned.

Depart, separate yourself from him/her, be ashamed before him who was made in the image of God and shaped by His hand. Fear the likeness of the incarnate God and no longer hide in His servant/handmaid_____; rather await the rod of iron, the fiery furnace of Tartars, the gnashing of teeth as reprisal for disobedience. Be afraid, be still, flee, neither return nor hide in him some other kind of evil, unclean spirits.

Depart into the uncultivated, waterless waste of the desert where no man dwells, where God alone vigilantly watches, Who shall bind you that dares with envy to plot against His image and Who, with chains of darkness shall hold you in Tartars, Who by day and night and for a great length of time has devised all manner of evils, O devil; for great is your fear of God and great is the glory of the Father, of the Son and of the Holy Spirit. Amen.

Third Prayer of Exorcism—St Basil the Great

Let us pray to the Lord.
Lord, have mercy.

O God of the heavens, God of Light, God of the Angels and Archangels obedient to Thine Authority and Power; O God Who art glorified in Thy Saints, Father of our Lord Jesus Christ, Thine Only-begotten Son, Who delivered the souls which were bound to death and Who enlightened them that dwelt in darkness; He Who released us from all our misery and pain and Who has protected us from the assaults of the enemy. And Thou, O Son and Word of God, has purposed us for immortality by Thy death and glorified us with Thy glory; Thou Who loosed us from the fetters of our sins through Thy Cross, rendering us pleasing to Thyself and uniting us with God; Thou Who didst rescue us from destruction and cured all our diseases; Thou Who set us on the path to heaven and changed our corruption to incorruption.

Hear Thou me who cry unto Thee with longing and fear, Thou before Whom the mountains and the firmament under the heavens do shrink; Thou Who makest the physical elements to tremble, keeping them within their own limits; and because of Whom the fires of retribution dare not overstep the boundary set for them but must await the decision of Thy Will; and for Whom all creation sighs with great sighs awaiting deliverance; by Whom all adverse natures have been put to flight and the legion of the enemy has been subdued, the devil is affrighted, the serpent trampled underfoot and the dragon slain; Thou Who has enlightened the nations which confess and welcome Thy rule, O Lord; Thou through Whom life hath appeared, hope hath prevailed, through Whom the man of the earth was recreated by belief in Thee. For Whom is like unto Thee, Almighty God? Wherefore we beseech Thee, O Father, Lord of mercies, Who existed before the ages and surpasses all good, calling upon Thy holy name, through the love of Thy Child, Jesus Christ, the Holy One, and Thine All-powerful Spirit.

Cast away from his/her soul every malady, all disbelief, spare him/her from the furious attacks of unclean, infernal, fiery, evil-serving, lustful spirits, the love of gold and silver, conceit, fornication, every shameless, unseemly, dark, and profane demon. Indeed, O God, expel from Thy servant/handmaiden _____ every energy of the devil, every enchantment and delusion, all idolatry, lunacy, astrology, necromancy, every bird of omen, the love of luxury and the flesh, all greed, drunkenness, carnality, adultery, licentiousness, shamelessness, anger, contentiousness, confusion, and all evil suspicion.

Yea, O Lord our God, breathe upon him/her the Spirit of Thy Peace, watch over him/her and produce thereby the fruits of faith, virtue, wisdom, chastity, self-control, love, uprightness, hope, meekness, longsuffering, patience, prudence and understanding in Thy servant/handmaiden that he/she may be welcomed by Thee in the name of Jesus Christ, believing in the coessential Trinity, giving witness and glorifying Thy dominion, along with the Angels and Archangels and all the heavenly host, guarding our hearts by them; for all things are possible to Thee, O Lord. Therefore, we ascribe glory to the Father, and to the Son and to the Holy Spirit, now and ever and unto the ages of ages. Amen.

PRAYERS OF DELIVERANCE AND EXORCISM-
ST. JOHN CHRYSOSTOM (344–407 A.D.)

First Prayer of St. John Chrysostom

O Eternal God, Who has redeemed the race of men from the captivity of the devil, deliver Thy servant/handmaid from all the workings of unclean spirits. Command the evil and impure spirits and demons to depart from the soul and body of your servant/handmaid and not to remain nor hide in him/her. Let them be banished from this the creation of Thy hands in Thine own holy name and that of Thine only begotten Son and of Thy life-creating Spirit, so that, after being cleansed from all demonic influence, he/she may live godly, justly and righteously and may be counted worthy to receive the Holy Mysteries of Thine only-begotten Son and our God with Whom Thou art blessed and glorified together with the all holy and good and life-creating Spirit now and ever and unto the ages of ages. Amen.

Second Prayer of St. John Chrysostom

O Thou Who hast rebuked all unclean spirits and by the power of Thy Word has banished the legion, come now, through Thine only begotten Son upon this creature, which Thou hast fashioned in Thine own image and deliver him/her from the adversary that holds him/her in bondage, so that, receiving Thy mercy and becoming purified, he/she might join the ranks of Thy holy flock and be preserved as a living temple of the Holy Spirit and might receive the divine and holy Mysteries through the grace and compassion and loving kindness of Thine only-begotten Son with Whom Thou art blessed together with Thine all-holy and good and life-creating Spirit now and ever and unto the ages of ages. Amen.

Third Prayer of St. John Chrysostom

We beseech Thee, O Lord, Almighty God, Most High, untempted, peaceful King. We beseech Thee Who has created the heaven and the earth, for out of

Thee has issued the Alpha and the Omega, the beginning and the end, Thou Who has ordained that the fourfooted and irrational beasts be under subjection to man, for Thou hast subjected them. Lord, stretch out Thy mighty hand and Thy sublime and holy arm and in Thy watchful care look down upon this Thy creature and send down upon him/her a peaceful angel, a mighty angel, a guardian of soul and body, that will rebuke and drive away every evil and unclean demon from him/her, for Thou alone are Lord, Most High, almighty, and blessed unto ages of ages. Amen.

Fourth Prayer of St. John Chrysostom

We make this great, divine, holy, and awesome invocation and plea, O devil, for thine expulsion, as well as this rebuke for your utter annihilation, O apostate! God Who is holy, beginningless, frightful, invisible in essence, infinite in power and incomprehensible in divinity, the King of glory and Lord Almighty, He shall rebuke thee, devil! — He Who composed all things well by his Word from nothingness into being; He Who walks upon the wings of the air. The Lord rebukes thee, devil! — He Who calls forth the water of the sea and pours it upon the face of all the earth. Lord of Hosts is His name. Devil: the Lord rebukes thee!

He Who is ministered to and praised by numberless heavenly orders and adored and glorified in fear by multitudes of angelic and archangelic hosts. Satan: the Lord rebukes thee! He Who is honored by the encircling Powers, the awesome six-winged and many-eyed Cherubim and Seraphim that cover their faces with two wings because of His inscrutable and unseen divinity and with two wings cover their feet, lest they be seared by His unutterable glory and incomprehensible majesty, and with two wings do fly and fill the heavens with their shouts of "Holy, holy, holy, Lord Sabaoth, heaven and earth are full of Thy glory!" Devil: The Lord rebukes thee!

He Who came down from the Father's bosom and, through the holy, inexpressible, immaculate and adorable Incarnation from the Virgin, appeared ineffably in the world to save it and cast thee down from heaven in His authoritative power and showed thee to be an outcast to every man. Satan: The Lord rebukes thee! He Who said to the sea, be silent, be still, and instantly it was calmed at His command. Devil: The Lord rebukes thee! He Who made clay with His immaculate spittle and refashioned the wanting member of the man blind from birth and gave him his sight. Devil: The Lord rebukes thee!

He Who by His word restored to life the daughter of the ruler of the synagogue and snatched the son of the widow out from the mouth of death and gave him whole and sound to his own mother. Devil: The Lord rebukes thee! The Lord Who raised Lazarus the four-days dead from the dead, undecayed, as if not having died, and unblemished to the astonishment of many. Satan: The Lord rebukes thee! He Who destroyed the curse by the blow on His face and by the lance in His immaculate side lifted the flaming sword that guarded Paradise. Devil: The Lord rebukes thee!

He Who dried all tears from every face by the spitting upon His precious expressed image. Devil: The Lord rebukes thee! He Who set His Cross as a support, the salvation of the world, to thy fall and the fall of all the angels under thee. Devil: The Lord rebukes thee! He Who spoke from His Cross and the curtain of the temple was torn in two, and the rocks were split, and the tombs were opened and those who were dead from the ages were raised up. Devil: The Lord rebukes thee!

He Who by death put death to death and by His rising granted life to all men. May the Lord rebuke thee, Satan! — that is, He Who descended into Hades and opened its tombs and set free those held prisoner in it, calling them to Himself; before Whom the gatekeepers of Hades shuddered when they saw Him and, hiding themselves, vanished in the anguish of Hades. May the Lord rebuke thee, devil! — That is, Christ our God Who arose from the dead and granted His Resurrection to all men.

May the Lord rebuke thee, Satan! — He Who in glory ascended into heaven to His Father, sitting on the right of majesty upon the throne of glory. Devil: May the Lord rebuke thee! He Who shall come again with glory upon the clouds of heaven with His holy angels to judge the living and the dead. Devil: May the Lord rebuke thee! He Who has prepared for thee unquenchable fire, the unsleeping worm and the outer darkness unto eternal punishment. Devil: May the Lord rebuke thee! For before Him all things shudder and tremble from the face of His power and the wrath of His warning upon thee is uncontainable. Satan: The Lord rebukes thee by His frightful name!

Shudder, tremble, be afraid, depart, be utterly destroyed, be banished! Thee who fell from heaven and together with thee all evil spirits: every evil spirit of lust, the spirit of evil, a day and nocturnal spirit, a noonday and evening spirit, a midnight spirit, an imaginative spirit, an encountering spirit, either of the dry land or of the water, or one in a forest, or among the reeds, or in trenches, or in a road or a crossroad, in lakes, or streams, in houses, or one sprinkling in the baths and chambers, or one altering the mind of man. Depart swiftly from this creature of the Creator Christ our God! And be gone from the servant/handmaid of God _____, from his/her mind, from his/her soul, from his/her heart, from his/her reins, from his/her senses, from all his/her members, that he/she might become whole and sound and free, knowing God, his/her own Master and Creator of all things, He Who gathers together those who have gone astray and Who gives them the seal of salvation through the rebirth and restoration of divine Baptism, so that he may be counted worthy of His immaculate, heavenly and awesome Mysteries and be united to His true fold, dwelling in a place of pasture and nourished on the waters of repose, guided pastorally and safely by the staff of the Cross unto the forgiveness of sins and life everlasting. For unto Him belong all glory, honor, adoration and majesty together with Thy beginningless Father and His all-holy, good and life-giving Spirit, now and ever, and unto ages of ages. Amen.

Fifth Prayer of St. John Chrysostom

Let us pray to the Lord.
Lord, have mercy.

Everlasting God, who delivered humankind from bondage to the Evil One, free this Your servant [N] from every action of unclean spirits. Command these evil and impure spirits and demons to withdraw from the soul and body of Your servant [N] and not to hide and indwell in him (her).

In Your Holy Name, and that of Your only-begotten Son and of Your Holy Spirit, let them be driven out of the work of Your hands, so that free of every satanic assault, he (she) may live a holy, righteous, and devout life, deserving of the sacred Mysteries of Your only-begotten Son and our God, with Whom You are blessed and glorified, together with Your all-Holy, Good and Life-Giving Spirit, now and always and forever and ever. Amen.

A BASIC FORM PRAYER FOR DELIVERANCE—PETER J. BELLINI

In the name of the Lord Jesus Christ, I bind you Satan and all the forces of darkness that have come against _Person's name . I take authority over the spirit of ___(name the spirits)_ and all curses, generational other otherwise, witchcraft, spells, incantations, caging, hexes, demonic activity, and words directed against __Person's name__ and everything that relates to the covenant, including but not limited to their family, friends, possessions, home, finances and their digital identity.

I break these demons and their strongholds by the power and authority of our Lord Jesus Christ. I cancel all demonic communications, strategies, and tactics devised against ___Person's name and everything that pertains to the covenant in the name of Jesus Christ. _Person's name repents of every sin known and unknown and resigns them to the cross where Christ condemns them in his body. He/she has made a decision to forever turn from their sins and turn to Christ. He/she renounces every demonic spirit attached to those sins and commands them to leave his/her spirit, soul, and body and be broken from his/her family and everything that pertains to the covenant. He/she renounce every unholy vow or alliance and bondage in the name of Jesus. May the power of your blood free him/her from sin, guilt, shame, and condemnation.

Satan, your legal power has been broken at the cross and is made effective with their repentance. I declare that each of these demons and their works have been judged by Jesus on the cross and can no longer legally stay. Every demon, evil spirit, and device of darkness has been denounced, deactivated, dismantled, destroyed, and judged and must come out now in the name of Jesus. He/She asks for forgiveness for their sins and opening the door to these spirits. Grant forgiveness O Lord according to your work on the cross. Seal their soul and every shut door with the blood of Jesus. Protect Person's name and all of us who pray with your blood and your holy angels. Fill Person's name with your Holy Spirit and power to overcome sin and evil. Cause them to grow in Christ and never look back from this moment. I pray all these things in the precious name of my Lord and Savior, Jesus Christ. Amen.

Bibliography

Amthor, Frank. *Neuroscience for Dummies*. Hoboken, NJ: Wiley, 2016.

Anderson, Neil. *Who I Am in Christ*. Minneapolis: Bethany, 2001.

Arnold, Clinton E. *Three Crucial Questions about Spiritual Warfare*. Grand Rapids, MI: Baker Academic, 1997.

Bainbridge, William Sims. *The Sociology of Religious Movements*. London: Routledge, 1997.

Basil St. and Chrysostom, John St. *Exorcism: Orthodox and Roman Rituals*. New Orleans: Society of Clerks Secular of St. Basil, 2009.

Bellini, Peter. *Truth Therapy*. Eugene, OR: Wipf and Stock, 2014.

———. *Unleashed!* Eugene, OR: Wipf and Stock, 2018.

———. *The Cerulean Soul*. Waco, TX: Baylor University Press, 2021.

Bench, Emily. "The High Street Evolution: Ohio State Developer Raising the Bar." Bizjournals.com, 6/8/2018. https://www.bizjournals.com/columbus/news/2018/06 /08/high-street-evolution-ohio-state-developer-raising.html.

Bercot, David W., ed. *A Dictionary of Early Christian Beliefs*. Peabody, MA: Hendrickson, 1998.

Calvin, John. *Institutes of the Christian Religion*. 1-vol. ed. Translated by Henry Beveridge. Grand Rapids, MI: Eerdmans, 1989.

Catechism of the Catholic Church. 2nd ed. New York: Random House, 1995.

Clark, Randy. *The Biblical Guidebook to Deliverance*. Lake Mary, FL: Charisma 2019.

Collins, Kenneth J., and Jason E. Vickers, eds. *The Sermons of John Wesley: A Collection for the Christian Journey*. Nashville: Abingdon, 2013.

Cox, Harvey. *The Secular City*. London: SCM Press, 1965.

Daunton-Fear, Andrew. *Healing in the Early Church: The Church's Ministry of Healing and Exorcism from the First to the Fifth Century (Studies in Christian History and Thought)*. Eugene, OR: Wipf and Stock, 2009.

"Dayton, Ohio, Mass Shooting: What We Know About the Victims." CBSNews.com, 8/5/2019. https://www.cbsnews.com/news/dayton-shooting-victims-what-we-know-about-injured-and-killed-ohio-mass-shooting-2019-08-05/.

Deferrari, Roy Joseph. Letters (83–130), ed., vol. 18. The Fathers of the Church. Translated by Wilfrid Parsons. Washington, DC: The Catholic University of America Press, 1953.

Eckhardt, John. *Deliverance and Spiritual Warfare Manual.* St. Mary, FL: Charisma House, 2014.

Fieldstadt, Elisha. "Oklahoma Teen Accused of Threatening School Shooting, Wanting to Shoot '400 People for Fun.'" NBCNews.com, 9/17/2019. https://www.nbcnews.com/news/us-news/oklahoma-teen-accused-threatening-school-shooting-wanting-shoot-400-people-n1055426.

Forcen, Carlos Espi. and Fernando Espi Forcen. "Demonic Possessions and Mental Illness: Discussion of Selected Cases in Late Medieval Hagiographic Literature" in *Early Science and Medicine,* 19:3, 2014.

Gill, Nicholas. "Missing: Campus Bars and Clubs." TheLantern.com, 5/5/2003. https://www.thelantern.com/2003/05/missing-campus-bars-and-clubs.

Gurnall, William. *The Christian in Complete Armor, reprint edition.* Peabody, MA: Hendrickson, 2010.

Hull, Bill. *The Complete Book of Discipleship.* Colorado Springs: Navigators, 2006.

Jennings, Daniel. *The Supernatural Occurrences of John Wesley.* Scotts Valley, CA: CreateSpace, 2012.

Leith, John H., ed. *Creeds of the Churches.* 3rd ed. Atlanta: John Knox, 1982.

MacNutt, Francis. *Deliverance from Evil Spirit.* Grand Rapids, MI: 2009.

Nikolovska, Hristina. "44 Alarming Addiction Statistics and Facts for 2021." Disturbmenot.co, 1/10/2021. https://disturbmenot.co/addiction-statistics/.

Otis, George. *Informed Intercession.* Ventura, CA: Regal, 1999.

Outler, Albert C., ed. *The Works of John Wesley.* Vol. 2, Sermons II: 34–70. Nashville: Abingdon, 1985.

Penn-Lewis, Jessie. *The Centrality of the Cross.* Fort Washington, PA: CLC, 1993.

———. *The Cross of Calvary.* Fort Washington, PA: CLC, 1979.

Silverstein, Jason. "There Were More Mass Shootings than Days in 2019." CBSNews.com, 1/2/2020. https://www.cbsnews.com/news/mass-shootings-2019-more-than-days-365/.

St. Theophan, the Recluse. *The Path to Salvation.* Translated by Seraphim Rose. Safford, AZ: St. Paisius Monastery, 1996.

Sumrall, Lester. *Demons: The Answer Book.* New Kensington, PA: Whitaker House, 2003.

Sweigart, Josh. "No Strip Clubs Operating on North Dixie Drive as Township Plans Rule Changes." Dayton Daily News, 11/20/2019. https://www.daytondailynews.com/news/local/strip-clubs-operating-north-dixie-drive-township-plans-rule-changes/JkbgxmKzoQXMmBDuDQBLmI/.

Twelftree, Graham. *In the Name of Jesus: Exorcism Among Early Christians.* Grand Rapids, MI: Baker, 2007.

United Methodist Hymnal, The. Nashville: Abingdon, 1989.

"University Square." CampusPartners.org. https://www.campuspartners.org/university square.

Venning, Ralph. *The Sinfulness of Sin.* Carlisle, PA: Banner of Truth, 1965.

Watson, Thomas. *The Doctrine of Repentance.* Carlisle, PA: Banner of Truth, 1987.

Webster, Robert, *Methodism and the Miraculous.* Lexington, KY: Emeth, 2013.

Wesley, John. *A Collection of Hymns for the Use of the People Called Methodist.* Salem, OH: Allegheny, 1984.

Wesley's Works. Kansas City, MO: Beacon Hill, 1986.

Wigglesworth, Smith. *Ever Increasing Faith*. Springfield, MO: Gospel, 1924.

Subject Index